The Royal Commission on Criminal Procedure

Chairman: Sir Cyril Philips

THE INVESTIGATION AND PROSECUTION OF CRIMINAL OFFENCES IN ENGLAND AND WALES: THE LAW AND PROCEDURE

Presented to Parliament by Command of Her Majesty
January 1981

LONDON

HER MAJESTY'S STATIONERY OFFICE

£7.50 net

Cmnd 8092–1

Introduction by the Chairman

In this volume we offer a description of the processes that lead up to a criminal trial in England and Wales. We have drawn together this account of the relevant law and procedure covered by our terms of reference in order to allow us to concentrate in our report on the analysis of the strengths and weaknesses of the existing arrangements and to develop our proposals.

There are areas of doubt and controversy in the relevant law and considerable variety in procedure in different parts of the country. We have not attempted to discuss or describe these in detail. The volume also deals only to a limited extent with practice, which is more fully covered in our research studies.

The main source we have used is the published evidence of the Home Office and we acknowledge with gratitude our debt to their work. We have updated and amended it where necessary and supplemented it with material from other sources.

Cyril Philips
October 1980

CONTENTS

CHAPTER 4

The enforcement of rights and duties

CHAPTER 5

The prosecution process

CHAPTER 6
Procedural aspects of bringing a case to trial

APPENDICES

Background

A. The main functions of the police

1. The Royal Commission on the Police, in its Final Report in 1962,[1] listed the main functions of the police as follows:

"First, the police have a duty to maintain law and order and to protect persons and property.

Secondly, they have a duty to prevent crime.

Thirdly, they are responsible for the detection of criminals and in the course of interrogating suspected persons they have a part to play in the early stages of the judicial process acting under judicial restraint.

Fourthly, the police in England and Wales (but not in Scotland) have the responsibility of deciding whether or not to prosecute persons suspected of criminal offences.

Fifthly, in England and Wales (but not in Scotland) the police themselves conduct many prosecutions for the less serious offences.

Sixthly, the police have the duty of controlling road traffic and advising local authorities on traffic questions.

Seventhly, the police carry out certain duties on behalf of Government Departments—for example, they conduct enquiries into applications made by persons who wish to be granted British nationality.

Eighthly, they have by long tradition a duty to befriend anyone who needs their help and they may at any time be called upon to cope with minor or major emergencies."

2. The terms of reference of the Royal Commission on Criminal Procedure require it to consider the powers and duties of the police[2] in relation in particular to the third, fourth and fifth of those functions. The law and procedure relating to them will be elaborated in this volume. It opens with a brief description of the constitutional position of the officers who perform these functions, from constable to chief constable, of the powers and duties of central and local government in relation to the police, and of the duties of citizens.

[1]London HMSO, Cmnd 1728, paragraph 59.
[2]Throughout this volume, except where otherwise specified, the term "the police" is used to cover the 43 police forces in England and Wales subject to the supervision of the Home Secretary under the Police Act 1964. Other police forces (for example the British Transport Police) are referred to where necessary.

Chapter 1

B. The constitutional position of the police

a. The status of the constable

3. In England and Wales the individual police officer holds the office of constable under the Crown. He is thus independent in that his legal status is not, strictly speaking, that of an employee. But he is subject to a code of discipline laid down in Regulations approved by Parliament and is supervised by his superior officers. Above all, he is subject to the law for the way he carries out his duties. The traditional view of policing arrangements stresses this independence and the integration of the police with the community they serve. The essence of it is to be found in the report of the Royal Commission on Police Powers and Procedure of 1929[1] (and approved by the Royal Commission of 1962):

> "The police of this country have never been recognised, either in law or by tradition, as a force distinct from the general body of citizens. Despite the imposition of many extraneous duties on the police by legislation or administrative action, the principle remains that a policeman, in the view of the common law, is only 'a person paid to perform, as a matter of duty, acts which if he were so minded he might have done voluntarily'.

> "Indeed a policeman possesses few powers not enjoyed by the ordinary citizen, and public opinion, expressed in Parliament and elsewhere, has shown great jealousy of any attempts to give increased authority to the police."

4. This is too simple a view of the position now. The police officer is, as already noted, subject to a statutory scheme of control by his senior officers in addition to the general criminal and civil law. He does have greater legal powers than the ordinary citizen, as will become clear from the later parts of this volume, and he is a member of a large, disciplined and technologically advanced service, with all the resources and authority that brings.

b. The position of the chief constable

5. Each of the 43 police forces in England and Wales is headed by a chief officer, known as the commissioner in the case of the two London forces, and elsewhere as the chief constable. Chief officers are responsible for the control of their forces in the enforcement of the law and, subject to regulations made by the Home Secretary, for appointments, discipline and promotions at chief superintendent level and below.[2] (The procedure for senior appointments is described at paragraph 9.) The Home Office view is that chief officers are answerable to police authorities and to the Home Secretary for the general efficiency of their forces, but are alone responsible for the way in which they decide to investigate and prosecute offences. The one qualification of the chief officer's independence in these matters is the right of the Director of Public Prosecutions to take over or conduct a prosecution and the requirement for the consent of the Attorney General or the Director to prosecution in certain classes of offences. The Director may also require a chief constable to report to him in any particular case, and complaints by the public against police officers

---

[1]London HMSO Cmnd 3297, paragraph 15.
[2]Police Act 1964, ss. 5 and 7; for the Metropolitan force, at commander level and below.

have to be reported to the Director unless the chief officer is satisfied that no criminal offence has been committed.

6. The case of *R v Metropolitan Police Commissioner ex parte Blackburn* (No 1)[1] has been seen as confirming that the decision to institute criminal proceedings rests primarily with the chief officer concerned. The constitutional principle that no branch of the executive or judiciary can direct a police officer to bring a prosecution (or not to do so) in a particular case has been re-stated by Lord Denning in the following terms:

"I hold it to be the duty of the Commissioner of Police of the Metropolis, as it is of every chief constable, to enforce the law of the land . . . He must decide whether or not suspected persons are to be prosecuted; and, if need be, bring the prosecution or see that it is brought. But in all these things he is not the servant of anyone, save of the law itself. No Minister of the Crown can tell him . . . that he must, or must not, prosecute this man or that one. Nor can any police authority tell him so. The responsibility for law enforcement lies on him. He is answerable to the law and to the law alone."[2]

This was not to be taken as implying, however, that the discretion not to prosecute was absolute. Lord Denning went on:

"[The chief officer] can also make policy decisions and give effect to them, as, for instance, was often done when prosecutions were not brought for attempted suicide. But there are some policy decisions with which, I think, the courts in a case can, if necessary, interfere."

Lord Denning gave as an example a hypothetical decision by a chief officer not to prosecute for thefts of goods under the value of £100. If such a decision were taken,

"I should have thought that the court could countermand it. He would be failing in his duty to enforce the law. . . . A question may be raised as to the machinery by which he could be compelled to do his duty . . . This duty can be enforced, I think, either by action at the suit of the Attorney General or by the prerogative writ of *mandamus* . . . No doubt the party who applies for *mandamus* must show that he has sufficient interest to be protected and that there is no other equally convenient remedy. But once this is shown, the remedy of *mandamus* is available, in case of need, even against the Commissioner of Police of the Metropolis."

7. This operational independence of chief officers from central government and local police authorities was preserved by the Police Act 1964. The Secretary of State and his advisers, in particular HM Inspectorate of Constabulary, and the local authority elected members and magistrates represented on the police authorities exercise responsibilities for the mainten-ance of efficient police forces and influence the general manner in which they

[1][1968] 2 QB 118.
[2]At p 136.

operate. But their role stops short of any responsibility for enforcing the law in individual cases.[1]

c. *Police forces and police authorities*

8. Under the Police Act 1964 the Home Secretary has ministerial responsibility for the 43 police forces in England and Wales. Except for the Metropolitan Police District, police forces are based on local authority or combined local authority areas. Each force is subject to general oversight by a police authority, which outside London is either a committee of the local authority or a separate body consisting of representatives of a number of authorities. In either case the authority is a statutory body independent of the local authority and, in addition to local authority members, one third of its members is drawn from magistrates for the area. In London, the Home Secretary is the police authority for the Metropolitan Police; the police authority for the City of London Police is the Common Council of the City of London. There are a number of other forces, for which the Home Secretary is not responsible, set up under legislation other than the Police Act. Their members have the powers of a constable within a limited jurisdiction; they include the Ministry of Defence Police, the British Transport Police, the UK Atomic Energy Authority Constabulary and various ports and parks police forces.

9. The duties and powers of the police authority are set out in the Police Act 1964. Its major duty is to maintain an adequate and efficient police force for its area. Some of its powers are exercised independently, and some are subject to the approval of the Home Secretary. Subject to his approval, it appoints and, if it should prove necessary in the interests of efficiency, dismisses the chief officer and his immediate subordinates; in respect of the Metropolitan Police the Home Secretary advises the Queen on such appointments. The police authority also determines the size of the force and the quantity of accommodation and equipment, and controls its expenditure, 50 per cent of which is met from local authority funds and 50 per cent from the Home Office vote.[2] It receives an annual report from the chief officer, and may also call for a report on any matter connected with the policing of the area; though, if the chief officer considers that it is not in the public interest to disclose the information or that it is not needed for the discharge of the functions of the police authority, the request falls unless confirmed by the Home Secretary. In addition, the police authority is under a statutory duty to keep itself informed about the handling of complaints in its area.

d. *Ministerial responsibility*

10. As noted above, the Home Secretary is the police authority for the Metropolitan Police, and his duties and powers as such towards the Metropoli-

---

[1]This wide view of the independence of chief officers from the control of central and local government has been challenged, particularly on its historical basis. See for example Geoffrey Marshall: *"Police Accountability Revisited"*, in *Policy and Politics, ed. D Butler and A H Halsey,* London, MacMillan Press Ltd, 1978.

[2]The "local" 50 per cent attracts an element of rate support grant, which is centrally financed. Overall, some 61 per cent of police expenditure was centrally financed in 1979–80.

tan Police Commissioner are broadly similar to those of other police authorities towards their chief constables.

11. But he also has more general responsibilities in relation to the policing of England and Wales. His primary function in relation to the police is, in the words of the Police Act 1964, to "exercise his powers ... in such manner and to such extent as appears to him to be best calculated to promote the efficiency of the police". The means at his disposal include the right to approve, or initiate, schemes for the amalgamation of police forces; to approve the decisions of police authorities regarding the size of forces and the appointment and removal of chief officers; and, subject to consultation with representative bodies and to Parliamentary approval, to make regulations governing the conditions of entry into the police service, the promotion procedure, the disciplinary code and the pay and conditions of service of police officers. In addition, he provides and maintains common police services such as initial training of recruits, telecommunications services, the Police National Computer, the Police College and Forensic Science Laboratories. The cost of these services is met by central government in the same proportion as is other local authority expenditure through the rate support grant system. The Home Secretary is advised in the discharge of these functions by the Chief Inspector of Constabulary and his staff, who inspect forces (other than the Metropolitan Police), report to him on their efficiency and make an annual report, which is laid before Parliament.

12. Under the provisions of the Police Act 1964, the Home Secretary may require a chief officer to submit a report to him on any matter connected with the policing of his area. He also has power to set up an inquiry into any matter connected with the policing of any area. If he is not satisfied that the service is being effectively maintained, he may either require the police authority to remove a chief officer or withhold the normal 50 per cent Government grant towards police expenditure until improvements are made. These powers are used very rarely but they underpin his efforts to foster uniform methods and standards of policing and cooperation between forces. In addition, the Home Secretary provides guidance on various aspects of the substantive and procedural criminal law and on good police practice by means of Home Office Circulars to the police.

c. The citizen and the enforcement of the criminal law

13. This section deals briefly with the part that the citizen can play in enforcing the criminal law. The citizen's rights when he is suspected or accused of an offence are described where relevant in the later parts of the volume.

14. The involvement of the individual and the local community in the enforcement of the law did not entirely disappear with the establishment of a professional police force. The private citizen continues to have a right to bring private prosecutions, although it is subject to considerable restriction and is relatively rarely exercised nowadays (see paragraph 171). Some powers of arrest are also still exercisable by the private citizen,[1] although these too are

[1]See, for example, Criminal Law Act 1967, subsections 2(2) and 2(3), which are reproduced at paragraph 44.

5

rarely exercised except in particular circumstances, such as the arrest of suspected shoplifters by store detectives. Once a citizen has effected an arrest he is required to deliver the arrested person to a constable or magistrate. He has no power to detain or charge him. In exercising his power to arrest or the right to prosecute, the citizen is, to some extent, protected by law. Otherwise, he might be liable for torts such as assault, false imprisonment or malicious prosecution. In the law of tort the citizen has a right to "abate a nuisance" which is causing injury to his property; necessity, self-defence (or defence of someone else) and defence of the common weal are recognised as justification for action taken.

15. It remains a breach of the common law for a citizen not to give assistance to a constable if called upon to do so. Halsbury's Laws of England[1] states that:

"A constable who sees a breach of the peace committed or who is assaulted or obstructed when making an arrest may, if there is reasonable necessity, call upon private persons for assistance; a person who refuses, without lawful excuse, to assist a constable [in these circumstances] commits an indictable offence.

"At a time of riot, it is the duty of magistrates to keep the peace and restrain the rioters, and to pursue and take them; to this end a magistrate may call upon any of The Queen's subjects to assist and they are bound to comply upon reasonable warning."

16. Prosecutions for this offence are rare. There was a case in Gwent in 1969, arising from an incident in which a constable attempting to arrest a man for being drunk and disorderly became involved in a struggle with him and a number of other men who came to his assistance. The officer appealed to a person present to assist him, but he refused. This person was subsequently charged with the offence, convicted and fined £50.

17. There are some further offences (leaving aside perjury and attempting to pervert the course of justice) which may be relevant to the duty of the citizen to assist or refrain from hindering the police. Very briefly, it is an offence:

(a) to accept or agree to accept anything in consideration for refraining from disclosing information concerning the commission of an arrestable offence (Criminal Law Act 1967, s. 5(1));

(b) to do anything without lawful authority or reasonable excuse with intent to impede the apprehension or prosecution of a person who has committed an arrestable offence (Criminal Law Act 1967, s. 4(1), replacing the offence of being an accessory after the fact to felony);

(c) to cause wasteful employment of the police by making a false report of an offence (Criminal Law Act 1967, s. 5(2)); and

(d) to make hoax bomb threats (Criminal Law Act 1977, s. 51(2)).

But apart from these exceptional cases, the private citizen is under no general and legally enforceable duty to assist the police to discover or apprehend an

[1] Fourth Edition, Vol 11, paragraph 105.

offender. It used to be the law that someone who knew that a felony had been committed and failed to bring it to the notice of the authorities committed an offence. This duty was abolished in 1967. The only surviving offence of this type relates to treason; it is punishable with life imprisonment.

18. For the purposes of the law, the citizen's duty to report crimes has thus almost entirely disappeared. His sole remaining duty is not to frustrate the investigation and punishment of such crimes by active concealment. There is a statement in the preamble to the Judges' Rules that the rules do not affect the principle "That citizens have a duty to help a police officer to discover and apprehend offenders ...". Professor Antony Allott, of the University of London,[1] has commented that "if by 'duty' the judges mean a legal duty, then there is no warrant whatever under the current law of England for this statement; there is no legal duty". This was firmly stated by Lord Parker, C.J., in the case of *Rice v Connolly*.[2] He said:

> "... the sole question here is whether the appellant had a lawful excuse for refusing to answer the questions put to him. In my judgment he had. It seems to me quite clear that though every citizen has a moral duty or, if you like, a social duty to assist the police, there is no legal duty to that effect, and indeed the whole basis of the common law is that right of the individual to refuse to answer questions put to him by persons in authority ... In my judgment there is all the difference in the world between deliberately telling a false story, something which on no view a citizen has a right to do, and preserving silence or refusing to answer, something which he has every right to do."

As the case illustrates, there is a distinction to be drawn between social or moral responsibility (not enforceable) and legal obligation (enforceable).

19. There are some specific respects in which the citizen is under a legal duty to provide information. They include provisions under the road traffic and public order legislation as well as more widely known requirements under tax law. For example, a person at a public meeting may be required to give his name and address to a police officer.[3] Another important exception is in the Prevention of Terrorism (Temporary Provisions) Act 1976. Section 11(1) of the Act provides that a person who has information which he knows or believes might be of material assistance in preventing an act of terrorism, or in securing the apprehension, prosecution or conviction of any person for an offence involving the commission, preparation or instigation of such an act of terrorism, and who fails without reasonable excuse to disclose that information as soon as reasonably practicable to a constable is guilty of an offence. Acts done to obstruct the police in the execution of their duty may be offences such as refusal to move away when told to do so by police trying to disperse a dangerous public assembly.[4] Refusal of information is not generally an obstruction of the police in the performance of their duty,[5] although giving false information may be.

---

[1] In a paper prepared for the Royal Commission on Criminal Procedure in 1978 (unpublished).
[2] [1966] 2 QB 414.
[3] Public Order Act 1936, s. 6.
[4] *Duncan v Jones* [1936] 1 KB 218.
[5] *Rice v Connolly* [1966] 2 QB 414; *Gelberg v Miller* [1961] 1 All ER 291.

Police powers and procedures outside the police station

A. Stop and search

20. The police have no general authority to search members of the public. They may only do so where the person concerned agrees or in certain limited circumstances prescribed by law. A search in the absence of authority or consent will constitute an assault, and an action in the civil or criminal courts may follow. There are two situations in which a person may lawfully be searched against his will: where there is specific statutory authority to stop and search short of arrest, and in certain circumstances where he has been arrested.

21. A number of statutory provisions give the police power to stop and search persons without arresting them (though arrest may follow if evidence justifying it is discovered during the search). A list of them is at Appendix 1. The provisions which apply throughout England and Wales may be distinguished from those of limited, or local, application. The national powers are concerned with a wide range of articles, from drugs and firearms to wild plants and birds, and depend on there being reasonable suspicion that the person concerned is in unlawful possession of an article of the type specified in the statute. The local powers are directed against persons reasonably suspected of being in possession of stolen or unlawfully obtained goods.

22. An example of a local provision is s. 66 of the Metropolitan Police Act 1839 which gives a constable power to "stop, search and detain . . . any person who may be reasonably suspected of having or conveying in any manner any thing stolen or unlawfully obtained". Powers of this kind have long existed in English law and were originally linked with provisions making it an offence to be unable to account for unlawful possession of the relevant article. For example, s. 24 of the Metropolitan Police Courts Act 1839 provided that:

> "Every person who shall be brought before any of the said magistrates charged with having in his possession or conveying in any manner any thing which may be reasonably suspected of being stolen or unlawfully obtained, and who shall not give an account to the satisfaction of such magistrate how he came by the same, shall be deemed guilty of a misdemeanour . . ."

Thus if a constable, having exercised the power under s. 66, found a person in possession of something which he reasonably suspected to have been stolen or unlawfully obtained, he could take him before a magistrate, and, if the person could not satisfy the magistrate that he was in lawful possession of the article, he would be convicted of an offence.

23. Except for one or two provisions of limited geographical application,[1] this is not now the law. The power to stop, search and detain remains, but the offence provision has been repealed. Parliament refused to renew s. 54(2) of the British Transport Commission Act 1949 (a provision broadly similar to s. 24 of the 1839 Act) when this came before it in 1976.[2] The main concern was that offences of this kind reversed the onus of proof, requiring the defendant to prove his innocence rather than the prosecution his guilt. The Government announced its intention to repeal all the similar provisions in public general legislation (including s. 24 of the Metropolitan Police Courts Acts 1839) as soon as an opportunity presented itself; and this was done in the Criminal Law Act 1977. Similar offences in local legislation will shortly lapse under the Local Government Act 1972 (unless Parliament were to agree to their renewal).

24. The repeal of s. 24 of the 1839 Act and other similar provisions does not affect such powers as the police have to stop, search and detain persons suspected of being in unlawful possession of stolen goods; but any subsequent charges now have to be brought under the Theft Act 1968 which requires the normal standard of proof.

25. The police have wide powers to stop motor vehicles (and pedal cycles) for example to examine the mechanical condition of the vehicle. The police officer is not required to have any prior suspicion that an offence has been committed. These powers are conferred by the road traffic legislation primarily to ensure conformity with that legislation. By s. 159 of the Road Traffic Act 1972, however, a police constable in uniform may require any person driving a motor vehicle to stop the vehicle, and this is a general power. The constable must be acting in the execution of his duty, that is to say his conduct must be authorised by statute or recognised at common law and not involve any unjustified use of the powers associated with the duty. In the case of *R v Waterfield*[3] it was stated that an attempt by a constable to require a stationary car not to move so the police could examine it in order to obtain evidence would be an invalid exercise of the power to stop under s. 159 of the 1972 Act. It was implied, however, that had the driver (or other person associated with the car) been arrested for an offence, detention of the car as prospective evidence would have been a proper exercise of the constable's duty. Of this case, Lord Denning, M. R.[4] said: "The decision causes me some misgiving ... My comment on the case is this: the law should not allow wrongdoers to destroy evidence against them when it can be prevented." There is no correspondingly general power to search vehicles, but there is a number of statutes which gives the police specific power to do so. Under these statutes, for example, the police may search a vehicle when a person is arrested on

---

[1]Port of London Act 1968, s. 157(2), and The Mersey Docks and Harbour (Police) Order 1975, Art. 5(2).
[2]Under the terms of the Act the provision was subject to a time limit which had previously been extended on a number of occasions since 1949.
[3][1964] 1 QB 164.
[4]*Ghani v Jones* [1970] 1 QB 693 at p 708.

suspicion of poaching or of possessing a controlled drug; also they may search a vehicle when a person is suspected of possessing stolen property either if he is stopped in certain places, for example railway premises, or under local legislation.[1] Uniformed officers also have powers to stop a vehicle and require its driver to take a breath test under the breathalyser provisions of the drink and driving law.[2]

26. Comprehensive statistics on the exercise of powers to stop and search are not collected centrally, except in the case of searches for controlled drugs under the Misuse of Drugs Act 1971. Statistics on the use of this power and its results are at Appendix 2. In addition, at the Royal Commission's request the Metropolitan Police provided information from its own records on the number of stops of persons and of vehicles made under s. 66 of the Metropolitan Police Act 1839. In two one month periods in 1978 and 1979 over 40,000 and 35,000 such stops were recorded respectively. The numbers of arrests which resulted were over 5,000 and 4,000, giving arrest rates of 13 per cent and 12 per cent. Detailed figures, broken down by district within the Metropolitan Police area, are at Appendix 3.

27. The power to search an arrested person in certain circumstances is a common law power. Halsbury's Laws of England[3] states the law as follows:

"There is no general common law right to search a person who has been arrested, but such a person may be searched if there are reasonable grounds for believing (1) that he has on his person any weapon with which he might do himself or others an injury or any implement with which he might effect an escape, or (2) that he has in his possession evidence which is material to the offence with which he is charged".

The availability of the power of arrest is not justification for such search; the arrest must have been effected.

"The right to a personal search is clearly dependent not upon the *right* to arrest, but the *fact* of arrest and that at the time of a search the person is *in custodia legis*."[4]

B. Entry to and search of premises and seizure

28. Unless affirmative justification exists in law, a police officer or any other person may not enter private premises without the permission of the occupier. This right was established by the cases of *Leach v Money*[5] and *Entick v Carrington*[6] in the mid-eighteenth century. Any entry without permission or lawful authority is a trespass, and the trespasser is liable to a civil action for damages. There are, however, a considerable number of circumstances in which entry may lawfully be made by police officers or officials of public authorities without the consent of the occupier. Appendix 4 sets out the more

---

[1]For a list of some of these statutory provisions see Appendix 1.
[2]Road Traffic Act 1972, ss. 5–12.
[3]Fourth Edition, Vol 11, paragraph 121. The cases cited as authority for this summary are *Bessell v Wilson* (1853) 20 LTOS 233, *Leigh v Cole* (1853) 6 Cox CC 329, *Dillon v O'Brien & Davies* (1887) 16 Cox CC 245, *Tyler & Witt v London & South Western Railway Company* (1884) Cab & E 1 285, and *Elias v Pasmore* [1934] 2 KB 164.
[4]*Barnett and Grant v Campbell* (1902) 2 NZLR 484, 493, *per* Cooper, J.
[5](1765) 19 State Tr 1001.
[6](1765) 19 State Tr 1029.

important statutory provisions giving powers of entry to officials of public bodies; some of these can be exercised by a constable as well as by the particular public official. Those which relate solely to the police are described in paragraphs 29 to 41 below.

a. On arrest

29. The law on whether a constable has power to search the premises of an arrested person is not certain. He is empowered to search areas under the immediate control of the prisoner, as the right to search on arrest described in paragraph 27 suggests. This certainly covers the room in which he is arrested.[1] Beyond this the law is unclear. There does, however, seem to be a right on arrest to search the premises of the arrested person even if the arrest took place elsewhere. But such a search is unlawful if there is no connection between it and the offence for which the prisoner was arrested.[2]

b. Under authority of a search warrant

30. Many statutory provisions give magistrates power to issue warrants authorising entry to and search of premises. Not all of these fall to be executed by the police, as Appendix 4 indicates. A list of statutory provisions empowering magistrates to issue search warrants which usually fall to be executed by the police is at Table 5.1 of Appendix 5. One of the provisions under which search warrants are most frequently issued is s. 26 of the Theft Act 1968, which may be taken as an example. It reads:

"(1) If it is made to appear by information on oath before a justice of the peace that there is reasonable cause to believe that any person has in his custody or possession or on his premises any stolen goods, the justice may grant a warrant to search for and seize the same; but no warrant to search for stolen goods shall be addressed to a person other than a constable except under the authority of an enactment expressly so providing . . .

"(3) Where under this section a person is authorised to search premises for stolen goods, he may enter and search the premises accordingly, and may seize any goods he believes to be stolen goods."

31. The decision whether or not to issue a warrant is a matter for the magistrate concerned. The Lord Chancellor has advised those responsible for the training of magistrates that:

(a) it is the duty of a magistrate before issuing a search warrant to satisfy himself that in all the circumstances it is right to issue it;

(b) a magistrate may question the person swearing the information to this end; and

(c) although a police officer who applies for a warrant should not be expected to identify his informant, the magistrate may wish to know whether the informant is known to the officer, and whether it has been

---

[1] *Dillon v O'Brien & Davies* (1887) 16 Cox CC 245.
[2] *Jeffrey v Black* [1978] 1 QB 490. (Though in line with other recent authorities, evidence obtained during the search in this case was admitted at trial despite the unlawfulness of the search.)

possible to make further enquiries to verify the information and, if so, with what result.

Chief officers of police have been informed that this advice has been given, and the Home Office has stressed the need to take all reasonable steps to check the reliability of information before applying for a search warrant.

32. There is no provision for recording why in any particular case the magistrate authorised a search. No form of information for a search warrant is prescribed by law. The following is a precedent suggested by *Oke's Magisterial Formulist*

> "Information for search warrant for stolen goods (Theft Act, 1968, s. 26(1)).
> In the [county of   Petty Sessional Division of
>]. The information of A.B. of   who upon oath [or affirmation] states that he has reasonable cause to believe that C.D. of
>   has in his custody or possession or on his premises at
>   certain stolen goods within the meaning of s. 24 of the Theft Act, 1968, namely, (specify stolen goods)."

This is a purely formal document as is the prescribed information for an offence set out in paragraph 177. It is not a deposition. In *Herniman v Smith*[1] the House of Lords disapproved an information in the technical language of the warrant; the better practice would be for the information to be taken in the form of a deposition stating shortly the facts (see further at paragraph 183).

33. A constable or some other person may be named as the person who may execute the search warrant. But whoever is named, the warrant may be executed by any constable acting within his police area by virtue of subsection 102(2) of the Magistrates' Courts Act 1952. The warrant (unlike a warrant of arrest) must be in the possession of the person executing it. A number of statutory provisions specifically authorise the use of force, but there is probably common law authority for the use of force to execute a search warrant provided admission has been demanded and refused.[2]

34. The law relating to the seizure of items of possible evidential value discovered in a search of premises is described in Archbold, *Pleading, Evidence and Practice in Criminal Cases*[3], as follows:

> "Where the police enter a person's house by virtue of a warrant, or arrest a man lawfully, with or without a warrant, it is settled law that the police are entitled to take any goods which they find in his possession or in his house which they reasonably believe to be material evidence in relation to the crime for which he is arrested or for which they enter. If in the course of their search they come on any other goods which show him to be implicated in some other crime, they may take them provided they act reasonably and detain them no longer than is necessary."

---

[1][1938] AC 305.
[2]*Launock v Brown* (1819) 2 B and Ald 592.
[3]40th Edition, paragraph 1410. Cases cited in support include *Chic Fashions (West Wales) Ltd v Jones* [1968] 1 All ER 229 and *Garfinkel and Others v Metropolitan Police Commissioner* [1972] Crim LR 44.

35. A more general power to seize items of possible evidential value was stated by the Court of Appeal in *Ghani v Jones*.[1] While re-affirming the common law rule against arbitrary search the court held that, where no person has been arrested or charged, property may be seized if the following conditions are satisfied:

1. the police must have reasonable grounds for believing

   (a) that so serious an offence has been committed that it is of the first importance that the offenders should be caught and brought to justice;

   (b) that the article is either the fruit of the crime or the instrument by which it was committed, or material evidence to prove its commission;

   (c) that the person in possession of the article has himself committed or is implicated or is an accessory to the crime or at any rate that his refusal to hand over the article is quite unreasonable;

2. the police must not keep the article or prevent its removal for any longer than is reasonably necessary, and if it is a document and a copy will suffice, one must be taken and the original returned;

3. the lawfulness of the conduct of the police must be judged at the time and not by what happens subsequently.

c. Under other forms of written authority

36. A number of statutory provisions gives the police power to enter premises under a form of written authority other than a warrant. These are listed in Table 5.2 of Appendix 5. Under most of the provisions the power to issue the relevant authority is conferred on senior police officers.

d. To execute a warrant of arrest

37. A constable has authority to enter premises (forcibly if need be) in order to effect an arrest under warrant in cases where the accused is known to be on the premises[2] but it is less clear whether he has that power if he only has reasonable cause to believe that the wanted person is on the premises.

e. To execute an arrest without warrant

38. No general power, either at common law or in statute, exists for a police officer to enter premises to make an arrest without warrant, but subsection 2(6) of the Criminal Law Act 1967 provides that:

> "For the purpose of arresting a person under any power conferred by this section a constable may enter (if need be, by force) and search any place where that person is or where the constable, with reasonable cause, suspects him to be."

The power of entry applies to all "arrestable offences" (defined in s. 2 of the Act, which is reproduced at paragraph 44). Other powers of arrest without

---

[1]*Ghani v Jones* [1970] 1 QB 693.
[2]*Launock v Brown* (1819) 2 B and Ald 592.

warrant do not generally carry a power of entry but there are one or two exceptions, for example certain offences of remaining or entering on property.[1]

f. Other statutory powers of entry without warrant

39. There is in addition a number of statutory powers of entry without warrant where the purpose is neither to search the premises for the proceeds of crime nor to arrest an offender. Most of these powers apply to special premises, such as cinemas and betting shops rather than dwelling houses, and many are linked to systems of licensing the premises for particular activities. They may be regarded as powers of entry for the purpose of inspection. In some cases the person given the power of entry is a constable (see Appendix 6), but in many others the power of entry is given to an official of the local authority or some other public body (see Appendix 4).

g. Other common law powers of entry

40. Police officers possess some further powers of entry at common law. Most of these apply to situations which by their nature require urgent action. They may be summarised as follows:

(a) to deal with or prevent a breach of the peace. The power of entry to deal with a breach of the peace was established by the early nineteenth century. Legal authority for the power of entry to prevent a breach of the peace was not however established until this century in the case of *Thomas v Sawkins*.[2]

(b) In fresh pursuit of an escaped prisoner. Entry is permitted only where there has been a lawful arrest and the constable is in immediate pursuit. In other cases a warrant of arrest must be obtained, unless the offence is an arrestable one and entry is permitted under the Criminal Law Act 1967 (see paragraph 44).

(c) To save life or limb, or to prevent serious damage to property. The power extends to persons other than constables and entry must be made in a reasonable manner.

41. As with stops and searches of persons and vehicles, there exists no centrally collated information on searches of premises. Nor, as far as could be ascertained, do police forces keep their own records of such searches. At the Royal Commission's request, ten forces conducted a special survey of all searches of premises carried out in specified areas within their force boundaries. Information was collected on, amongst other things, the type of offence under investigation at the time the search was made; whether the search was conducted on warrant; and whether evidence was discovered which implicated the suspect in the offence under investigation, or any other offence. Nearly three-quarters of the searches were carried out in connection with offences of theft and handling or burglary, and approximately one-tenth in relation to drugs offences. The remainder were for a range of offences, some of them very serious and involving violence, and others relatively minor. Over half the searches were conducted before arrest with the consent of the suspect or

[1]Criminal Law Act 1977, Part II, particularly s. 11.
[2][1935] 2 KB 249.

householder or after arrest but without a warrant. A third or so of the searches were backed by a warrant issued by a magistrate, but superintendents' warrants were rarely used. In all, a little over two-fifths of the searches were successful in the sense of uncovering evidence implicating the suspect in an offence, whether that under investigation or another offence, or, in a small number of searches, resulting in material linking other persons to an offence. Fuller details of the method and results of the survey are given in Appendix 7.

C. Arrest

42. Arrest is the deprivation of liberty, a denial of personal freedom. In its ordinary sense, "arrest" distinguishes between the situation where a person is free to go as he pleases and that where he has been told he is in custody. Confusing and sometimes contradictory statements are to be found in the case law as to the meaning of arrest. For example, arrest has been described as the beginning of imprisonment.[1] Whether or not a person has been arrested has been said to depend not on the legality of the arrest but on whether he has been deprived of his liberty.[2] But it has also been said that while every arrest involves the deprivation of liberty the converse is not necessarily true. Arrest can only lawfully be effected in the exercise of an asserted authority. If a person is put under restraint arbitrarily or for some expedient motive, he is imprisoned. He may think he is under arrest if the restraint is exercised by a police officer. In the case of *R v Brown*, where two police officers detained a person who fled from them, thereby arousing their suspicions, Shaw, L. J. said:[3]

> "The officers concerned reacted to what they regarded as suspicious conduct by imprisoning him for so long as might be necessary to confirm their general suspicions or to show them to be unfounded. In the first event they could then arrest him on a specific charge; in the second event they would be bound to release him. In either case, they may have rendered themselves liable to pay damages for trespass and false imprisonment."

43. In 1978, 24 per cent of those proceeded against for indictable offences were brought before the court by way of summons and 76 per cent following arrest and charge. The corresponding figures for non-indictable offences were 87 per cent (summons) and 13 per cent (arrest and charge).[4] These figures, however, give a misleading picture of the proportions of defendants who are arrested; proceedings by way of summons may often be instituted following the arrest and release of a suspect.[5] The figures for non-indictable offences are heavily influenced by motoring offences, for the majority of which no power of arrest exists.

[1] See *Christie v Leachinsky* [1947] AC 573 where Lord Du Parcq said at p 600: "Arrest (as is said in Dalton's Country Justice, 1727 ed. at p 580) may be called the beginning of imprisonment."
[2] See Lord Dilhorne in *Spicer v Holt* [1977] AC 987 at p 1000, and Winn, L. J. in *R v Sadler* [1970] 1 WLR 416 at p 423.
[3] [1977] 64 Cr App R 231 at pp 234 ff.
[4] See Appendix 8 for breakdown by offence.
[5] For further elaboration of this point see R Gemmill and R F Morgan-Giles: *Arrest, Charge and Summons—Current Practice and Resource Implications*, (Royal Commission on Criminal Procedure Research Study No 8, London HMSO 1980). For further information on the institution of proceedings generally, see Chapter 6.

Chapter 2

a. Arrest without warrant

44. The most important general powers of arrest without warrant are set out in s. 2 of the Criminal Law Act 1967 which provides as follows:

"(1) The powers of summary arrest conferred by the following subsections shall apply to offences for which the sentence is fixed by law or for which a person (not previously convicted) may under or by virtue of any enactment be sentenced to imprisonment for a term of five years, and to attempts to commit any such offence; and in this Act, including any amendment made by this Act in any other enactment, 'arrestable offence' means any such offence or attempt.

(2) Any person may arrest without warrant anyone who is, or whom he, with reasonable cause, suspects to be, in the act of committing an arrestable offence.

(3) Where an arrestable offence has been committed, any person may arrest without warrant anyone who is, or whom he, with reasonable cause, suspects to be, guilty of the offence.

(4) Where a constable, with reasonable cause, suspects that an arrestable offence has been committed, he may arrest without warrant anyone whom he, with reasonable cause, suspects to be guilty of the offence.

(5) A constable may arrest without warrant any person who is, or whom he, with reasonable cause, suspects to be, about to commit an arrestable offence.

(6) For the purpose of arresting a person under any power conferred by this section a constable may enter (if need be, by force) and search any place where that person is or where the constable, with reasonable cause, suspects him to be.

(7) This section shall not affect the operation of any enactment restricting the institution of proceedings for an offence, nor prejudice any power of arrest conferred by law apart from this section."

The definition of "arrestable offence" in subsection (1) covers most, but not all, serious offences including, for example, murder, wounding, theft, arson and other offences of criminal damage. Some serious offences not covered by this definition carry specific powers of arrest[1] (see further paragraph 46 and Appendix 9), but others such as indecent assault on a woman (under s. 14 of the Sexual Offences Act 1956) do not carry any power of arrest without warrant. It should be noted that the powers conferred on a constable by subsections (4) and (5) are wider than the powers conferred, by subsections (2) and (3), on "any person" (which means either a constable or a private citizen). Under the latter provisions a citizen may arrest a person only if that person is in the act of committing an arrestable offence or, in effect, only where an arrestable offence has clearly been committed. Subsection (7) preserves powers of arrest contained in other statutes (again see paragraph 46 and Appendix 9) and common law powers of arrest. The only common law power of arrest remaining is where a breach of the peace has been committed

---

[1] For example firearms offences, carrying an offensive weapon, and going equipped for theft or burglary.

16

(or is reasonably apprehended) and there are reasonable grounds for apprehending its continuance or immediate renewal.

45. Further powers of arrest are available in respect of certain offences against children or young persons specified in Schedule 1 to the Children and Young Persons Act 1933. By subsection 13(1) of that Act a constable may arrest without warrant:

(a) any person who within his view commits any of the offences mentioned in Schedule 1 to the Act if the constable does not know and cannot ascertain his name and residence;

(b) any person who has committed, or whom a constable has reason to believe has committed, any of the offences mentioned in Schedule 1 if the constable has reasonable ground for believing that he might abscond or does not know and cannot ascertain his name and address.

Some of the offences mentioned in Schedule 1 to the 1933 Act are arrestable offences under s. 2 of the Criminal Law Act 1967 (see paragraph 44), for example murder and manslaughter of a person under 17. The powers under s. 2 of the 1967 Act are presumably available in respect of such offences. But the limited power of arrest in subsection 13(1) of the 1933 Act may be contrasted with the additional power to detain under subsection 13(2) of the Act (see paragraph 67).

46. Many statutory provisions also expressly confer powers of arrest without warrant for particular offences even though their maximum penalty is less than the Criminal Law Act standard of five years' imprisonment. Some of them confer powers of arrest on persons other than, or in addition to, the police, for example the powers of arrest under s. 5 of the Sexual Offences Act 1967, s. 11 of the Prevention of Offences Act 1951, and s. 11 of the Coinage Offences Act 1936 are exercisable by anyone, not only a police officer. In other cases powers of arrest are conferred on particular persons, for example an immigration officer (Immigration Act 1971, Schedule 2) or a customs officer (Customs and Excise Act 1952, s. 274). A list of powers conferred on the police is at Appendix 9. As the list shows, the provisions vary considerably. Some apply only where a person is seen or found committing the offence specified, others where there is reasonable suspicion that the relevant offence is being or has been committed. A number of powers of arrest may be exercised only if the name and address of the suspected offender cannot be ascertained to the satisfaction of the police officer. In some of these cases the power of arrest is also (or alternatively) linked to suspicion that the person may abscond.[1]

b. Arrest under warrant

47. Several statutory provisions[2] enable magistrates to issue warrants of arrest for offences. The most frequently used is s. 1 of the Magistrates' Courts Act 1952, which reproduced earlier provisions. Subsection (1) of that section provides, in part, that:

---

[1]Not all offences lacking any power of arrest without warrant are necessarily technical or trivial, for example the offence of indecent assault on a woman mentioned in paragraph 44.
[2]Including the Magistrates' Courts Act 1952, s. 77, Extradition Act 1870, s. 8 and the Fugitive Offenders Act 1967, s. 6.

"Upon an information being laid before a justice of the peace for any county that any person has, or is suspected of having, committed any offence, the justice may . . .

(b) issue a warrant to arrest that person and bring him before a magistrates' court . . .

Provided that the justice shall not issue a warrant unless the information is in writing and substantiated on oath."

A limitation has since been added by subsection 24(1) of the Criminal Justice Act 1967, which provides that:

"A warrant for the arrest of any person who has attained the age of seventeen shall not be issued under section 1 of the Magistrates' Courts Act 1952 . . . unless

(a) the offence to which the warrant relates is an indictable offence or is punishable with imprisonment or

(b) the address of the defendant is not sufficiently established for a summons to be served on him."

48. This provision has three intentions: first, that where a person is alleged to have committed a minor offence the normal procedure for bringing him before a court should be by summons, rather than by arrest; second that, in general, offences which are not punishable by imprisonment should not attract arrest, which is "the beginning of imprisonment", but third, that an arrest can be justified where the summons procedure will not be effective in bringing an alleged offender before the courts.

49. Where there is power to issue a warrant, the procedure is for a police officer (or any other person) to "lay an information" before a magistrate.[1] The decision whether or not to issue a warrant is then a matter for the discretion of the magistrate. This discretion is not reviewable.[2] If the magistrate decides that it is proper to issue a warrant, he must then further consider whether or not to endorse it for bail.[3] If the warrant is so endorsed, the police are required to release the accused (subject to any conditions of bail stated in the endorsement) to appear before a magistrates' court as specified in the endorsement. If the warrant does not authorise the police to release the accused on bail then he must be brought before the magistrates' court named in the warrant immediately.[4]

c. *Execution of a power of arrest*

50. The mode of exercising a power of arrest is not prescribed by statute, but the courts have laid down certain requirements. Halsbury's *Laws of England*[5] summarises the law on the act of arrest as follows:

---

[1]Laying an information is discussed in paragraphs 175 to 183.
[2]See further paragraph 183, where the law and practice on issuing a warrant are discussed in more detail.
[3]Magistrates' Courts Act 1952, s. 93.
[4]See the prescribed form of warrant, form 3 in the Schedule to the Magistrates' Courts (Forms) Rules 1968.
[5]Fourth Edition, Vol 11 paragraph 99

"Arrest consists in the seizure or touching of a person's body with a view to his restraint; words may however amount to an arrest if, in the circumstances of the case, they are calculated to bring, and do bring, to a person's notice that he is under compulsion and he thereafter submits to the compulsion."

51. In *Alderson v Booth*[1] Lord Parker C. J. said:

"There are a number of cases both ancient and modern, as to what constitutes an arrest, and, whereas there was a time when it was held that there could be no lawful arrest unless there was an actual seizing or touching, it is quite clear that that is no longer the law. There may be an arrest by mere words, by saying 'I arrest you' without any touching, provided of course that the defendant submits and goes with the police officer. Equally it is clear, as it seems to me, that an arrest is constituted when any form of words is used which in the circumstances of the case were calculated to bring to the defendant's notice, and did bring to the defendant's notice, that he was under compulsion and thereafter he submitted to that compulsion."

52. An arresting officer must therefore make it clear to the person arrested, either by action or words, that he is under arrest and ensure that he is aware of the ground of the arrest. Here the leading case is *Christie v Leachinsky*[2], where, in the course of his judgment, Viscount Simon set out the rules as follows:

"(1) If a policeman arrests without warrant upon reasonable suspicion of felony, or of other crime of a sort which does not require a warrant, he must in ordinary circumstances inform the person arrested of the true ground of arrest. He is not entitled to keep the reason to himself or to give a reason which is not the true reason. In other words a citizen is entitled to know on what charge or on suspicion of what crime he is seized. (2) If the citizen is not so informed but is nevertheless seized, the policeman, apart from certain exceptions, is liable for false imprisonment. (3) The requirement that the person arrested should be informed of the reason why he is seized naturally does not exist if the circumstances are such that he must know the general nature of the alleged offence for which he is detained. (4) The requirement that he should be so informed does not mean that technical or precise language need be used. The matter is a matter of substance, and turns on the elementary proposition that in this country a person is, *prima facie*, entitled to his freedom and is only required to submit to restraints upon him if he knows in substance the reason why it is claimed that this restraint should be imposed. (5) The person arrested cannot complain that he has not been supplied with the above information as and when he should be, if he himself produces the situation which makes it practically impossible to inform him, eg by immediate counter attack or by running away."

53. If arrest is resisted, force may have to be used. It has long been the law that in making an arrest a police officer is entitled to use force, but no more

---

[1] [1969] 2 QB 216 at p. 220.
[2] [1947] AC 573 at pp 587–588.

force than is necessary. The common law principle is now contained in subsection 3(1) of the Criminal Law Act 1967, which reads as follows:

"A person may use such force as is reasonable in the circumstances . . . in effecting or assisting in the lawful arrest of offenders or suspected offenders or of persons unlawfully at large."

The subsection applies both to arrest under warrant and to arrest without warrant.

54. In exceptional cases, in order to restrain an arrested person, it may be necessary to use handcuffs. On this the Home Office has issued the following guidance to chief officers of police:[1]

"Whether a prisoner should be handcuffed must depend on the particular circumstances, as for instance the nature of the charge and the conduct and temper of the person in custody. Handcuffing should not be resorted to unless there is fair ground for supposing that violence may be used or an escape attempted. Handcuffing cannot be justified unless there are good special reasons for resorting to it."

55. Where the police act in execution of a magistrate's warrant they are protected under the Constables Protection Act 1750 from a successful civil action. This does not apply to an action in respect of the manner of execution of a warrant where this is unlawful.

d. Detention on arrest

56. Where a private citizen effects an arrest, he must either take the arrested person before a magistrate as soon as reasonably practicable or hand him over to the police without unreasonable delay.[2] The normal (and virtually exclusive) practice today is to hand the arrested person over to the police. Where a constable arrests a person without warrant the position is governed by s. 38 of the Magistrates' Courts Act 1952 (see paragraphs 65 and 66). Where a constable arrests on warrant, he must comply with the terms of the warrant which will require either the production of the accused at court immediately or his release on bail.[3]

D. Other powers and procedures in the investigation of crime

a. Surveillance by the police

57. In essence, surveillance amounts to no more than a more intensive form of observation and/or hearing undertaken by the police as a means of confirming or dispelling a suspicion. There is in this country no specific law which prevents a person from maintaining observation upon or from seeking to overhear the activities of another person, except to the extent that the law of trespass may apply. In principle therefore the use of surveillance by the police (or by any private citizen) is not in itself unlawful; and the law does not confer

---

[1]*Consolidated Circular to the Police on Crime and Kindred Matters,* 1977 edition, paragraph 4.65.

[2]Archbold, 40th edition, paragraph 2806; *John Lewis and Co v Tims* [1952] AC 676.

[3]See form 3 in the Schedule to the Magistrates' Courts (Forms) Rules 1968. The requirement to bring the accused (if not bailed) before the court immediately is not qualified in any way. See further paragraph 49.

on the police particular powers or privileges which would assist them in their surveillance activities.

58. The courts will admit evidence of what an officer may have seen or heard with the aid of technical equipment which enables him to observe or hear an offence being committed by a person who is unaware of his presence. There have been a number of cases in which the courts have held that evidence obtained by eavesdropping is admissible. In *R v Ali and Hussain*[1] the police used a tape recorder to eavesdrop upon conversations between two prisoners. The Court of Criminal Appeal held that the evidence was properly admitted:

> "The method of the informer and of the eavesdropper is commonly used in the detection of crime ... the method of taking the recording cannot affect the admissibility as a matter of law although it must remain very much a matter for the discretion of the judge."

Similarly, in *R v Stewart*[2] the Court of Appeal held that evidence of a police officer who had eavesdropped on a conversation between two suspects by sitting in a neighbouring cell was properly admitted. In *R v Keeton*[3] the court held that the evidence of a police officer who had listened to a telephone conversation which the defendant made while detained at the police station was properly admitted. There has also been a number of cases in which the courts have accepted evidence obtained by equipment used in visual surveillance. For example in a case in 1975 in which a number of workers at Billingsgate Market were convicted of stealing fish, evidence of criminal offences which took place at night-time was obtained by means of video and light amplification equipment.

59. The principles which the police should apply to the use of surveillance equipment have been developed in consultation between the Home Office, HM Inspectors of Constabulary and chief officers of police. These guidelines were commended to the police in a Home Office Circular in October 1978. As an example of how police forces have instituted procedures for the issue and use of surveillance equipment an extract from the general orders of one force is given at Appendix 10.

b. *The interception of communications*

60. The Government has recently reviewed the arrangements for the interception of letters and telephone calls, and has published a White Paper *"The Interception of Communications in Great Britain"*[4] which brings up to date the review by the Committee of Privy Councillors under the Chairmanship of Lord Birkett in 1957.[5] The Home Secretary's announcement in April 1980 of the publication of the White Paper is at Appendix 11.

---

[1] [1965] 2 All ER 464.
[2] (1970) 54 Cr App R 210.
[3] (1970) 54 Cr App R 267.
[4] London HMSO Cmnd 7873.
[5] London HMSO Cmnd 283.

Police powers and procedures at the police station

A. The legal basis of detention at the police station

a. The general rule on detention

61. The relevant law is clear and is summarised in the introduction to the Judges' Rules (reproduced at Appendix 12) which states the principle:

> "that police officers, otherwise than by arrest, cannot compel any person against his will to come to or remain in any police station."

This does not preclude a person from deciding, or agreeing, to go to a police station voluntarily. But if, in such a case, the person changes his mind, it is in law open to him to leave the police station. The courts have held that if he does so and is prevented from leaving, or told that he will be prevented, he is to be regarded as being under arrest; but if it is not made clear to him that he is under arrest, then he is not to be so regarded and is entitled to leave the police station, using reasonable force to do so.[1]

62. The courts have held that powers of arrest may be exercised only where the requisite grounds of suspicion already exist, and not for the purpose of establishing such grounds. In *R v Lemsatef*[2] (a case involving customs officers) Lord Justice Lawton stressed this point:

> "it must be clearly understood that neither customs officers, nor police officers, have any right to detain somebody for the purposes of getting them to help with their enquiries."

In *R v Houghton and Franchiosy*[3] the Court of Appeal again in the person of Lawton L. J. reiterated the point. The Court wished to state

> "in the clearest possible terms that police officers can only arrest for offences. If they think that there is any difference between detaining or arresting, they are mistaken. They have no power, save under the Prevention of Terrorism (Temporary Provisions) Act 1976, to arrest anyone so that they can make enquiries about him ... Maybe the police should have powers to detain for inquiries in cases such as this. They have not got them now. Parliament might have to decide whether they should have them. The courts cannot do so."

---

[1] *R v Inwood* [1973] 2 All ER 645. See further, D N Clarke and D Feldman: *"Arrest by Any Other Name"*, [1979] Crim LR 702.
[2] [1977] 2 All ER 835.
[3] (1978) 68 Cr App R 197.

In short, save for the special case of the prevention of terrorism legislation, no-one may be arrested solely in order to enable the police to question him.

b. Restrictions on detention; police bail

63. When an arrested person is brought to the police station, the station officer should enquire whether the arrest is justified. If it is not, the person should be released. If there is no power to make an arrest (for example because there are insufficient grounds of suspicion to do so), the police officers concerned may be held liable in a subsequent action for damages for false imprisonment. During the period of detention, an application for a writ of *habeas corpus* may be made on the person's behalf, although in 1977 there were only 55 and in 1978 24 such applications and a large proportion of these related to detention under the immigration legislation.

64. There are restrictions on the period a person may be detained in police custody.[1] The person who is arrested under warrant on a criminal charge must be taken before the court issuing the warrant (unless it is endorsed for bail) immediately.[2] In the case of a person arrested without warrant, there are five possible outcomes.[3] First, he may be released without charge if, after making the arrest, the police discover evidence which exculpates the suspect, or they decide there is insufficient evidence to justify his prosecution.[4] Second, he may be released, the question of prosecution being still under consideration (the intention being, if he is prosecuted, that this will be by way of summons). Third, he may be released on bail to attend at a specified police station if the inquiries into the offence cannot be completed forthwith. Fourth, he may be released on bail to appear before a magistrates' court. Fifth, he may be retained in custody and brought before a magistrates' court as soon as practicable.[5] In the case of a juvenile retained in custody the requirement is to bring him before the court within 72 hours (see paragraph 91).

65. The procedure for police bail and the retention of an arrested person in custody are regulated by s. 38 of the Magistrates' Courts Act 1952 as amended by the Bail Act 1976, which states that:

"(1) On a person's being taken into custody for any offence without a warrant, a police officer not below the rank of inspector, or the police officer in charge of the police station to which the person is brought, may, and if it will not be practicable to bring him before a magistrates' court within 24 hours after his being taken into custody, shall, inquire into the case and, unless the offence appears to the officer to be a serious one, grant him bail in accordance with the Bail Act 1976 subject to a duty to appear before a magistrates' court at such time and place as the officer appoints.

(1A) Where a person has been granted bail under subsection (1) above, the magistrates' court before which he is to appear may appoint a later

---

[1]For restrictions on the power of private citizens to detain after arrest see paragraph 56.
[2]See paragraph 56.
[3]See Gemmill and Morgan-Giles, *op cit.*
[4]*Wiltshire v Barrett* [1966] 1 QB 312, and subsection 28(4) of the Children and Young Persons Act 1969.
[5]Magistrates' Courts Act 1952, subsections 38(1), (2) and (4), see paragraph 65.

time as the time at which he is to appear and may enlarge the recognizances of any sureties for him to that time.

(2) Where, on a person's being taken into custody for an offence without a warrant, it appears to any such officer as aforesaid that the inquiry into the case cannot be completed forthwith, he may grant him bail in accordance with the Bail Act 1976 subject to a duty to appear at such a police station and at such a time as the officer appoints, unless he previously receives a notice in writing from the officer in charge of that police station that his attendance is not required; and the recognizance of any surety for that person may be enforced as if it were conditioned for the appearance of that person before a magistrates' court for the petty sessions area in which the police station named in the recognizance is situated.

(3) [repealed].

(4) Where a person is taken into custody for an offence without a warrant and is retained in custody, he shall be brought before a magistrates' court as soon as practicable."

66. Where a person is not bailed or otherwise released, and is retained in custody, subsection (4) requires him to be brought before a court as soon as practicable. Subsections (1) and (4) taken together distinguish between serious and less serious cases. In both types of case the police must bring the arrested man before a magistrates' court "as soon as practicable" but in the latter they are subject to the additional requirement that they must release the man on bail if it will not be practicable to bring him before a court within 24 hours. There is, however, no definition of the terms "serious offence" or "as soon as practicable" and no reference to the proper reasons for not releasing the arrested person.

67. An additional power to detain in custody is provided by subsection 13(2) of the Children and Young Persons Act 1933. Under that provision, where a person is arrested for an offence mentioned in Schedule 1 of that Act, he shall be released on bail unless his release would tend to defeat the ends of justice or cause injury or danger to the child or young person against whom the offence is alleged to have been committed. The offences mentioned in Schedule 1 to the 1933 Act include murder and manslaughter of a child or young person and various sexual offences and offences of violence committed against a child or young person.

B. Questioning by the police and the right of silence

a. Questioning and the Judges' Rules

68. It has always been an essential part of the criminal justice system that there was some official body or person to inquire into offences. At one time it was the jury; by 1700 the function had passed to the justices of the peace, and by the early part of the nineteenth century the *de facto* power was in the hands of the police. This inquiry involved questioning people who might have knowledge of the offence, one or more of whom might well turn out to be a suspect. The questioning of suspects by the police included those who had been

arrested and were being kept in custody. Although a person cannot be arrested merely for the purpose of questioning,[1] the police may question someone who has been lawfully arrested and is in police custody. This power has never been statutorily stated, though judicial guidance has been given in decided cases and in the Judges' Rules and Administrative Directions to the Police.[2]

69. Early authoritative statements as to the powers of the police to question were made by Channell, J. who in *R v Knight and Thayer*[3] said:

> "When [a constable] has taken anyone into custody ... he ought not to question the prisoner ... I am not aware of any distinct rule of evidence that, if such improper questions are asked, the answers to them are inadmissible, but there is clear authority for saying that the judge at the trial may in his discretion refuse to allow the answers to be given in evidence."

In *R v Booth and Jones*[4] the same judge said that police officers were entitled to ask questions for information, as to whether to charge a person. But the moment a police officer had decided to charge a person or to take him into custody, he ought not to question him.

> "A magistrate or judge cannot do it, and a police officer certainly has no right to do so."

These two statements were quoted with approval by Lord Sumner in *Ibrahim v R.*[5] A similar view was stated by Lord Brampton (formerly Hawkins, J.) in his Preface to Vincent's Police Code in 1882, though he also said there:

> "[A constable] ought not, by anything he says or does, to invite or encourage an accused person to make any statement *without first cautioning him* that he is not bound to say anything tending to incriminate himself, and that anything he says may be used against him." (Emphasis added.)

And the first set of Judges' Rules, issued in 1912, make it clear that a suspect could be questioned provided he was first cautioned. The caution is:

> "You are not obliged to say anything unless you wish to do so but what you say may be put into writing and given in evidence."[6]

70. The present Rules (which are prefaced by an important note stating certain principles not affected by the Rules) were issued to the police in 1964 following a review of the earlier Rules by the judges. Appended to them is a set of Administrative Directions to the Police, drawn up by the Home Office and approved by the judges. These are concerned with particular detailed

---

[1]See paragraphs 42 ff; the arresting officer must have reasonable cause to suspect that the arrested person is guilty of an offence.
[2]These are at Appendix 12.
[3](1905) 20 Cox CC 711.
[4](1910) 5 Cr App R 177.
[5][1914] AC 599.
[6]An account of the history of the Judges' Rules is at Appendix 13. For research on the operation of the Rules in practice see Softley and others: *Police Interrogation: An Observational Study in Four Police Stations* (Royal Commission on Criminal Procedure Research Study No 4, London HMSO 1980); Barrie Irving with Linden Hilgendorf: *Police Interrogation: A Case Study of Current Practice* (Royal Commission on Criminal Procedure Research Study No 2, London HMSO 1980).

25

points arising from the Rules, including the keeping of records, the provision of refreshment, and the circumstances in which juveniles and mentally handicapped persons should be interviewed. A re-issue of the document in June 1978 incorporated some minor changes in the Administrative Directions. The general effect of the Rules may be summarised as follows. A police officer may question a suspect whether in custody or not (Rule I). He need not caution the suspect unless and until he has enough evidence to suspect that he has committed an offence (Rule II). In Rule II the word "evidence" means information of a nature that would be admissible as evidence in court: *R v Osborne*.[1] The suspect is not required to answer questions put to him by the police. As Lord Parker, C. J. said in *Rice v Connolly*[2] ". . . the whole basis of the common law is the right of the individual to refuse to answer questions put to him by persons in authority . . ." Accordingly, the caution should have a number of effects. In addition to advising him of his "right of silence" it informs the suspect that he may be in peril of prosecution; and it tends to help in showing the voluntariness of any statement subsequently made. But the Rules place no limit on the questions which may be put to a suspect before charge. And neither the Rules nor any common law principle require that if the suspect indicates that he wishes to remain silent no more questions may be asked. Further, evidence of the questions posed and the fact that the suspect did not answer, or gave an evasive answer, is admissible (see paragraph 81).

71. As soon as a police officer has enough evidence to charge the suspect (that is, enough to establish a *prima facie* case)[3] he should cause him to be charged without delay and thereafter may not question him about the offence charged (paragraph (d) of the Introduction to the Judges' Rules and Rule III). When a person is charged, or informed that he may prosecuted, he is again cautioned. The caution is similar to that quoted in paragraph 69 except that the suspect is told that anything he says will (as distinct from may) be taken down in writing (Rule III(a)).

72. If, at any stage, the suspect wishes to make a written statement, the Rules prescribe the form it should take. The statement may be written either by the person himself or by a police officer. The Rules state that in either event the statement should be in the suspect's own words, without prompting or questioning and the suspect is required to write and sign a declaration indicating that he has been cautioned and makes the statement of his own free will (Rule IV).

b. Breach of the Judges' Rules

73. The introductory note to the Rules, the Rules themselves, and the Administrative Directions are usually included together in a reference to "the Judges' Rules", and this wide meaning of the Rules applies in particular to references to a breach of the Rules. It is clear that the Rules are not rules of law.[4] It is also clear that an admission obtained in breach of them is not

[1] [1973] 1 QB 678.
[2] [1966] 2 QB 414.
[3] This is a higher standard than enough information to found a reasonable suspicion, see Lord Devlin in *Hussein v Chong Fook Kam* [1970] AC 942.
[4] *R v Voisin* (1918) 13 Cr App R 89; *R v Wattam* (1952) 36 Cr App R 72; *R v Prager* [1972] 1 WLR 260.

necessarily thereby rendered inadmissible. But, as the introductory note to the Rules states:

> "Non-conformity with these Rules may render answers and statements liable to be excluded from evidence in subsequent criminal proceedings."

The judge (or magistrates' court) has a discretion to exclude a confession or admission obtained in breach of the Rules. It was stated in *R v Prager*[1] that non-observance of the Rules "may, and at times does, lead to the exclusion of an alleged confession; but ultimately all turns on the judge's decision whether, breach or no breach, it has been shown to have been made voluntarily."

74. In the introductory note to the Judges' Rules it is stated that the Rules do not affect the principle:

> "That is a fundamental condition of the admissibility in evidence against any person, equally of any oral answer given by that person to a question put by a police officer and of any statement made by that person, that it shall have been voluntary, in the sense that it has not been obtained from him by fear of prejudice or hope of advantage, exercised or held out by a person in authority, or by oppression."[2]

75. This principle requires that a statement (which includes a confession or admission)[3] be free and voluntary and not preceded by any inducement held out by a person in authority.[4] Mere exhortations to tell the truth, or to tell what he (the suspect) knows, have been held to render an admission involuntary and therefore inadmissible. A person in authority is, in effect, anyone whom the suspect might reasonably suppose to be capable of influencing the course of the prosecution, and this will obviously include a constable.[5] An inducement made by a person not, in this sense, in authority but in the presence of a constable may render a confession inadmissible. Examples of confessions held to be inadmissible for this reason are:

(a) Where a surgeon told the suspect "you are under suspicion and you had better tell all you know".[6]

(b) Where the suspect's father said to him "Put your cards on the table. Tell them the lot. If you did not hit him they cannot hang you".[7]

(c) Where a social worker said to the suspect (who was a juvenile) "Do not admit anything you have not done. But it is always the best policy to be honest. If you were at the house, tell the officers about it. If you were concerned, tell him about it and get the matter cleared up."[8]

---

[1][1972] 1 WLR 260 at p 266.
[2]This was approved as a correct statement of the law in *Commissioners of Customs and Excise v Harz and Power* [1967] 1 AC 760; and *R v Prager* [1972] 1 WLR 260.
[3]*Commissioners of Customs and Excise v Harz and Power* [1967] 1 AC 760, 817.
[4]See Cave, J. in *R v Thompson* [1893] 2 QB 12.
[5]See *Cross on Evidence*, 5th edition, p 541.
[6]*R v Kingston* (1830) 172 ER 752.
[7]*R v Cleary* (1963) 48 Cr App R 116.
[8]*The Times* January 18 1978.

76. The principle also requires that any statement obtained from a suspect must be voluntary in the sense that it has not been obtained from him by oppression.[1] In *R v Priestley*[2] Sachs, J. said that oppression:

". . . in the context of the principles under consideration imports something which tends to sap, and has sapped, that free will which must exist before a confession is voluntary . . . Whether or not there is oppression in an individual case depends upon many elements. I am not going into all of them. They include such things as the length of time of any individual period of questioning, the length of time intervening between periods of questioning, whether the accused person had been given proper refreshment or not, and the characteristics of the person who makes the statement. What may be oppressive as regards a child, an invalid or an old man or somebody inexperienced in the ways of this world may turn out not to be oppressive when one finds that the accused person is of a tough character and an experienced man of the world."

And in an address to the Bentham Club in 1968, Lord MacDermott described "oppressive questioning" as:

"questioning which by its nature, duration, or other attendant circumstances (including the fact of custody) excites hopes (such as the hope of release) or fears, or so affects the mind of the subject that his will crumbles and he speaks when otherwise he would have stayed silent."

Both of these descriptions were adopted by the Court of Appeal in *R v Prager*.[3] It must follow that an admission obtained by torture, physical or psychological, cannot be voluntary and is therefore inadmissible.

c. The right of silence

77. The so-called right of silence is, in fact, another way of stating the common law principle that no man can be required (that is compelled) to incriminate himself. In *R v Sang*[4] Lord Diplock said:

"The underlying rationale of this branch of the criminal law, though it may originally have been based on ensuring the reliability of confessions is, in my view, now to be found in the maxim, *nemo debet prodere se ipsum*, no one can be required to be his own betrayer, or in its popular English mistranslation 'the right to silence'."

The concept is succinctly stated in the following extract from the decision of the US Supreme Court in *Miranda v Arizona:*[5]

"The privilege against self-incrimination, which has had a long and expansive historical development, is the essential mainstay of our adversary system and guarantees to the individual 'the right to remain silent unless he chooses to speak in the unfettered exercise of his own free will',

---

[1] The reference to oppression was added to the introduction to the Judges' Rules in 1964 following the observations of Lord Parker C. J. in *Callis v Gunn* (1963) 48 Cr App R 36 at p 40 condemning confessions obtained in an oppressive manner.
[2] (1966) 50 Cr App R 183.
[3] [1972] 1 WLR 260.
[4] [1979] 2 All ER 1222 at p 1230.
[5] 384 US 436 (1966).

during a period of custodial interrogation as well as in the courts or during the course of other official investigations."

78. In this country this right, or privilege, is currently enforced by means of rules of evidence. As outlined above, if an admission or confession is not proved to be voluntary it is inadmissible and if obtained in breach of the Judges' Rules or otherwise unfairly, it may, at the discretion of the court, be excluded. The basic and crucial reason for the rules requiring confessions to be voluntary and refusing to allow adverse inferences to be drawn from silence (insofar as they achieve this) is the courts' awareness of the vulnerability of the suspect when questioned by the police. The rules exemplify the courts' concern that evidence of statements made by the accused to the police should be reliable and should not be the result of undue pressure.

79. Research shows that only a minority of suspects do in fact exercise the right to say nothing. Most give some kind of statement or an explanation for their conduct.[1] If a suspect does exercise his right to say nothing the prosecution may not make any adverse comment on the fact and there are limits to the comments the judge may make to the jury.

80. Nevertheless if a suspect chooses to say nothing in answer to police questions, his silence may be incriminating. A distinction must be drawn between the consequences to an accused of his silence before a caution under the Judges' Rules has been administered and afterwards. Silence before the caution has been given cannot of itself constitute proof of guilt but it may form part of the circumstances which the court has to take into account when assessing the evidence. However, once a person has been cautioned, that is told by the police that he need say nothing, the law is that it must be unsafe to use his silence against him for any purpose whatever. As regards questioning before the caution has been administered, Lawton, L. J. said in *R v Chandler*:[2]

"The law has long accepted that an accused person is not bound to incriminate himself; but it does not follow that a failure to answer an accusation or question when an answer could reasonably be expected may not provide some evidence in support of an accusation."

That case also quoted as the law the principle stated by Lord Atkinson in *R v Christie*[3] that:

"the rule of law undoubtedly is that a statement made in the presence of an accused person, even upon an occasion which should be expected reasonably to call for some explanation or denial from him, is not evidence against him of the facts stated save so far as he accepts the statement, so as to make it, in effect, his own. If he accepts the statement in part only, then to that extent alone does it become his statement. He may accept the statement by word or conduct, action or demeanour, and it is the function of the jury which tries the case to determine whether his words, action,

---

[1] The types of statements or explanations given are discussed in Softley and in Irving *op cit*. For information on statements made by defendants tried in the Crown Court, see J Baldwin and M McConville: *Confessions in Crown Court Trials* (Royal Commission on Criminal Procedure Research Study No 5, London HMSO 1980).
[2] [1976] 1 WLR 585.
[3] [1914] AC 545 at p 554.

conduct, or demeanour at the time when a statement was made amounts to an acceptance of it in whole or in part. It by no means follows, I think, that a mere denial by the accused of the facts mentioned in the statement necessarily renders the statement inadmissible, because he may deny the statement in such a manner and under such circumstances as may lead a jury to disbelieve him, and constitute evidence from which an acknowl-. edgement may be inferred by them."

81. Evidence may be given of questions put to the accused by a police officer and the accused's response thereto. The response (in addition to a straightforward answer) may be a statement to the effect "I am not prepared to comment" or it may be silence, that is, no answer at all. Where the accused exercises his right of silence in this way, it is not the law that no adverse inference may be drawn. It is clearly the law that the mere exercise of the right of silence is not *of itself* evidence of guilt; but it is equally clearly the law that the fact of the exercise of the right is admissible evidence and forms a part of the whole of the case, and it becomes part of the facts which the jury or magistrates have to consider.

82. The nature of the comment the judge may make as to silence in response to questioning before trial has been the subject of considerable and conflicting case law and has attracted much academic and other controversy.[1] The most recent case on the nature of the comment a judge may make on the accused's silence before trial is *R v Gilbert*,[2] in which the Court of Appeal (comprising in this instance two Law Lords and a *puisne* judge) noted that it was not possible to reconcile all of the earlier cases but stated:

> "It is in our opinion now clearly established ... that to invite a jury to form an adverse opinion against an accused on account of his exercise of his right to silence is a misdirection."

The court indicated concern at the present state of the law and said:

> "It is not within our competence sitting in this Court to change the law. We cannot overrule the decisions to which we have referred. A right of silence is one thing. No accused can be compelled to speak before, or for that matter, at his trial. But it is another thing to say that if he chooses to exercise his right of silence, that must not be the subject of any comment adverse to the accused. A judge is entitled to comment on his failure to give evidence. As the law now stands, he must not comment adversely on the accused's failure to make a statement."

83. The case law is concerned only with what the judge may say to the jury about the accused's silence. It does not, indeed it cannot, prevent a jury or bench of magistrates from drawing an adverse inference. In *R v Sullivan*[3] Salmon, L. J. quoted from the judge's summing-up:

> "Sullivan refused to answer any questions. Of course bear in mind that he was fully entitled to refuse to answer questions ... But you may think that if he was innocent he would be anxious to answer questions."

---

[1] For an account of this see Home Office evidence to the Royal Commission on Criminal Procedure, Memorandum IX, Parts I and III (Home Office 1978). See, for instance, the article critical of the present rules by Professor Sir Rupert Cross, at [1973] Crim LR 329.
[2] (1977) 66 Cr App R 237.
[3] (1966) 51 Cr App R 102.

This was held to be a misdirection, but of it Salmon, L. J. said:

"It seems pretty plain that all the members of the jury, if they had any common sense at all, must have been saying to themselves precisely what the learned judge said to them."

In *R v Gilbert*[1] Viscount Dilhorne said:

"As the law now stands, although it may appear obvious to the jury in the exercise of their common sense that an innocent man would speak and not be silent, they must be told that they must not draw the inference of guilt from his silence."

84. The accused cannot be compelled to give evidence at his trial and the prosecution may not comment on his failure to do so. The judge, however, may, in his discretion, comment on the accused's failure to give evidence; and although the judge must exercise his discretion to ensure that the trial is fair, in some cases the interests of justice may call for strong comment.[2] The Court of Appeal has concluded[3] that the comment by the judge should in almost every case follow the statement by Lord Parker C. J. in *R v Bathurst*[4] that if the judge were minded to comment to the jury this should be to the effect that:

"the accused is not bound to give evidence, that he can sit back and see if the prosecution have proved their case, and that, while the jury have been deprived of the opportunity of hearing his story tested in cross-examination, the one thing they must not do is assume that he is guilty because he has not gone into the witness box."

C. Access to legal advice and to other persons

a. Access to legal advice

85. Although there are no statutory provisions conferring on suspected persons any entitlement to see or consult a solicitor, paragraph (c) of the introduction to the Judges' Rules states the principle:

"That every person at any stage of an investigation should be able to communicate and to consult privately with a solicitor. This is so even if he is in custody provided that in such case no unreasonable delay or hindrance is caused to the processes of investigation or the administration of justice by his doing so."

According to paragraph 7(a) of the Administrative Directions appended to the Rules:

"*(a)* A person in custody should be supplied on request with writing materials. Provided that no hindrance is reasonably likely to be caused to the processes of investigation or the administration of justice:

  (i) he should be allowed to speak on the telephone to his solicitor or to his friends;

  (ii) his letters should be sent by post or otherwise with the least possible delay;

---

[1] (1977) 66 Cr App R 237.
[2] *R v Sparrow* [1973] 1 WLR 488.
[3] *R v Mutch* [1973] 1 All ER 178.
[4] [1968] 2 QB 99.

(iii) telegrams should be sent at once, at his own expense.

(b) Persons in custody should not only be informed orally of the rights and facilities available to them, but in addition notices describing them should be displayed at convenient and conspicuous places at police stations and the attention of persons in custody should be drawn to these notices."

In addition s. 62 of the Criminal Law Act 1977 states that:

"Where any person has been arrested and is being held in custody in a police station or other premises, he shall be entitled to have intimation of his arrest and of the place where he is being held sent to one person reasonably named by him, without delay or, where some delay is necessary in the interest of the investigation or prevention of crime or the apprehension of offenders, with no more delay than is so necessary."

This section is relevant here because the person in custody might use the entitlement conferred by s. 62 to request that his solicitor be notified of his arrest.

86. Two points in particular should be noted about these provisions. First, they do not recognise any right for a solicitor to be present when a person in custody is being questioned. Second, the rights which are recognised, to have information about the arrest sent to another person (who may be a solicitor) and to consult and communicate, by various means, with a solicitor, are all subject to the provisos set out in paragraph 85 whose exercise is a matter for police discretion. Unless these provisos apply, the Judges' Rules envisage that an arrested person should not as a matter of routine be prevented from obtaining legal advice if he wishes to do so.

87. The available research shows that relatively few suspects ask to consult with a solicitor while they are in police custody. The Home Office study of police interrogation found that about one in ten did so; a third of these requests were refused by the police. The rate increased to one in five at one station where suspects were told of their right to contact a solicitor.[1] Research based on interviews with defendants tried on indictment indicates a rather higher rate of requests, but even so these occur in only a minority of cases. Such defendants frequently claimed that their requests were refused by the police.[2]

b. Access to other persons

88. As noted in paragraph 85, s. 62 of the Criminal Law Act 1977 sets out formally the entitlement of a person in custody to have information about his arrest and the place of his detention conveyed to a reasonably named person. But it provides that the execution of this entitlement may be delayed where this is necessary (but no longer than is so necessary):

"in the interest of the investigation or prevention of crime or the apprehension of offenders."

A copy of the relevant sections of the Home Office circular to chief constables about the implementation of this provision is at Appendix 14.

---

[1] See Softley, *op cit,* Chapter 3.
[2] See J Baldwin and M McConville: *Police interrogation and the right to see a solicitor* [1979] Crim LR 145; and M Zander: *Access to a solicitor in the police station* [1972] Crim LR 342.

89. Statistical information about the operation of s. 62 is limited. The fullest material deals only with the numbers of those whose requests to have someone notified of their arrest were refused after four and 24 hours and does not indicate what percentage of arrested persons made such a request (see Appendix 15). The Home Office study of police interrogation indicates that half the adult suspects observed did not want anyone informed of their whereabouts.[1]

D. Special provisions in relation to certain categories of suspect

a. Juveniles

90. Subsection 29(1) of the Children and Young Persons Act 1969, as amended, provides that where a juvenile (that is, a person under the age of 17) is arrested, with or without warrant, and cannot be brought immediately before a magistrates' court, the police officer in charge of the police station to which he is brought or another police officer not below the rank of inspector shall forthwith enquire into the case, and shall release him unless:

    (a) the officer considers that he ought in his own interest to be further detained; or

    (b) the officer has reason to believe that he has committed homicide or another grave crime or that his release would defeat the ends of justice or that if he were released (in a case where he was arrested without a warrant) he would fail to appear to answer to any charge which might be made.

Where a juvenile is arrested, the person who arrested him must take such steps as may be practicable to inform at least one parent or guardian (s. 34 of the Children and Young Persons Act 1933 as amended). Where a juvenile is released, his parent or guardian, if he consents to be surety for the juvenile, may be required to comply with any conditions of his release, one of which may be that the parent or guardian attend court with the juvenile (subsection 29(2) of the 1969 Act as amended and subsection 3(7) of the Bail Act 1976).

91. Where a juvenile is not released after arrest, he must be brought before a magistrates' court within 72 hours. Further, the police must make arrangements for him to be taken into the care of the local authority unless the officer who enquires into the case certifies:

    (a) that it is impractical to make such arrangements, or

    (b) that the juvenile is of so unruly a character that it is inappropriate to do so.

(Children and Young Persons Act 1969, subsections 29(3) and (5).)

92. Where it is necessary to take juveniles into police custody they are not usually placed in the cells. The Home Office has issued the following guidance:

> "When a juvenile has to be kept in a police station the degree of security needed will depend on a number of factors, including his age and behaviour and the reason he is in police custody. There may sometimes be no need to keep him in a secure room. Juveniles should not be placed in police cells, unless they are so unruly that they are likely to cause damage

---

[1]Softley, *op cit,* Chapter 3.

33

in a detention room or other accommodation. Secure accommodation, not in police cells, should therefore be available at any station where it may be necessary to detain juveniles overnight. Where no room can, or need, be set aside permanently for the purpose, one should be allocated to be taken into use when required."[1]

Administrative Direction 4 appended to the Judges' Rules provides that:

"As far as practicable children and young persons under the age of 17 years (whether suspected of crime or not) should only be interviewed in the presence of a parent or guardian, or in their absence some person who is not a police officer and is of the same sex as the child. . ."[2]

b. *Mentally handicapped persons*

93. In the last few years, partly as a result of one or two individual cases, concern has been expressed about the position of mentally handicapped persons in police custody. The substance of a circular issued by the Home Office in 1976 is now consolidated in Administrative Direction 4A to the Judges' Rules. This advises that officers should take particular care in putting questions to and accepting the reliability of answers from a person who appears to have a mental handicap. As far as practicable, such persons should be interviewed only in the presence of a parent or other independent person.

c. *Suspects requiring an interpreter*

94. Special provision is also made for two further groups, namely those who do not speak English (Administrative Direction 5) or who suffer from deafness (Appendix C to the Judges' Rules). In the case of the former, an interpreter is to be present who should take down the statement in the language in which it is made. This should be signed by the person making it. An official translation is to be made which will if necessary be proved as an exhibit with the original statement. When the suspect is a deaf person, Appendix C notes that it may be necessary to have a competent interpreter present. Agreement has been reached with the Royal National Institute for the Deaf and the Association of Directors of Social Services for the Director of Social Services to designate a point of contact through which arrangements can be made locally to secure the services of interpreters.

E. Powers to take photographs and fingerprints

95. There is a distinction in law to be made between photographing and fingerprinting. While fingerprinting will almost certainly require some physical contact between the police officer responsible and the person being finger-printed, photography does not. Accordingly, whereas fingerprinting without statutory authority or the consent of the person concerned may constitute an assault, the English courts have never held the photographing of a suspect by a police officer to be unlawful, even where there is no consent or statutory authority. What statute law there is on these matters has to be seen against this background.

---

[1] *Home Office Consolidated Circular to the Police on Crime and Kindred Matters* 1977 edition, paragraph 4.70.

[2] For descriptions of the operation of these safeguards in practice, see Softley, *op cit*, Chapters 2 and 3.

96. The police may only take a person's fingerprints, even if he is suspected of crime, with the person's consent or if there is specific authority to do so. If a person refuses to be fingerprinted, the police may apply to a magistrates' court for a fingerprint order. The application is made under s. 40 of the Magistrates' Courts Act 1952. Subsection (1) of that section, as extended by s. 33 of the Criminal Justice Act 1967, provides that the court may, if it thinks fit, on the application of a police officer not below the rank of inspector, order the fingerprints or palmprints (or both) of certain persons to be taken by a constable. The section applies to persons not less than 14 years old who either (a) have been taken into custody and charged with any offence before a magistrates' court or (b) appear before a magistrates' court in answer to a summons for an offence punishable by imprisonment. No criteria are laid down indicating the circumstances which the court should take into account in such an application. It seems the matter is left solely to the discretion of the court (see *George v Coombe*).[1] The Home Office has indicated that it may not always be possible for the police to give reasons because this might inferentially inform the court of the accused's previous convictions or of the fact that it was desired to use his fingerprints to determine whether these are identical with fingerprints found at the scene of other offences.[2] By s. 39 of the Criminal Justice Act 1948 a previous conviction may be proved against any person in criminal proceedings by showing that his fingerprints (or palmprints) and those of the person convicted are the fingerprints or palmprints of the same person.

97. Where an order is made for the taking of fingerprints (or palmprints) s. 40 of the Magistrates' Courts Act 1952 goes on to provide:

"(2) Fingerprints taken in pursuance of an order under this section shall be taken either at the place where the court is sitting or, if the person to whom the order relates is remanded in custody, at any place to which he is committed; and a constable may use such reasonable force as may be necessary for that purpose.

(3) The provisions of this section shall be in addition to those of any other enactment under which fingerprints may be taken.

(4) Where the fingerprints of any person have been taken in pursuance of an order under this section, then, if he is acquitted or the examining justices determine not to commit him for trial or if the information against him is dismissed, the fingerprints and all copies of them shall be destroyed."

It will be noted that the effect of the terms of subsection (4) as to the destruction of fingerprints (or palmprints) is such that it does not apply to fingerprints (or palmprints) given voluntarily. Although to take the fingerprints of a suspect without such an order or his consent is *prima facie* a trespass, the prints may still be admitted in evidence.[3]

98. Section 5 of the Children and Young Persons Act 1969, which is not yet in force, provides that the prosecution of juveniles aged 14 or more will have to be preceded by a reference to the local authority for observations as to the

---

[1] [1978] Crim LR 47.
[2] *Home Office Consolidated Circular to the Police on Crime and Kindred Matters,* 1977 edition, paragraph 4.15.
[3] *Callis v Gunn* [1964] 1 QB 495.

suitability of criminal proceedings. Such a reference is intended to take place at the point where the police would normally charge or lay an information. Linked with this provision is s. 8 of the 1969 Act, which is also not yet in force, enabling the court to make a fingerprint (or palmprint) order, on application, before the prosecution is begun, that is before charge or summons. This is because the charge or information would in effect be deferred.

99. The police also have power under two particular statutes to take the photographs and fingerprints of persons in custody on their own authority. The Immigration Act 1971 (Schedule 2, paragraph 18(2)) gives "any immigration officer, constable or prison officer, or any other person authorised by the Secretary of State" power to "take all such steps as may be reasonably necessary for photographing, measuring or otherwise identifying" a person detained under the Act, pending his examination and pending a decision to give or refuse him leave to enter the United Kingdom. The Prevention of Terrorism (Temporary Provisions) Act 1976 (Schedule 3, paragraph 5 (3)) gives a similar power to "any examining officer, constable or prison officer, or any other person authorised by the Secretary of State" in respect of any person detained under the Act.

F. Identification procedures

100. The law and procedures relating to the holding of identity parades and the prosecution of cases involving disputed identity are detailed and complex. They are now to be found in Home Office Circular No 109/1978,[1] the guidelines applied by the Director of Public Prosecutions,[2] and in the judgment of the Court of Appeal in *R v Turnbull*.[3] These developments follow the report of the *Departmental Committee on Evidence of Identification in Criminal Cases* published in 1976[4] which was set up following public concern over several cases where convictions had resulted from mistaken identification.

G. Other aspects of the treatment of persons in police custody

a. Supervision and documentation

101. Although the detailed arrangements for the supervision and documentation of a person in custody at a police station vary from force to force and, because of the size and business of stations, from station to station, there are common features throughout the country. The account that follows reflects general good practice. The primary responsibility for the care and safekeeping of persons detained in custody rests with the station officer, who has general responsibility for the running of the station. It may happen with large and busy stations that a charge sergeant is available who has no other responsibility than the cell block and persons lodged there. Either of these officers is ultimately responsible to the divisional commander, through the sub-divisional commander.

102. The station officer is responsible for receiving the arrested person on his arrival at the police station, for recording details of the arrest and arrival,

[1] *Identification parades and the use of photographs for identification.*
[2] Written Answer by the Attorney General, House of Commons Official Report 27 May 1976 [cols 287–289].
[3] (1976) 63 Cr App R 132.
[4] 27 April 1976 HC 338 HMSO.

for searching him and recording his property, for checking on his physical condition, and for notifying him of his right under s. 62 of the Criminal Law Act 1977. This information is placed upon a document of record (variously known as a detention sheet, charge sheet or reception sheet) which is also used to record, among other things, all visits to the person (he will be seen by the station officer or one of his staff at least once an hour and every half hour if he is drunk) and the provision of meals. If he is taken from the cell for interview or to see a visitor (a friend or solicitor) that is also recorded.

b. Secure accommodation at police stations

103. Some form of secure accommodation is provided in all police stations, the extent of the provision depending on operational need. In all but the smallest stations, the complex of accommodation comprises a charge room and annexe, surgeon's room, matron's room, interview room, cells and detention rooms. In new buildings, police authorities are expected to follow the advice on specifications for cells in the Home Office *Memorandum on the Planning of Police Buildings 1966*. The detailed design of cells in older buildings sometimes varies from these recommendations, but in general they broadly meet the required specifications. In a few large urban areas, prisoners are detained locally only for a short period pending transfer to a main bridewell, which sometimes contains as many as 75 cells.

c. Refreshments

104. The police are required to provide food and drinks to persons in custody. Administrative Direction 5 appended to the Judges' Rules emphasises that:

> "Reasonable arrangements should be made for the comfort and refreshment of persons being questioned."

d. Property

105. Details of all property which comes into police possession as a result of a person being arrested is entered on the charge sheet or other record. When the property is listed the prisoner is invited to sign it as a true record. It is then countersigned by the officer in the case or the station officer. Property which is the subject of a charge or is likely to be produced in evidence is listed separately from the prisoner's property, but usually on the same document. The property is then placed in a container and locked away. During the time a prisoner is in police custody he is permitted to dispose of property provided this will not interfere with the course of justice. There is no clear statutory authority for this procedure, and the position at common law is uncertain. There is case law to the effect both that it is and is not lawful. Some of the cases deal with the common law power to search on arrest, which is limited to the circumstances described in paragraph 27 above and is not to be used as a matter of routine. One further provision is relevant. Under s. 39 of the Magistrates' Courts Act 1952 (which reproduced an earlier provision), the court has power to return property seized to the accused where it is of opinion that this can be done consistently with the interests of justice and the safe custody of the prisoner. But it is not clear what the effect of this provision is.

37

Certainly it does not explicitly purport to validate the seizure of any wider class of property than could be seized at common law.

106. A prisoner who is placed in a cell is allowed to retain his own clothing while in custody except that any item with which he could harm himself or another is taken away from him, for example ties, braces, belts, shoelaces (to prevent suicide by hanging), and footwear if this is heavy (to minimise the risk of attack on police officers who may visit him). If it is necessary to remove his clothing for scientific examination he is provided with alternative dress. Changes of clothing are permitted if available. In a recent case,[1] the Divisional Court held that the police had to have a very good reason for removing clothing or depriving a prisoner of property. It was their duty to take all reasonable measures necessary to ensure that the prisoner did not escape, or injure himself or others, destroy or dispose of evidence or commit some further crime (such as malicious damage to property). But where such measures involved removal of clothing, considerable justification was required. There would have to be some evidence either that all suspects of that particular category had, or that the suspect himself had shown, a tendency to use the clothing to inflict injury.

107. When a person is released from police custody, either on bail or to a court, his property is returned to him against his signature which is again countersigned by the officer releasing him. It is the usual practice to hand back to the person all that is legitimately his, but he is not given property which is subject to a charge or which may be required for evidence. Two further considerations which the police have to bear in mind in deciding whether to return property are the provisions of s. 39 of the Magistrates' Courts Act 1952, which requires police to provide the court with a list of property taken from a person who is appearing before it so as to enable the court to direct the return of the property to the accused or his nominee if this is consistent with the interests of justice and subsections 28(1) and (3) of the Theft Act 1968, which enables a court, after conviction, to order in appropriate cases that money found in a prisoner's possession on his apprehension be paid in compensation to a third party.

e. Medical examinations

108. Guidance on medical examinations of persons in police custody is contained in the *Home Office Consolidated Circular to the Police on Crime and Kindred Matters*. The relevant paragraphs are at Appendix 16. It will be noted that the guidance covers the particular position of persons who are ill or drunk and may be in need of care or attention.

---

[1]*Lindley v Rutter*, The Times 1 August 1980.

The enforcement of rights and duties

Introduction

109. It is clear that the powers of the police in the investigation of crime are considerably greater than those of private citizens. Accordingly correspondingly greater safeguards are required. Allegations of improper behaviour by the police (whether by misusing or exceeding their powers) can arise in a number of ways: out of supervision by other police officers; through a member of the public; in the course of an inspection by the Inspectorate of Constabulary; or during the giving of evidence in a criminal trial. If proved, improper behaviour can be dealt with in a number of ways. This chapter describes the way in which police conduct is regulated and redress is provided for breaches of the rules. Statistical material on the exercise of the various remedies and procedures has been assembled at Appendix 17, except for civil proceedings in respect of which there are no centrally collected figures.

A. Internal discipline and police complaints procedures

a. Police discipline and control by the chief officer

110. Police officers are bound by the requirements of the criminal law and the police discipline code. In addition, each force has general orders prescribing in considerable detail the practice and procedures to be followed in the force. The discipline code is a statutory document, made under the authority of the Police Act 1964 and subject to Parliamentary approval. General orders by contrast are not public documents. They vary from force to force, although to a large extent they contain common material, extracted from, among other things, Home Office Circulars (including that which contains the Judges' Rules and Administrative Directions). They are issued on the authority of the chief officer and do not possess the status of law. The senior officers of the force are responsible for ensuring that knowledge of general orders is disseminated throughout the force. Failure to comply with general orders may amount to a disciplinary offence.

111. The discipline code (extracts from which are at Appendix 18) has traditionally proscribed a very wide range of offences, including discreditable conduct; disobedience to orders; neglect of duty; corrupt or improper practice; abuse of authority (defined as including incivility to members of the public); and criminal conduct (that is being found guilty of any act or omission prohibited by the criminal law). These offences cover most aspects of a

constable's duties (and to some extent his private life) and in theory almost any misconduct, neglect or even carelessness in carrying out his duties is potentially a disciplinary offence.

112. The law and procedure governing police discipline is complex. It is set out in detail in Home Office Circular 63/1977 and some extracts from this are at Appendix 19. In general, unless the Police Complaints Board is involved (see paragraphs 113 ff) discipline is an internal force matter and it is for the deputy chief constable to decide whether to bring a disciplinary charge. It is long established practice, however, that formal disciplinary action is normally reserved for more important matters, others being disposed of without recourse to a disciplinary hearing, for example by way of advice to or admonition of the officer concerned.

b. Complaints

113. The complaints system is the traditional means by which members of the public who are dissatisfied with the behaviour of a particular police officer have sought a remedy. Section 49 of the Police Act 1964 initiated the present system of recording and investigating complaints and a leaflet telling members of the public how they could make a complaint was first issued in 1965. The text of the latest version of this leaflet is at Appendix 20. A complaint may lead to disciplinary action against the officer concerned. The leaflet discusses, *inter alia*, the definition of a complaint, the procedure to be followed when one has been made and the role of the Police Complaints Board.

114. The complaints procedures came under increasing criticism in the 1960s and 1970s from sections of the public who felt that a system in which the investigation and consideration of complaints were undertaken by the police left them as judge and jury in their own cause and because, having made the complaint, the complainant did not, as of right, play any part in its resolution; from the police as involving a vast amount of time and effort, often on matters which were essentially trivial; and, in a narrower field, from those who argued that complaints against police officers by accused persons should normally be investigated before and not after the relevant trial or appeal (see paragraph 122). Various proposals for change were put forward in the early 1970s and in the event the system established by the 1964 Act was modified in the Police Act 1976 which, among other changes, established the Police Complaints Board.

115. The Board's functions are outlined in paragraphs 64ff of the Circular 63/1977 (which are reproduced at Appendix 19). The nature of the Board's role is shown by the following extract from its 1977 report:

> "The Board have no power to conduct investigations into complaints, although they may seek further information from the police about complaints cases submitted to them. The Board cannot take action on complaints sent to them direct except to send them straight on to the chief officer of police concerned. Nor do the Board have power to deal with questions of criminal proceedings against police officers following a complaint against them, although the Board may ask for information relating to a possible criminal offence by a police officer which comes

officially to their notice to be sent to the Director if they have reason to believe that such information has not been supplied to him.

". . . To sum up, the Police Complaints Board have no positive part to play in the handling of a complaint until it has been recorded and investigated by the police and until it has been referred, if necessary, to the Director of Public Prosecutions. The Board cannot question the decision of the Director on criminal proceedings. Where the deputy chief constable decides to prefer disciplinary charges, the Board have no power to vary these charges: in such a case they are solely concerned, where the charges are denied, to decide whether or not the charges should be heard before a disciplinary tribunal. But where the deputy chief constable decides not to prefer disciplinary charges the Board, if they disagree, have power to recommend and if necessary direct that charges are nevertheless preferred. It is not the Board's function, however, to give a judgment on the merits of a complaint or to say, for example, whether or not the police officer or the complainant was at fault; and the Board cannot deal with questions of compensation or redress. Furthermore, where a justifiable complaint is found to result from a defect in procedures rather than from the actions of an individual police officer, it will be apparent that the Board's decision solely on the question whether or not disciplinary proceedings should be taken against the officer concerned can provide only a very limited response to the substance of the complaint."

116. Section 49(3) of the Police Act 1964 requires that unless a chief officer is satisfied that no criminal offence has been committed, he must send to the Director of Public Prosecutions the report of all investigations into complaints by members of the public against a police officer. Further details of this procedure are at paragraphs 47 to 50 of Circular 63/1977; paragraphs 51 to 57 set out the procedures and considerations in a case which has both criminal and disciplinary aspects (see Appendix 19). One of the major problems is that of double jeopardy: that is, whether and in what circumstances an officer should be subject to a disciplinary charge when he has already been prosecuted (and either convicted or acquitted) for a substantially similar criminal offence, or where the evidence necessary to prove the disciplinary offence has been held insufficient to justify criminal prosecution for a similar offence. By s. 11 of the Police Act 1976, he is not liable to disciplinary proceedings in the former case, and according to paragraph 56 of Circular 63/1977 he should not normally be liable in the latter case, although there are some important exceptions to this rule. For example, where money has been misappropriated by a police officer there might be insufficient evidence to justify prosecuting him under the Theft Act but adequate evidence to charge him with the disciplinary offence of failing to account properly for the money. In such circumstances, where there are additional elements involved in the disciplinary offence, the Circular advises that it would be right to deal with the matter as a disciplinary charge. There are other examples in the extracts from the Circular at Appendix 19.

117. The Police Complaints Board, in its report for 1978, drew attention to the marked variations in practice by deputy chief constables in referring complaints to the Director. In cases on the margins of criminal conduct, for example where the alleged conduct infringed some law which was no longer

41

enforced, the Director might be expected to decide not to prosecute, but the effect would be to preclude disciplinary action for which the facts of the case might otherwise provide justification. In its triennial review report,[1] the Board again referred to the "double jeopardy" rule and the variation of practice in referring cases to the Director. It pointed out that the "double jeopardy" rule had certain consequences. Where a case was referred to the Director, he took, for practical purposes, the decision about disciplinary action in many serious allegations. This was undesirable for the reason that the decision was not taken in a disciplinary context but on an assessment of the likely outcome of criminal proceedings. The guidance on when the same evidence as was insufficient for prosecution could properly be used to found disciplinary action appeared to be interpreted differently in different forces. The Board went on to recommend that consideration be given to removing the requirement to send cases to the Director where specified minor offences only were alleged. It also stated that, pending such a revision of the procedure, it would welcome some interim means of securing greater consistency of practice among forces in referring complaints and reports of minor infringements.

118. The Board remarked the continuing pressure from particular quarters for the creation of an independent body to investigate complaints against the police, on the grounds that independent investigators would bring greater thoroughness and impartiality to the task. The Board's experience indicated that in general the police do investigate complaints thoroughly and impartially. The Board saw considerable practical objections to a proposal for all complaints to be investigated by a body independent of the police, but it also saw room for improvement of certain aspects of the complaints procedure. It identified the main focus of discontent as unexplained injuries sustained during the course of arrest or in police custody and recognised a need to set misgivings at rest in that area. It proposed that an independent investigative body comprising experienced and well-qualified police officers on two to three year secondments and answerable to an independent lawyer be given responsibility for investigating such complaints.

B. Criminal and civil proceedings

119. This section examines briefly the application of criminal and civil law to police misconduct, including the problems which may arise when the substance of a complaint or discipline investigation is related to pending or possible criminal proceedings.

a. The criminal law

120. The criminal courts provide various checks on the activities of police officers. First, there is the general sanction of the criminal law. A police officer can be charged and convicted for offences arising out of his work, for example corruption, assault on a prisoner, careless driving in a police car, as well as for an offence not arising out of his work. For a police officer to be convicted of a criminal offence, whether or not connected with his work, is of itself a disciplinary offence. He will be subject to disciplinary sanctions and, in certain cases, may be dismissed or required to resign. Where a police officer is

[1]*Police Complaints Board Triennial Review Report 1980* London HMSO Cmnd 7966.

suspected of or charged with a criminal offence, he is entitled to the same safeguards as any other person in this situation.

121. The conduct of a police officer may also be relevant to criminal proceedings against an accused person. There can be a variety of reasons for an acquittal most of which do not represent a criticism of the police officer concerned in the case. There are some instances, however, in which the fact that the police have followed the appropriate procedures has to be established before a case can be proved. For example, a charge of assaulting an arresting officer in the execution of his duty will not succeed if it can be shown that the initial arrest was unlawful. In order to prove that a person has committed the offence of driving with more than the permitted level of alcohol, the prosecution is required to show that the police have correctly followed the procedures laid down for use of the breathalyser and for requesting a specimen for a laboratory test. The court may exclude statements which were obtained in contravention of the Judges' Rules and must exclude those where voluntariness is not established (see paragraphs 74–76). Or it may disbelieve oral confessions ("verbals") which it is alleged were invented by the police.

122. In these ways there is an in-built tendency for criminal charges against suspects to be associated with allegations or complaints from those suspects of misconduct by individual police officers. Under s. 49 of the Police Act 1964 such complaints are required to be recorded straight away, but if they are closely associated with criminal proceedings against the complainant or someone else and those charges are to be heard in court, the investigation of the complaint will not normally begin until after the court proceedings are complete. The reasons for this are set out at paragraph 39 and Annex F to Home Office Circular 63/1977, which are among the extracts from the Circular at Appendix 19. The Police Complaints Board, again, has drawn attention to the problems arising from this rule but it was unable to suggest a remedy for them. Cases affected by the rule in 1979 took over twice as long to reach the Board as other cases. The defendant may, however, request that the investigation of his complaint not be delayed pending his trial (see paragraph 9 of Annex F to the Circular). Where there is conflicting evidence it will be left to the courts to decide, either in a "trial within a trial" or in the course of the main proceedings. After his trial has been concluded, the defendant may tell the police that he does not wish his complaint to be further pursued. If so, the end of the court proceedings will normally be the end of the matter so far as the individual police officer is concerned. But, where such an allegation or complaint is pursued, it will be dealt with under the normal complaints procedure including any necessary reference to the Director of Public Prosecutions.

123. The Royal Commission on the Police, in its final Report in 1962,[1] recommended that in any case where the court criticises the conduct of a police officer, this criticism should be brought to the attention of his superior officer for consideration of possible advice to the officer or for possible criminal or disciplinary action. This recommendation was brought to the attention of chief officers by Home Office Circular 103/1963.

[1]London HMSO Cmnd 1728.

124. A further possible consequence of misconduct by a police officer is a private prosecution by the complainant. In practice, this is rare. Most of those which do occur are for common assault. Such a prosecution may follow the acquittal of the complainant on a charge of assaulting a police officer or obstructing a police officer in the execution of his duty, but it is also possible for a defendant accused of assault himself to apply for a summons against the police officer concerned alleging an assault. It is for the court to decide whether the two summonses should be tried together.

b. The civil law

125. The general civil law applies equally to the acts of police officers as to those of other citizens and, accordingly, an action for damages may lie. By s. 48 of the Police Act 1964, the chief officer is vicariously liable for such acts committed by officers "under his direction and control" when acting in the course of their duties. He is liable to be sued jointly, and any costs or damages which he is obliged to pay (including, with the approval of his police authority, out of court payment of compensation) are met from the police fund.

126. The sort of case to be brought might include a claim for damages for assault or for false imprisonment following an arrest which the plaintiff alleges to be unlawful. It is open to a person who has been prosecuted and acquitted to allege that the prosecution was launched for improper motives and claim damages for malicious prosecution. A claim for damages for trespass may be brought to challenge the legality of a police search of premises. The legality of police detention of property can be challenged in the courts by a plaintiff claiming to be entitled to possession of the property.

127. A successful claim in civil proceedings against a police officer may have wider consequences than the satisfaction of the plaintiff's claim. The court's ruling on the law may make clear the extent of police powers about which there has been some dispute and the conduct of the particular officer concerned will come to the notice of his chief officer and the police authority.

C. The work of the Inspectorate of Constabulary

128. HM Inspectors of Constabulary are appointed by the Crown on the recommendation of the Home Secretary from among the most senior officers in the police forces of England and Wales. Because of their seniority in the service they spend on average only a few years in post as Inspectors. The first Inspectors were appointed under the provisions of the County and Borough Police Act 1856. The governing statute at present is the Police Act 1964. In addition to the Chief Inspector, there are currently five Inspectors based in separate regions of England and Wales. They inspect 42 forces of the mainland, including the City of London but excluding the Metropolitan Police (the arrangements for which are dealt with in paragraph 130). By invitation they also inspect the police force for Northern Ireland (the Royal Ulster Constabulary) and the three Island forces. They are occasionally asked to advise overseas governments and other government departments in the United Kingdom on police matters.

129. In a note to the Royal Commission in 1979 the then Chief Inspector (Sir Colin Woods) described the work of the Inspectorate as follows:

"The general statutory duties of HM Inspectors of Constabulary, as set out in Section 38 of the Police Act 1964, are to inspect and report to the Secretary of State on the efficiency of all the police forces in their area and to carry out such other duties for the purpose of furthering police efficiency as the Secretary of State may from time to time direct. In practice, however, their duties extend far beyond these requirements.

"Clearly the Inspectors' primary concern is the efficiency of the maintained forces with which they sustain a close liaison and formally inspect once a year. They must also be ready to advise the Secretary of State on all matters of discipline, appeals, awards for gallantry, administration and finance, including those matters arising in connection with the Exchequer Grant in aid of police expenditure; furthermore they should always be ready to assist police authorities with all the information and advice they may require in respect of any arrangements connected with the police force of the area.

"[The main duties of the Inspectorate now include:]

   (a) Planning and developing arrangements for promoting collaboration between forces particularly in the field of common ancillary services, for example regional crime squads, higher training;

   (b) Ensuring that the results of central research are properly disseminated to forces and that new developments of science and technology are being applied;

   (c) Forming an opinion about the adequacy of buildings, equipment and manpower provided by each police authority and advising the Police Department of any shortcomings and on the priorities which should be adopted in the allocation of resources;

   (d) Monitoring the manner in which complaints from members of the public are dealt with;

   (e) Reporting any misgivings they might have about the competence of individual chief police officers to the proper authorities;

   (f) Advising the Secretary of State about the respective merits of candidates for senior police appointments;

   (g) Advising on recommendations for gallantry and distinguished service awards;

   (h) Serving as members of police disciplinary tribunals and generally advising on appeals against disciplinary findings;

   (i) Acting as chairmen of various selection boards for higher training as well as being members of a wide range of committees;

   (j) Being consulted about answers to parliamentary questions, policy for the criminal justice system and new legislation, relations between the police and the public, community relations and so on.

". . . [The Inspectorate serves the needs of the partnership between local and central government] mainly by being a channel of communication between local government and local forces on the one hand and central government (Police Department) and Ministers on the other. Through its position in the Home Office Police Department and regular formal and informal meetings with its senior officials the Inspectorate is kept in touch with latest policies and can draw the attention of officials to causes for concern or action which come to the Inspectorate's notice.

"HM Chief Inspectors of Constabulary visit police forces frequently but inspect rarely; their job generally is to coordinate the work of their inspectors who each has the responsibility of inspecting a number of forces in one or more of the regions. They finalise the Inspectorate advice at the national level. The HMCIC is, of course, available for urgent advice to Ministers over the whole range of professional police matters as and when immediate problems arise.

"There are four Assistants to HM Chief Inspector for England and Wales each with a broadly based specialist function as follows:

> *(a)* Traffic, training and community relations;
>
> *(b)* Computers, communications, management information systems and research;
>
> *(c)* Integration and employment of women;
>
> *(d)* Crime and kindred matters.

"The Assistants and their Staff Officers work in close collaboration with Inspectors and their staffs as well as with policy divisions. A specialist Staff Officer deals with recruitment, particularly of graduates, to the police service. They are perhaps of particular value through their availability to their colleagues in the Police Department for informal discussions of current matters."

130. Different arrangements apply for the inspection of the Metropolitan Police. It is an internal service, the Inspector being a serving Deputy Assistant Commissioner of the force. The arrangements are described in Appendix 21.

D. The exclusion of evidence improperly obtained

131. To what extent do the courts seek to control and regulate police conduct by excluding evidence irregularly obtained? The basic rule is that if evidence is relevant it is admissible. In *R v Leatham*[1] Crompton, J. said:

> "It matters not how you get it; if you steal it even, it would be admissible."

In *Kuruma v R*[2] Lord Goddard, C. J. said:

> "the test to be applied in considering whether evidence is admissible is whether it is relevant to the matters in issue. If it is, it is admissible, and the court is not concerned with how the evidence was obtained."

There is, however, the important exception to this basic rule relating to confessions and admissions, which to be admissible in evidence must be voluntary (see paragraphs 74–76). In addition the judge[3] has a discretion to exclude evidence. He may do so when a confession or admission is obtained in breach of the Judges' Rules. He may also exclude evidence that the accused

[1] (1861) 8 Cox CC 498 at p 501.
[2] [1955] AC 197 at p 203.
[3] In this and the following paragraph the word "judge" should be read to include magistrates.

has been convicted of other crimes (similar fact evidence) when this would otherwise be admissible to rebut a defence of accident *etc*, and may prevent cross-examination of the accused as to his previous convictions when this is permissible because the accused has attacked the character of a prosecution witness. In both these instances the judge may exclude the evidence if he is of opinion that its prejudicial effect is likely to outweigh its probative value.[1]

132. There are cases where it has been suggested that evidence improperly obtained may be excluded at the discretion of the judge. In *Kuruma v R*,[2] Lord Goddard, C. J. said:

> "No doubt in a criminal case the judge always has a discretion to disallow evidence if the strict rules of admissibility would operate unfairly against the accused . . . . If, for instance, some admission of some piece of evidence, eg a document, had been obtained from a defendant by a trick, no doubt the judge might properly rule it out."

In *Callis v Gunn*[3] Lord Parker, C. J. said:

> ". . . in considering whether admissibility would operate unfairly against a defendant, one would certainly consider whether it had been obtained in an oppressive manner, by force or against the wishes of an accused person."

And, he said, the overriding discretion:

> "would certainly be exercised by excluding the evidence if there was any suggestion of it having been obtained oppressively, by false representations, by a trick, by threats, by bribes, anything of that sort."

In *Jeffrey v Black*[4] Lord Widgery C. J. said:

> "If the case is such that not only have the officers entered without authority, but they have been guilty of trickery, or they have misled someone, or they have been oppressive, or they have been unfair, or in other respects they have behaved in a manner which is morally reprehensible, then it is open to the justices to apply their discretion and decline to allow the particular evidence to be let in as part of the trial."

These statements are high authority for saying that the courts should be concerned not only with fairness at the trial but also with the fairness of the police before trial. On this reasoning evidence could be excluded because of the misconduct of the police irrespective of its evidential value, and the judicial discretion to exclude evidence could be used to express disapproval of police behaviour and as a disciplinary measure.

133. But in a recent case this was specifically rejected by the House of Lords. In *R v Sang*[5] Lord Diplock said:

> "It is no part of a judge's function to exercise disciplinary powers over the police or prosecution as respects the way in which evidence to be used at

---

[1]For a statement of these principles see the judgment of Lord Diplock in *R v Sang* [1979] 2 All E R 1222 at pp 1227–1228.
[2][1955] AC 197 at p 203.
[3][1964] 1 QB 495.
[4][1978] QB 490.
[5][1979] 2 All ER 1222, at p 1230.

the trial is obtained by them. If it was obtained illegally there will be a remedy in civil law; if it was obtained legally but in breach of the rules of conduct for the police, this is a matter for the appropriate disciplinary authority to deal with. What the judge at the trial is concerned with is not how the evidence sought to be adduced by the prosecution has been obtained, but with how it is used by the prosecution at the trial."

Although their Lordships were not unanimous as to the extent of the judicial discretion to exclude evidence, none disagreed with the principle stated by Lord Diplock above. Furthermore, each of their Lordships agreed with the following propositions:

(1) A trial judge in a criminal trial always has a discretion to refuse to admit evidence if in his opinion its prejudicial effect outweighs its probative value.

(2) Save with regard to admissions and confessions and generally with regard to evidence obtained from the accused after the commission of an offence, he has no discretion to refuse to admit relevant admissible evidence on the ground that it was obtained by improper or unfair means. The court is not concerned with how it was obtained.

The prosecution process

Introduction

134. Prior to the nineteenth century, it was generally the task of the private citizen to bring alleged offenders to the notice of the court; there was no official designated as public prosecutor. Thus it was open to any individual to seek to commence proceedings against any other. During that century, the police came to handle the majority of prosecutions, more as the result of a gradual historical development than of any deliberate decision to give them that duty. But that development did not confer on the police in England and Wales any special power in law as prosecutors. In Scotland, by contrast, the right of private prosecution was already regarded as fallen into disuse by the early nineteenth century, and the special position of the public prosecutor (the procurator fiscal) was clearly established.

135. This historical view of private prosecution in England and Wales does not correspond to present practice for three main reasons. First, there is a public prosecutor in the person of the Director of Public Prosecutions, who is under a duty to "institute, undertake or carry on criminal proceedings in any case which appears to him to be of importance or difficulty or which for any other reason requires his intervention."[1] Second, a variety of statutes restricts the prosecution of offences by requiring the consent of the Director, Attorney General, High Court Judge or other body to the institution or continuance of proceedings.[2] Third, most prosecutions are in practice brought by the police and a large number of the rest by other public agencies.

A. Prosecution by the police

136. Chapter 1 discussed the constitutional position and accountability of the police, dealing briefly with the police discretion to prosecute and its limits. Certain points should be noted. None of the statutes setting up police forces in England and Wales made any mention of their prosecutorial role. The police are under no duty to prosecute except that deriving from their general duty to enforce the law. According to Lord Denning, the chief officer is answerable only to the law for the decision to prosecute (see paragraph 6). This discretion is potentially reviewable by means of prerogative writ if the way the chief

---

[1] Prosecution of Offences Regulations 1978, Regulation 3; see also s. 2 of the Prosecution of Offences Act 1979.
[2] For a full list of these provisions, see K W Lidstone, Russell Hogg and Frank Sutcliffe: *Prosecutions by Private Individuals and Non-Police Agencies* (Royal Commission on Criminal Procedure, Research Study No 10, London HMSO 1980) (The Sheffield Study).

officer exercises it amounts to failure in his duty to enforce the law. Notwithstanding the lack of any formal duty, the present position is that the great majority of prosecutions in England and Wales are brought by the police. This section is concerned primarily with who prosecutes on behalf of the police and how decisions in relation to prosecution are taken.

a. The formal responsibility for prosecution

137. Informations[1] are usually laid in the name of the officer who, formally at least, has made the decision to prosecute. In some forces they will be in the name of the chief constable; in others, the officer in charge of the force prosecuting department or the head of the division or sub-division. In yet others (the Metropolitan Police for instance) it is usual for informations to be laid in the name of the reporting or arresting officer. This variation has little practical effect, as was illustrated in the recent case of *Hawkins v Bepey*.[2] In that case the Divisional Court held that the death of a chief inspector before the hearing of an appeal against the dismissal of an information which he had laid did not mean that the appeal thereby lapsed. The Court held that the information had been laid on the instruction of the chief constable and, therefore, the prosecutor in the case was either the chief constable or the force of which he had command.

b. Police decisions on prosecution

138. There is a number of decisions involved in bringing a person before a court to face a criminal charge. The way these are taken can vary according to how serious the offence is, the circumstances in which it first comes to light, whether there is a power of arrest, whether the suspect is an adult or a juvenile and the evidential complexity of the case. What follows deals with police decisions and is a somewhat simplified account of them.

139. The first decision is whether to follow up an incident which may amount to a criminal offence. Following up all such incidents would clearly be impossible. The officer on the street therefore takes decisions about what to pursue. The discretion to take no formal action is more likely to be exercised the more minor is the conduct involved. The way in which other early decisions on prosecution are made (assuming some further action is to be taken) depends first on whether the offence is one which carries a power of arrest. If it does not, the officer may report the matter to a senior officer. (He will tell the individual concerned that he is being reported for consideration of prosecution.) The choice then lies between no further proceedings, administering a formal caution (see paragraphs 150–154) or prosecution. This decision is normally ratified at chief inspector level or above, either in the force prosecutions department or by the commander of the division or sub-division (usually a chief superintendent or superintendent). If the decision is that there should be a prosecution, the proceedings will be commenced by way of summons. If the offence carries a power of arrest, the officer concerned may choose either to arrest the person or to report the matter with a view to prosecution. If the

---

[1]The laying of an information is described at paragraphs 175–177. Procedural aspects of bringing a case to trial are discussed in Chapter 6.
[2][1980] 1 WLR 419.

latter course is adopted, the procedure will then be the same as that described above in respect of a non-arrestable offence. If an arrest is made, the person is taken to the station where after such further investigation as may be necessary, if any, the station officer (usually the station or charge sergeant but occasionally an inspector) decides whether to accept or refuse the charge. The range of outcomes is described at paragraph 64, but essentially the choice lies between no proceedings, a caution or prosecution. Whether or not an arrest has been made, in the more serious or complicated cases or in cases which are likely to attract publicity or where a complaint is likely to be made against the police, senior officers may be involved in the decision whether to prosecute: the divisional commander, or in rare instances an assistant chief constable or even the chief constable.

140. Arrested juveniles are usually released so that the police may consult with the local authority social services department and the probation service (some forces also consult with the school and the educational welfare service) before making the decision on whether the offence will be dealt with by prosecution, caution or by taking no further action. Police forces have a variety of arrangements for dealing with juvenile offenders. About half of them have established specialised juvenile bureaux and, in the majority of the remainder, juvenile liaison officers are assigned to deal with juvenile matters at divisional or sub-divisional level.

c. Obtaining legal advice

141. After the decision to prosecute has been taken, the next stage is preparation for trial. Whether and at what point legal advice is sought will naturally vary with the gravity and complexity of the offence, as well as the practice of the force concerned. For example, no legal advice will be needed in a case of "simple" drunkenness where a guilty plea is expected, and little or no legal advice may be needed in a case of simple theft, but in a fraud case legal advice might well be needed before even the charges can be decided upon. In the latter type of case a lawyer may have been consulted before the police decide to arrest. The arrangements for obtaining legal advice vary from force to force.[1] The basis for the practice in most forces is the recommendation made by the Royal Commission on the Police in 1962 that consideration be given to the appointment of a prosecuting solicitor for every force to give legal advice in deciding upon prosecutions and preparing cases for trial.[2] The position at June 1980 is that thirty-one police forces have prosecuting solicitors' departments of some kind.[3] In addition the Metropolitan force has its own Solicitor and the City of London force is understood to obtain advice from the legal staff of the Common Council. In several of the ten forces without a department of any kind, the chief constable has in the past requested a department. Those forces without a prosecuting solicitor employ private firms *ad hoc.*

---

[1] For an account of these various arrangements, see Mollie Weatheritt: *The Prosecution System: Survey of Prosecuting Solicitors' Departments* (Royal Commission on Criminal Procedure Research Study No 11, London HMSO 1980).
[2] London HMSO Cmnd 1728 paragraph 380.
[3] See Appendix 22.

142. There are no nationally prescribed standards for the organisational arrangements of prosecuting solicitors' departments. The prosecuting solicitor and his staff may be employed by the police authority itself, or they may be on the staff of the local auuthority (perhaps with other duties to perform on behalf of that authority). There is little uniformity in their terms and conditions of service and no unified career structure throughout the country. Similarly, there are wide variations in the type and amount of work done by the prosecuting solicitors' departments and the way the work is handled. They range in size from less than half a dozen legally qualified staff to more than 50 in the large metropolitan areas. Some are highly centralised, with. solicitors going out from one office to the various courts; others are decentralised, with one or two solicitors permanently attached to one area of the force. In some cases the prosecuting solicitor is employed full time on police work, in others he may also occasionally prosecute on behalf of the local authority or agencies such as the British Transport Police; and the police may also make use of private firms of solicitors. The kind and proportion of cases in which the prosecuting solicitor is asked for advice, the stage at which he is called in, and the proportion of summary cases in which he conducts the prosecution case also vary. But broadly, the functions of prosecuting solicitors may be summarised as the conduct of prosecutions in magistrates' courts, briefing counsel in trials on indictment and advising the police on prosecution matters. They have no responsibility for investigations.

143. The relationship between the solicitor and the police is not precisely defined, and much depends on the cooperation and understanding of the individuals concerned. Basically it is a client/solicitor relationship, whether the solicitor is a member of a prosecuting solicitor's department or a private firm. The solicitor may offer advice but the final decision on who shall be prosecuted and for what offence rests with the police. This is equally true if any question arises whether a prosecution should be withdrawn at any stage, for example if further evidence comes to light. This may. be contrasted with the position of the Director of Public Prosecutions who (through his various powers, on which see paragraphs 158 ff) may override police decisions over prosecution.

d. Representation at court

144. Practice varies from force to force over representation of the police in the magistrates' court. The following is an account of general practice.[1] Whether the police are legally represented in cases tried summarily depends on the complexity or importance of the case, as well as on such other factors as whether the defence is also represented and whether a plea of not guilty is expected. The Royal Commission on the Police in 1962 regarded it as "undesirable" that police officers should appear as prosecutors except for minor cases. If the police are legally represented in the magistrates' court, it may be by a member of a prosecuting solicitor's department, by a private solicitor or by a barrister.

145. In cases which go to the Crown Court there is of course no question of police advocacy, nor in general do solicitors have a right of audience there.

[1]For a full account see Weatheritt, *op. cit.*

The choice of barrister in cases heard on indictment rests either with the prosecuting solicitor or with the police or, in cases which he has taken over, with the Director of Public Prosecutions. Since rather more than 25 per cent of serious crime committed in England and Wales each year is committed in London, the requirements of London in respect of criminal prosecutions are very demanding and a permanent group of prosecuting counsel—the only one in the country—has been established there. They are called Treasury Counsel and number at present seven senior and ten junior counsel appointed by the Attorney General at the Central Criminal Court. The Director of Public Prosecutions has first call upon them to conduct his prosecutions. In addition there is a supplementary list of 25 leading and 25 junior counsel who can be instructed at any time making a total of 67 counsel of different seniority immediately available to undertake advisory and trial work for the Director. The Metropolitan Police also maintains a list of approved counsel. In the provinces the Director's cases are dealt with by counsel nominated by the Attorney General from a list of counsel practising on the relevant circuit.

e. Constraints upon police discretion in the decision to prosecute

146. As indicated in paragraphs 139 and 140, the police exercise a discretion at several different points in the prosecution process and at several different levels within the force. But while there is internal supervision over the exercise of this discretion by junior officers, there is little explicit guidance in force orders or elsewhere on how the discretion should be exercised. The extent to which such guidance is known to be available is discussed in the following paragraphs.

147. In the case of traffic offences, forces operate on the basis of written guidance, scheduled to force orders, outlining which offences merit prosecution and which can be disposed of by a written caution. The guidance is drawn up at regional conferences of the Association of Chief Police Officers, following a recommendation by the Royal Commission on the Police in 1962[1] that chief officers should formulate consistent policies in relation to prosecution of traffic offences.

148. Adults suspected of an offence other than a traffic offence are normally prosecuted unless the circumstances suggest an alternative approach. The most obvious reason for not prosecuting is that there is no reasonable prospect of conviction because the evidence is insufficient or of poor quality. But there are many other considerations which may lead the police to decide that despite the existence of a case strong enough to go to trial it would not be in the public interest to prosecute. Although much depends on the circumstances of each case, a number of broad principles can be discerned. If the offence committed was merely a trivial or technical infringement it could be oppressive to enforce the letter of the law. Humanitarian considerations may operate in cases where the offender is either very young or very old, or suffering from serious illness or mental disorder. The "public interest" in the broad political sense may play a part in deciding whether prosecution or non-prosecution will best promote the maintenance of law and order. Finally there are some areas of the law where

[1] *op. cit.*

a degree of discretion is particularly desirable, such as obsolete or archaic offences, or especially controversial or unpopular laws.

149. Where the police decide to prosecute their decision will be subject to the scrutiny of the courts, which may, if the circumstances appear to warrant it, comment adversely upon a prosecution that has been improperly brought. If a conviction is recorded, but the court regards the prosecution as unnecessary or oppressive, it may grant the accused an absolute discharge or impose a nominal penalty, and it may refuse to award costs to the prosecution. If the accused is acquitted the court has power to award costs against the prosecution. Decisions not to prosecute are not subject to the same scrutiny by the courts, although according to Lord Denning a chief officer's policy decision not to prosecute particular types of offence could be challenged before the courts (see paragraph 6).

f. Cautioning

150. Cautioning is used as an alternative to prosecution and reflects the exercise of police discretion not to prosecute detected offenders. There is a distinction to be made between the informal guidance or warning which a person, especially a juvenile or a motorist, may receive from a police officer on the street and a formal caution. The latter should be given only if the police are satisfied that the offence is capable of proof.

151. Although the practice of cautioning has been given recognition in two statutes (the Street Offences Act 1959 and the Children and Young Persons Act 1969[1]), it has never been specifically authorised by statute and no precise date can be assigned to its origin.[2] In addition, it seems to have aroused little judicial comment. This is not entirely surprising, since offences for which cautions are given are, by definition, not prosecuted, and (except in juveniile courts) it is not the practice to cite a caution if the person cautioned is subsequently convicted of some other offence. Where a reference has been made to cautioning it seems to have been regarded as a matter within the discretion of the police. Thus, for example, in *R v Metropolitan Police Commissioner, ex parte Blackburn and another (No 3)*[3] the procedure of cautioning a person and inviting him to sign a disclaimer of any interest in material seized under the Obscene Publications Act was described in the judgment as a convenient and effective procedure because of the courts' unpredictable attitudes to alleged obscenity and the time involved in referring cases to them.

152. In proportionate terms, cautions are most frequently given to juveniles. Formal cautioning has grown considerably in recent years: in 1978, of all juveniles cautioned or found guilty of indictable offences, 49 per cent were cautioned.[4] The practice of cautioning juveniles follows a deliberate policy recommended by the Home Office not to prosecute juveniles if this can be

---

[1]The relevant subsection (5(2)) of the 1969 Act has, however, not been brought into force.
[2]For information on the history of the practice, see Home Office Evidence to the Royal Commission on Criminal Procedure, Memorandum No VI, paragraphs 7–10 (Home Office 1979).
[3][1973] 1 QB 241.
[4]See Appendix 23, which shows cautioning rates by police force area.

avoided. A juvenile will be cautioned only if he admits the alleged offence and he and his parent or guardian agree to the caution. A caution will not normally be considered suitable if the juvenile has previously been cautioned or prosecuted. Other factors such as the wishes of the complainant (if any) and the views of the local authority social services department may be taken into account. A caution is cited in the same way as a previous conviction if the juvenile is subsequently found guilty of another offence. When a juvenile is cautioned, he and his parents will be required to attend at a police station and the caution will be formally given by a senior police officer.

153. Motoring offenders are commonly cautioned. The caution is given in writing by way of a letter sent through the post. It is not required that the motorist admit the offence, and the fact that he has been cautioned may not be referred to in any way if the motorist is subsequently convicted of a further offence.

154. Adults who have committed offences other than motoring offences are comparatively infrequently cautioned. In 1978 of all adults cautioned or found guilty for indictable offences, 4 per cent were cautioned.[1] Most decisions to caution appear to be taken on humanitarian grounds, for example old age or ill-health. As with juveniles a formal caution will, it is said, be given only if the adult admits the offence. But it does not follow invariably that he will be prosecuted if he denies it. In these cases, as with motoring offenders, the fact that the person has been cautioned may not be referred to in court if he is subsequently convicted of another offence.

B. The Director of Public Prosecutions

a. The Director's office and functions

155. The creation of the Office of Director of Public Prosecutions resulted from pressure throughout the middle years of the nineteenth century for a system of public prosecution. The Prosecution of Offences Act 1879 provided for the establishment of a Director of Public Prosecutions to be appointed by the Home Secretary though the Director's duties were to be exercised under the superintendence of the Attorney General. The Director's powers and duties were defined in very broad terms, the details being left to regulations made under the Act. He was "to institute, undertake, or carry on such criminal proceedings ... and to give such advice and assistance to chief officers of police, clerks to justices and other persons ... as may be for the time being prescribed by regulations under this Act, or may be directed in a special case by the Attorney General". The 1880 Regulations referred, *inter alia*, to cases "which appear to the Director of Public Prosecutions to be of importance or difficulty, or in which special circumstances seem to him to render his action necessary to secure the due prosecution of an offender".

156. The Act also provided for the appointment of Assistant Directors who were to be responsible for particular areas or districts but nothing was done to implement this provision, which was in fact the last vestige of earlier unsuccessful schemes for a network of local prosecutors, and the Director's staff have always been based in London. The department has an authorised

[1]See Appendix 23.

establishment of 57 legally qualified staff. In addition a Deputy Director, two Principal Assistant Directors and nine Assistant Directors are appointed by the Home Secretary.

157. The Director's office was first established as a separate entity by the Prosecution of Offences Act 1908. The present functions of the Director are based on the three Acts of 1879, 1884 and 1908 (which were consolidated in the Prosecution of Offences Act 1979) and the Prosecution of Offences Regulations 1978.

b. *The power to take over proceedings*

158. The Director is empowered by the 1979 Act to assume responsibility for the further conduct of any prosecution including discontinuing it at any stage if he sees fit. Thus although the right of a member of the public to institute or carry on criminal proceedings is expressly preserved by the 1979 Act (as it had been by the Acts of 1879 and 1908) the Director is given an important supervisory role by this provision. Taken with the power to require cases—or certain classes of case—to be referred to him, it in effect gives him the potential for imposing particular prosecution policies on other prosecutors. But the provisions have not been seen by successive Directors as appropriate to be used in that way. The power to take over prosecutions has been exercised on extremely few occasions, for example where the prosecution is malicious.

c. *Consents to prosecution*

159. In certain classes of case, however, the Director is required to become involved, particularly in recent years, by Parliament enacting that certain offences can be prosecuted only by or with the consent of the Director or the Attorney General.[1] The theoretical basis to the requirement for consent to be given before prosecution was analysed in the Home Office Memorandum to the Departmental Committee on s. 2 of the Official Secrets Act 1911,[2] which was cited by the Director in his evidence to the Royal Commission as follows:

"Put at its most general, the basic ground for including in a statute a restriction on the bringing of prosecutions is that otherwise there would be a risk of prosecutions being brought in inappropriate circumstances. There are several kinds of reason which may lead to the conclusion that such a risk exists. These reasons are not wholly distinct from each other, and more than one of them may well be present in any particular case but for purposes of exposition they may conveniently be distinguished as follows:

  (a) to secure consistency of practice in bringing prosecutions, eg where it is not possible to define the offence very precisely, so that the law goes wider than the mischief aimed at or is open to a variety of interpretations;

  (b) to prevent abuse, or the bringing of the law into disrepute, eg with the kind of offence which might otherwise result in vexatious private prosecutions or the institution of proceedings in trivial cases;

---

[1] There are also offences which require the consent of a Government department or some other official body.

[2] London HMSO Cmnd 5104, pp 125–26.

(c) to enable account to be taken of mitigating factors, which may vary so widely from case to case that they are not susceptible of statutory definition;

(d) to provide some central control over the use of the criminal law when it has to intrude into areas which are particularly sensitive or controversial, such as race relations or censorship;

(e) to ensure that decisions on prosecution take account of important considerations of public policy or of a political or international character, such as may arise, for instance, in relation to official secrets or hijacking.

"Subject to what is said above about the absence of a clear and long-established general policy [underlying the requirements for consent], recent practice would suggest that a control over prosecutions introduced on grounds (a), (b) or (c) above would normally be thought appropriate to the Director of Public Prosecutions, a control on ground (e) would normally be thought appropriate to the Attorney General, and a control on ground (d) might be given to either, depending on the particular circumstances. Where important political or international considerations may be involved, the Crown's senior Law Officer who is directly answerable in Parliament for his decisions and who is in a position to consult Ministerial colleagues directly if need be, is regarded as the proper person to carry the responsibility. Official Secrets Act cases apart, the case of Leila Khaled[1] provides a good recent illustration of this kind of situation. Similarly, with sensitive subjects like race relations Parliament may feel that they would like to hold the Attorney directly responsible for a personal decision rather than relying on his general superintendence of the Director."

Appendix 24 is a further memorandum submitted by the Director in response to an invitation from the Royal Commission. It discusses the question of consents to prosecution and gives statistics for 1977 on the number and type of cases submitted to the Director and Attorney General for consent or *fiat* and the number where this was withheld.

d. *The Director's prosecution activity and policies*

160. There were 17,738 applications to the Director in 1978. Proceedings were brought by the Director against 2,242 persons in 1,178 cases involving a total of 7,353 charges or counts. In the remaining cases he gave advice to the police or other authority, but it was left to the authority to prosecute as necessary. In his evidence to the Royal Commission, the Director described in some detail the factors which he takes into account when deciding whether to prosecute or to give his consent to a prosecution. This part of his evidence is reproduced at Appendix 25. The first criterion is whether there is a reasonable prospect of conviction. This is a higher standard than merely sufficient evidence to constitute a *prima facie* case. It has been described as whether a conviction is more likely than an acquittal. It takes into account such factors as the credibility which the jury is likely to attach to a witness. Even if this criterion

---

[1] The Palestinian terrorist who was deported instead of being prosecuted.

is met, the Director will not automatically prosecute. He then goes on to consider other factors, for example whether acquittal would have unfortunate consequences, the likely expense and duration of the trial compared with the gravity of the offence, and grounds of public policy. How the Director interprets these grounds is set out in Appendix 25. The Director also has a role to play in encouraging consistency of prosecution policy and practice between police forces in England and Wales. He has described these in a short note supplementary to his evidence to the Royal Commission. This is at Appendix 26.

e. *Allegations of criminal offences against police officers*

161. An additional responsibility for the Director is dealing with allegations that a criminal offence has been committed by a police officer. Under s. 49 of the Police Act 1964, complaints by the public against the police have to be reported to the Director unless the chief officer is "satisfied that no criminal offence has been committed". The Director comments in his evidence:

> "In practice almost every chief officer is extremely anxious to divest himself of responsibility for deciding whether one of his officers should be prosecuted, however trivial the allegation, so that there can be no suspicion of improper bias.

> "Hence they normally report all cases involving an officer even if the evidence is virtually non-existent and regardless of whether the complaint has been made by a member of the public. They will also report cases involving cadets and special constables who do not, strictly speaking, come within s. 49."

C. The functions of the law officers in relation to the prosecution system

162. The Attorney General, assisted by the Solicitor General (both of whom are Members of Parliament and appointed to their offices by the Government of the day), is the chief legal adviser to the Government and is ultimately responsible for all crown litigation. Apart from the occasions on which the Attorney or Solicitor General actually conduct a prosecution in court, the Law Officers have two important powers in respect of particular prosecutions. First, the Attorney General possesses the common law power to enter a *nolle prosequi* in cases tried on indictment, which has the effect of terminating the proceedings. This is analogous to the power of the Director of Public Prosecutions to take over a case and offer no evidence (see paragraph 158). But the Director's power may be exercised in respect of both summary and indictable cases, whereas the *nolle prosequi* is used only in respect of cases to be tried on indictment.

163. The Attorney General's other major power is to give or withhold his *fiat* to prosecution in those offences where his consent is necessary before a prosecution can be brought. By the Law Officers Act 1944, the Solicitor General may exercise this function if the Attorney General is absent or incapacitated or if he specifically authorises him to do so. This provision was discussed in relation to the similar powers of the Director of Public Prosecutions at paragraph 159. Statistical material on its use also is at Appendix 24.

164. Apart from these two special powers, the Attorney General carries Ministerial responsibility (and is thus answerable to Parliament) for his decisions as to the institution and conduct of criminal proceedings. This responsibility extends to the actions and decisions of the Director of Public Prosecutions, since the latter may be directed by the Attorney General to prosecute in a particular case (though this power is rarely used).[1] By tradition, the Attorney General can be asked to account for his decisions only *ex post facto*, and it is for him to decide how much of his reasoning to disclose. Indeed it is a well understood constitutional principle that the Attorney General's decisions on particular cases must be his alone. The position, as stated in 1959 by the then Prime Minister, is that "it is an established principle of government in this country, and a tradition long supported by all political parties, that the decision as to whether any citizen should be prosecuted, or whether any prosecution should be discontinued, should be a matter, where a public as opposed to a private prosecution is concerned, for the prosecuting authorities to decide on the merits of the case without political or other pressure". He went on to say that the Attorney General should "absolutely decline to receive orders from the Prime Minister or Cabinet or anybody else that he should prosecute".[2]

D. Prosecutions by non-police agencies

165. Substantial numbers of prosecutions are brought by government departments, nationalised industries, local authorities and a variety of other public bodies for criminal offences falling within their fields of responsibility.[3] Many of these are offences created by the statute relating specifically to the duties of that organisation, for example the Health and Safety at Work Act 1974 which established the Health and Safety Executive. Some of these statutes name the department or body concerned as the sole prosecutor, or one of a number of alternative prosecutors. For example s. 19 of the Prevention of Oil Pollution Act 1971 provides that proceedings may be brought only by the Attorney General, a harbour authority, the Secretary of State or a person authorised by him.

166. Of the offences commonly prosecuted by central government bodies the majority relate to the collection of various forms of revenue, the expenditure of public money (such as fraudulent claims to rebates or benefits) or contravention of regulatory requirements (such as factories legislation). Many of the departments and public bodies concerned have their own specialist investigation departments as well as their own legal advisers. As an example, in 1976 the Post Office Investigation Division comprised some 300 staff and prosecuted some 3,500 persons, the prosecutions largely being conducted by the Post Office Solicitor's Department. Some bodies handle even larger numbers of prosecutions. In 1975 the Department of the Environment (which was at that time the Vehicle Licensing Authority for England and Wales) and the local authorities which acted as its agents for vehicle licensing purposes

---

[1]Prosecution of Offences Act 1979, subsection 2(1).
[2]HC Debates Vol 600, col 31, 16 February 1959.
[3]Prosecutions by non-police governmental agencies are fully discussed in Chapter Three, and prosecutions by public utilities and local authorities in Chapter Six, of the Sheffield study, *op. cit.*

considered over one million reports of apparently unlicensed vehicles, which resulted in over 150,000 prosecutions for offences relating to vehicle excise duty.[1] But by no means all the offences charged by these bodies are of such a specialised nature. The Department of Health and Social Security in seeking to minimise benefit fraud will make use of the various offences under the Theft Act 1968. Clearly in many cases there is a degree of overlap with the responsibilities of the police, but there is generally an understanding as to their respective fields of operation. Thus the police are likely to deal with cases of violent robbery from Post Office premises or transport but offences involving savings frauds are more likely to be prosecuted by the Post Office itself.

167. Many of the functions of government which are performed by local authorities include law enforcement responsibilities, often under statutes specifically naming a local authority or one of its officials. For example, s. 51 of the Weights and Measures Act 1963 provides that proceedings under the Act shall not be instituted except by or on behalf of a local weights and measures authority or a chief officer of police. These specific statutory powers are in addition to the general power conferred by s. 222 of the Local Government Act 1972 for any local authority to prosecute in any legal proceedings where it is considered expedient for the promotion or protection of the interests of the inhabitants of the area. Section 223 of the Act enables a member or official of a local authority to exercise the power under the previous section on its behalf. Out of the wide range of duties which local authorities discharge, those which frequently involve prosecutions are public health and environmental duties generally, child welfare and education, consumer protection (for example under the Trade Descriptions Act 1968) and highways and parking matters.[2]

168. It should be noted that securing convictions for breaches of the law may not be the major aim of those public bodies which are also prosecuting authorities. For example, those concerned with the collection of revenue give a higher priority to maximising the amount of revenue collected, and those involved in the welfare or education of children see the child's needs as their major concern. Many of these bodies have a wide range of alternatives to prosecution such as care proceedings, mitigated penalties, warnings, cautions, prohibition notices, seizure of goods, or the cancellation or suspension of licences.

E. Private prosecutions

169. Under this heading are included prosecutions by private agencies, such as the NSPCC and RSPCA,[3] and by private individuals and retail stores.[4] The right of private prosecution is frequently described as an important constitutional principle. Traditionally the courts have been anxious to protect this right and in a number of leading cases have rejected defence submissions that a

---

[1]For further statistics on prosecutions by these agencies, see Appendices 3.1–3.7 to the Sheffield study, *op. cit.*
[2]See also the tables in Chapter Six of the Sheffield study, *op. cit.*
[3]For a discussion of these, see Chapter Four of the Sheffield study, *op, cit.*
[4]*Ibid*, at Chapter Five.

private person had no title to prosecute. For example, it was established in *Smith v Dear*[1] that it was no bar to prosecution by a third party that the victim of a crime was satisfied with compensation received from the offender. The general principle was stated by Channell, J. in *R v Kennedy*[2] thus:

" . . . as it is put in the form of a criminal offence, it appears to me that a private individual is entitled to prosecute for it."

As Lord Wilberforce said in *Garret v Union of Post Workers*:[3]

"The individual, in such situations, who wishes to see the law enforced has a remedy of his own: he can bring a private prosecution. This historical right which goes right back to the earliest days of our legal system, though rarely exercised in relation to indictable offences, and though ultimately liable to be controlled by the Attorney General (by taking over the prosecution and, if he thinks fit, entering a *nolle prosequi*) remains a valuable constitutional safeguard against inertia or partiality on the part of authority."

170. There is in practice, however, a number of constraints upon the individual prosecutor. First, there is the cost. Since legal aid is not available to meet the cost of bringing a prosecution, the private prosecutor has to find the money to obtain legal advice and, where necessary, representation. If the prosecution results in a conviction, the prosecutor may be awarded his own costs at the discretion of the court, but if the accused is acquitted the prosecutor may well have to bear part or the whole of the defence costs as well as his own. If the prosecution was frivolous or vindictive, the prosecutor may be sued by the defendant for malicious prosecution, with the possibility of damages being awarded if the action is successful. Furthermore, as has been noted, there is a large number of statutory offences for whose prosecution the consent of the Director of Public Prosecutions or Attorney General is necessary. Lastly there are the powers of the Director to take over any case at any point, and those of the Attorney to enter a *nolle prosequi* in an indictable case. The courts may also refuse to allow an unsatisfactory prosecution to be initiated (whether by private individuals or by the police). It has been held that "justices may, in the exercise of their discretion, refuse to issue a summons, even if there was evidence of the offence before them, if they considered that the issue of a summons would be a vexatious and improper proceeding".[4]

171. In practice, private prosecutions are nowadays numerically significant in only two categories of cases, shoplifting and common assault. As regards shoplifting, many of the larger stores have their own detective staff, and one or two police forces leave the firm to prosecute if it wishes. Various reasons have been suggested for this policy. For example, where the offence has been detected and the arrest carried out by trained personnel, there may not be the same practical need for police involvement, especially if the store concerned is accustomed to bringing its own prosecutions. While, however, the precise policy of the police on prosecution of shoplifters varies from force to force (as

[1] (1903) 20 Cox CC 458.
[2] (1902) 20 Cox 230 CC at 242.
[3] [1977] 3 All ER 70.
[4] See Lord Alverstone L. C. J. in *R v Bros* (1901) 66 JP at p 55.

a study by a Home Office Working Party[1] has shown) some steps have been taken towards greater uniformity of prosecution practice. The present position is that the Metropolitan Police encourage supermarkets and other large businesses to conduct their own prosecutions where they are willing to do so, while other police forces in England and Wales normally conduct all prosecutions for shoplifting, unless the company concerned wishes to undertake the prosecution itself.[2]

172. The other offence for which private prosecutions are brought is a common assault charged under s. 42 of the Offences Against the Person Act 1861. By the terms of that section the proceedings are to be brought "by or on behalf of the party aggrieved". By virtue of these words it has been held that the police may not prosecute, save in the most exceptional circumstances, for example where the victim is so feeble, old and infirm as to be incapable of instituting proceedings or is not a free agent but under the control of the person committing the assault.[3] Further, by virtue of s. 45 of the 1861 Act a person prosecuted for common assault under s. 42 of the Act is released from all further proceedings, civil or criminal, for the same cause. This applies whether he is convicted or acquitted.

173. The 1861 Act contains a variety of provisions relating to acts of violence. These include assault occasioning actual bodily harm (s. 47) and inflicting grievous bodily harm (s. 20) each punishable on conviction on indictment with five years imprisonment or on summary conviction with six months imprisonment and a fine of £1,000. There is also a common law offence of common assault; this is punishable on conviction on indictment with 12 months imprisonment (s. 47 of the 1861 Act) or on summary conviction with six months imprisonment and a fine of £1,000 (s. 28 of, and paragraph 5(h) of Schedule 3 to, the Criminal Law Act 1977). None of these offences is caught by the restriction on prosecution imposed by s. 42 of the 1861 Act or by the provisions of s. 45 of that Act preventing civil proceedings. Consequently, the police may prosecute for any assault, so long as the proceedings are not brought as a common assault under s. 42 of the 1961 Act. Notwithstanding the possibility of prosecuting under these provisions, it is now a widely adopted practice for the police not to prosecute for common assault. Indeed, it appears to be an accepted, though not necessarily correct, view of the law, that the police should not prosecute for a minor assault, because it is thought to prevent civil proceedings.[4]

174. The situations giving rise to private prosecutions for common assault are not easy to classify.[5] They frequently involve parties known to each other (for example neighbours) and they sometimes form part of a wider dispute. Sometimes violence may be used by both parties. Sometimes violence by one party may have been provoked, for example by abuse or annoyance and

---

[1]*Shoplifting and thefts by shop staff. Report of the Working Party on Internal Shop Security* (1973).

[2]For a discussion of the prosecution of shoplifting by stores and of the policies of different police forces see the Sheffield study, *op. cit.*

[3]*Nicholson v Booth* (1888) 52 JP 662; *Pickering v Willoughby* [1907] 2 KB 296.

[4]The Sheffield study, *op. cit.*

[5]For a discussion of this offence, see the 14th Report of the Criminal Law Revision Committee: *Offences against the Person*, London HMSO 1980, Cmnd 7844.

disturbance. Sometimes the violence used is trivial, but this is not always the case. The "accepted view of the law" referred to above can lead to the police taking no action, leaving the complainant to institute a private prosecution even where the assault is neither trivial nor provoked.

Procedural aspects of bringing a case to trial

A. The institution of proceedings

a. Laying an information

175. As a matter of strict legal theory all criminal proceedings are begun by the "laying of an information"; yet this is not the actual situation. Where the accused has been arrested and charged there is no step in the proceedings which can be regarded as the laying of an information. Where the proceedings are begun by way of summons, although there is a step which could be so described, what is actually done usually bears no relation to what the law requires.

176. The word "information" is not statutorily defined but it has been described as "nothing more than what the word implies, namely the statement by which the magistrate is informed of the offence for which the summons or warrant is required".[1] An information is not necessarily a document, for it need not be in writing[2] except where a warrant is issued.[3]

177. When it is in writing the form of an information is prescribed[4] and is as follows:

... Magistrates' Court

Date: *[date information laid]*

Accused: *[name of accused]*

Address:

Alleged offence:

The information of: *[name of person laying the information]*

Address:

who [upon oath][5] states that the accused committed the offence of which particulars are given above.

Taken [and sworn][5] before me

J.P.　　Justice of the Peace

[J.C.　　Justices' Clerk]

---

[1] See Huddleston, B in *R v Hughes* (1879) 4 QBD 614 at p 633.
[2] Magistrates' Courts Rules 1968, Rule 1.
[3] When it must also be substantiated on oath, Magistrates' Courts Act 1952, s. 1.
[4] Magistrates' Courts (Forms) Rules 1968, Form 1 in the Schedule.
[5] These words will be deleted unless the information is for a warrant.

An information is, under r. 83 of the Magistrates' Courts Rules, required to do no more than describe the offence in ordinary language; it need not state all the elements of the offence so long as it gives reasonable information of the nature of the charge and, where appropriate, quotes the statutory provision creating the offence. An information which is not on oath (that is, an information for a summons) may be laid either before a magistrate or (by virtue of the Justices' Clerks Rules 1970) before a justices' clerk. An information for a warrant (which must be on oath) may be laid only before a magistrate. It will be noted that although the prescribed form requires the signature of the magistrate or justices' clerk before whom it is laid, it does not require the signature of the informant.

b. Methods of bringing a person before a court

178. There are two main methods by which persons are brought before a court for the purpose of proceedings.

(a) The prosecutor may lay an information as described in the foregoing paragraphs and request the issue of a summons which is then served on the accused and which informs him of the offence(s) with which he is charged and the date on which he is summoned to appear before the magistrates' court.

(b) In the case of an offence for which a power of arrest without warrant exists the police may arrest the person for the offence without first laying an information and applying for a warrant. Following the arrest, the person is normally charged at the police station with the offence. The law requires that if it will not be practicable to bring the person before a magistrates' court within 24 hours he should be released on bail for surrender to a magistrates' court at a later date. If he is retained in custody, he must be brought before a magistrates' court "as soon as practicable".[1]

179. It is also possible (although this procedure seems rarely to be used) for the prosecutor to lay an information in writing and substantiated on oath, and to request the issue of a warrant to arrest the accused and bring him before the magistrates' court. A warrant may not be issued unless the offence is indictable or is punishable by imprisonment or unless the address of the accused is not sufficiently established for a summons to be served on him.[2]

c. Information for summons

180. When a summons is sought, laying an information requires the informant (that is, the prosecutor) to tell the magistrate or justices' clerk that he alleges that the accused has committed a specified offence. The magistrate or justices' clerk is required to go through the judicial exercise of deciding whether a summons ought to be issued or not.[3] He has a (judicial) discretion to refuse to issue a summons if he is of opinion that the prosecution is

[1] See paragraph 65.
[2] Criminal Justice Act 1967, subsection 24(1).
[3] *R v Brentford JJ* [1975] 1 QB 455; *R v West London JJ* [1979] 2 All ER 221.

vexatious[1] or that there will not be enough evidence to prove the allegation.[2] At the very least the magistrate or justices' clerk should ascertain:

> *(a)* whether the allegation is an offence known to the law and if so whether the ingredients of the offence are *prima facie* present;
>
> *(b)* that the offence alleged is not "out of time";
>
> *(c)* that the court has jurisdiction;
>
> *(d)* whether the informant has the necessary authority to prosecute.[3]

181. In practice, however, where a summons is applied for by the police or other recognised prosecution agencies[4] no consideration is given as to whether or not a summons should be issued. It is even common practice for them to prepare their own informations and summonses. If such a prosecutor makes a mistake or error of judgment leading to the case being dismissed then he may be ordered to pay costs and these will normally be paid without delay. The same is not necessarily true of a private prosecutor. Where a private person lays an information a magistrate or justices' clerk will seek to ensure the propriety of the prosecution and the technical correctness of the information and summons.

d. Information when accused arrested and charged

182. Where proceedings follow an arrest without warrant and the accused is charged by the police there is, as a matter of law, an "information" which has been "laid".[5] This, however, is a legal fiction. In such a case, the only relevant document prepared will be the police charge sheet which will contain all the particulars required for an information (see paragraph 177). The charge sheet will be delivered by the police to the court by way of the justices' clerk's office and the justices' clerk's staff will prepare the court register from the charge sheet. At no stage is the allegation put to a magistrate or the justices' clerk so that he may go through the judicial exercise of deciding whether or not there should be a hearing and ensure that the information (that is, the charge) is technically correct.[6] So, even though the charge sheet contains all the particulars required for an information, there is no point at which an information can be said to be "laid". The information is usually regarded as having been laid on the day the accused is bailed to attend court (whether or not he actually attends) or on the day an accused in custody is brought to court.

e. Information for arrest warrant

183. On an application for a warrant the magistrate should be satisfied that a warrant, as distinct from a summons, should be issued. The essential principle is that a warrant ought not to be issued when a summons would be

---

[1] *R v Bros* (1901) 66 JP 54, quoted with approval in *R v West London JJ* (above).
[2] *R v Mead* (1916) 80 JP 382.
[3] *R v West London JJ* (above).
[4] For example, government departments and local authorities.
[5] This is clear from a variety of statutory provisions including the Magistrates' Courts Act 1952, s. 14, the Magistrates' Courts Rules 1968, r. 10 and the Costs in Criminal Cases Act 1973, s. 12, all of which envisage the existence of an information.
[6] Compare the position prescribed by law on the laying of an information for a summons, paragraph 180.

equally effectual.[1] The information must be in writing and substantiated on oath[2] but it is usually no more than the purely formal document set out in paragraph 177. Nevertheless in a note of long standing to s. 1 of the Magistrates' Courts Act 1952 *Stone's Justices' Manual* states in relation to an information for a warrant:

> "It is customary to take an information in the form of deposition, stating shortly the facts: a formal information in the technical languge of the warrant was disapproved by the House of Lords in *Herniman v Smith* [1938] AC 305."

Despite this editorial opinion and high judicial guidance, it is extremely rare for an information for a warrant to be in the form of a deposition. A deposition is properly defined as a statement made on oath before a magistrate, taken down in writing, and signed by the person making the statement and by the magistrate. However carefully and thoroughly the magistrate may enquire into the matter, there will therefore be no record indicating why he issued a warrant (and not a summons). The application will, by its very nature, be *ex parte*. Historically, informations were laid in open court and the allegations made were liable to be reported in the press.[3] Today it is regarded as the better practice for informations to be laid in private. If the accused is aggrieved and claims that his arrest and detention was unjustified, his remedy will be by way of a civil action. The propriety of the issue of the warrant will be irrelevant in the criminal proceedings it commences. But, in the absence of a written record of what is an *ex parte* private hearing, it will be difficult, if not impossible, for him to commence such an action, for he will not know and will be unable to ascertain why a warrant was issued. The decision of a magistrate to issue a warrant is not subject to review; yet it is a decision which results in the deprivation of a person's liberty.

B. Committal proceedings

a. Historical background

184. Before the establishment of regular police forces it was the duty of magistrates to pursue and arrest offenders and it was the magistrates who could be referred to as "detectives and prosecutors".[4] They had responsibility for the taking of depositions as long ago as the 16th century. These were equivalent to the statements taken from witnesses by the police today. The examination of the witnesses took place in private and the accused had no right to be present. In the early part of the 19th century the responsibility for enquiring into offences began to pass to the police. In 1848 changes were made in the procedure. The Administration of Justice (No 1) Act of that year set out to consolidate the law relating to the duties of magistrates in relation to the functions of investigating and inquiring into offences, with such changes as were deemed necessary. The most important change was a provision whereby the accused was entitled, for the first time, to be present at the examination of the witnesses against him. But the inquiry was not required to be in open

---

[1] *O'Brien v Brabner* (1885) 49 JPN 227.
[2] Magistrates' Courts Act 1952, s. 1.
[3] *Kimber v Press Association* [1893] 1 QB 65.
[4] For a fuller account see *Report of Departmental Committee on Proceedings before Examining Justices* London HMSO 1958, Cmnd 479 (the Tucker Report).

court, that is in public. The nature of the inquiry by the magistrates was changing before 1848 and continued to do so after that year. During this transitional period, the position of the police as investigators and prosecutors was becoming more clearly established. During the same period, the magistrates' inquiry became a judicial instead of an investigative function. Indeed, by 1848, or soon after, the magistrates' examination (that is committal proceedings) usually took place in open court. As a result of these changes there became grafted onto the system a preliminary judicial hearing.

b. Committal proceedings today

185. This preliminary judicial hearing continues today, with modifications, as committal proceedings.[1] The link with the magistrates' former investigative functions is evidenced by the statutory reference to committal proceedings as an inquiry into an offence by examining justices;[2] and by the procedure which envisages that the charge will not be formulated until after the "examining justices" have heard the evidence of the prosecution and that it is the magistrates who will decide upon what charge the accused will be committed for trial.[3] These terminological and procedural relics have no practical effect today. As the police became the principal investigators of crime, so the magistrates' inquiry became a judicial function with the object of ensuring that there was sufficient evidence for the accused to stand trial. In 1848 when this practice was codified[4] all crimes proper were triable only at assizes or quarter sessions (now the Crown Court);[5] so it may be said that the normal criminal procedure envisaged a preliminary judicial hearing before a person could be put on trial.

186. From 1848 until the present time there has been a continuous tendency to confer jurisdiction on magistrates' courts to try criminal offences. Today, those courts try as many as 80 per cent of all indictable offences.[6] Consequently, a preliminary judicial hearing is held in only the 20 per cent of such cases which are committed for trial at the Crown Court.

c. Purpose of committal proceedings

187. The purpose of committal proceedings now is to ensure that no person shall stand trial at the Crown Court unless there is a *prima facie* case against him. It is not a purpose of committal proceedings that the defence may hear all the prosecution witnesses, or any particular witness or witnesses, give their evidence in chief or that such witnesses shall be made available for cross examination. The prosecution are not required to call all their witnesses at committal proceedings; if they can make out a *prima facie* case without calling any particular witness or witnesses, even an important witness, they are entitled

---

[1]It is possible to dispense with committal proceedings by preferring a voluntary bill of indictment but this procedure is rarely used.

[2]Magistrates' Courts Act 1952, ss. 4, 6 and 7, which, in this context, are simply repeating the wording of 19th century statutes.

[3]See s. 7 of the 1952 Act and r. 4 of the Magistrates' Courts Rules 1968 (repeating the effect of 19th century legislation).

[4]In the Administration of Justice (No 1) Act 1848.

[5]Only very minor offences could be dealt with by magistrates' courts. No indictable offence could be dealt with by them.

[6]If all offences are included in the calculation, the proportion dealt with by magistrates' courts is as high as 97 per cent.

to do so and neither the defence nor the court can require any witness to be called.[1] It follows that committal proceedings are not necessarily a means whereby the defence may obtain full disclosure of the prosecution case before trial. In most cases, however, the prosecution do present all their evidence at the committal proceedings, and if they do not, they should give notice before the trial of any additional evidence they propose to call.

d. Form of committal proceedings

188. Committal proceedings may take one of two forms, either:

(a) a hearing under s. 7 of the Magistrates' Courts Act 1952, or

(b) a committal for trial without consideration of the evidence by the magistrates under s. 1 of the Criminal Justice Act 1967.

These different types of committal are discussed in the following paragraphs. The general rule is that all stages of committal proceedings, whichever form they take, must take place in the presence and hearing of the accused. There are limited exceptions. These are where the accused is so disorderly as to make it impractical for evidence to be given in his presence or he is absent for reasons of health but is legally represented and has consented to evidence being given in his absence (Criminal Justice Act 1967, s. 45).

189. Since 1967 most committals are made under s. 1 of the Criminal Justice Act 1967. This provides that where all the evidence before the court (whether for the prosecution or the defence) consists of written statements,[2] tendered with or without exhibits, the magistrates may commit the accused for trial at the Crown Court without consideration of the contents of those statements, unless:

(a) the accused or one of them is not legally represented; or

(b) counsel or a solicitor for the accused or one of them has asked the court to consider a submission that the statements disclose insufficient evidence to put that person upon trial by jury for the offence.

190. The other form of committal proceedings, under s. 7 of the Magistrates' Courts Act 1952, requires the magistrates' court[3] to consider the evidence.[4] The procedure is laid down in s. 4 of the Magistrates' Courts Rules 1968 whereby the oral evidence of each witness[5] must be put into writing. It is then read to the witness, signed by him, and authenticated by the magistrate (or one of the magistrates). Evidence so recorded is known as a deposition.

191. The procedure involving the recording of the oral evidence of each witness as a deposition may be modified by allowing a written statement[6] of a

---

[1]*R v Epping and Harlow JJ ex parte Massaro* [1973] 1 QB 433; *R v Grays JJ ex parte Tetley* (1980) 80 Cr App R 11.

[2]These must comply with the provisions of s. 2 of the Criminal Justice Act 1967 and r. 58 of the Magistrates' Courts Rules 1968, see footnotes 1 and 2 to paragraph 191.

[3]The court may be comprised of a single magistrate for this purpose.

[4]Magistrates sitting for a committal hearing are statutorily (and archaically) referred to as "examining justices".

[5]Including any evidence given by or on behalf of the accused but not any witness of his merely as to character.

[6]This must be in the prescribed form, r. 58 of the Magistrates' Courts Rules 1968 and form 8 of the Magistrates' Courts (Forms) Rules 1968. It will be based on the original statement made to the police but excluding prejudicial and inadmissible matter and where the prosecution has a legal representative should be prepared by him and not a police officer, *Practice Note* [1969] 3 All ER 1033.

witness to be admitted in evidence in accordance with s. 2 of the Criminal Justice Act 1967. Such a statement may be admitted in evidence only if, amongst other conditions,[1] the accused (or each of them) does not object and the court does not require the witness to attend and give evidence. An advantage of this modification of the procedure is that a witness whom the defence do not wish to cross-examine at the committal proceedings need not be called to give evidence at those proceedings. A statement so admitted as evidence must be read out[2] at the committal hearing and forms part of the evidence upon which the court will decide whether or not to commit the accused for trial.

192. At a committal hearing under s. 7 of the Magistrates' Courts Act 1952 the court must, if it is of the opinion that there is sufficient evidence to put the accused on trial by jury, commit him for trial; if it is not so satisfied it must discharge him. The function of magistrates at a committal hearing is to decide whether there is "such evidence that, if it be uncontradicted at the trial, a reasonably minded jury may convict upon it".[3] In no sense are they attempting to determine whether or not the accused is guilty of the offence.

193. There is no information kept nationally of the use made of committals under s. 1 of the Criminal Justice Act 1967 as opposed to those under s. 7 of the Magistrates' Courts Act 1952. It is generally thought that the proportion of the latter to the former is extremely small and the limited research information that is available bears out this impression. In a study of cases committed for trial by Sheffield magistrates' court during 1972, only one case out of a total of 356 had full committal proceedings.[4] And of 2,406 cases sent for trial in the Crown Court at Birmingham during 1975 and 1976, only four had full committals; in 18 others some of the evidence had been given orally.[5]

C. Disclosure of evidence by the prosecution

a. In cases tried on indictment

194. In cases tried at the Crown Court the evidence of the prosecution may be disclosed to the defence in any one or more of three ways. First, (and this is the most common way) where the prosecution propose to adduce evidence at the committal proceedings by way of written statement, a copy of the statement will be given to the defence at or before those proceedings (see paragraph 191). Second, where, at the committal proceedings, oral evidence is recorded as a deposition, the Crown Court is responsible for supplying the defence with a copy of the deposition (see paragraph 190). Third, where the prosecution propose to call evidence in addition to that given at the committal proceedings, they should give notice to the defence of their intention to call such evidence

---

[1] These other conditions are (a) the statement purports to be signed by the person who made it, (b) it contains a declaration that it is true to the best of that person's knowledge and belief, and (c) that a copy has been served on the accused or each of the accused.

[2] If the court so directs, the contents of the statement may be summarised instead of being read out in full.

[3] *R v Governor of Brixton Prison, ex parte Bidwell* [1937] 1 KB 374.

[4] A E Bottoms and J D McClean: *Defendants in the Criminal Process*, London, Routledge and Kegan Paul, 1976.

[5] We are grateful to Drs John Baldwin and Michael McConville of the Institute of Judicial Administration, University of Birmingham, for allowing us to quote these findings from their study of acquittals at the Crown Court in advance of publication.

and a copy of the evidence they propose to call ought to be served on the defence. It seems there is no procedure whereby the prosecution can be required to serve a copy of such additional evidence, but if the accused is taken by surprise he may apply for an adjournment. The defence is normally given full advance disclosure of the evidence the prosecution propose to call. The duty of the prosecution to disclose to the defence any other material in their possession has elements of uncertainty and is discussed in the following paragraphs.

195. It is clear that where the prosecution have taken a statement from a witness who they know can give material evidence, but whom they do *not* intend to call as a witness, they are obliged to make that witness available to the defence by supplying his name and address.[1] Failure to discharge this obligation may amount to a denial of natural justice and result in the conviction being quashed.[2]

196. Where a prosecution witness gives evidence which conflicts with a previous statement made by him, prosecuting counsel is expected to show defence counsel the statement so that he may cross examine on it.[3] It is doubtful if the prosecution are under any greater duty than that and in *R v Howes*[4] the Lord Chief Justice said, "If the prosecution are putting forward a case in which it is necessary for them to tender a witness . . . whose evidence is vital to the material issue, it would not be right for them if they had a statement from that witness conflicting with the evidence he is afterwards giving in the box, that they should not supply a copy of his previous statement or inform the defence of that fact."

197. Where a prosecution witness is of known bad character it appears to be the rule that the defence should be informed of the fact[5] or, at least, informed of convictions affecting the credibility of the witness.[6]

198. Details of previous convictions of the accused must be supplied by the police to the defence solicitor or, if no solicitor is instructed, to defence counsel on request.[7] The purpose of this requirement is to prevent the defence inadvertently putting the character of the accused at issue without realising that he is vulnerable on this score.

199. There are certain kinds of expert or technical evidence which the prosecution must make available to the defence. For example, the prosecution must supply a copy of any statement or report made by any prison medical officer who can give evidence as to insanity, and must make such a witness available to the defence.[8] More generally, it is a recognised principle that the

[1] *R v Bryant and Dickson* (1946) 31 Cr App R 146. In *Dallison v Caffery* [1965] 1 QB 348, Lord Denning M. R. suggested at p 369 that the prosecution should not only supply the name and address of the witness but also a copy of his statement; in the same case, however, Diplock, L. J. stated at p 376 that the duty on the prosecution was confined to making the witness available.
[2] *R v Leyland JJ ex parte Hawthorne* [1979] 2 WLR 28.
[3] *R v Clarke* (1930) 22 Cr App R 58; *Baksh v R* [1958] AC 167.
[4] March 27 1950 (unreported).
[5] *R v Collister and Warhurst* (1955) 39 Cr App R 100.
[6] See Lord Devlin in *Connelly v DPP* [1964] AC 1254 at p 1348.
[7] *Practice Direction* [1966] 1 WLR 1184.
[8] *R v Casey* (1947) 32 Cr App R 91. Nowadays such reports are sent direct to the court, which then supplies copies to both the prosecution and defence.

results of any examination carried out at a Home Office Forensic Science laboratory should be made available to the defence where such results may have a bearing on the case, even if the prosecution has neither tendered such results in evidence nor intends to do so.[1]

200. A recent development which, while not the primary purpose of the scheme, involves an element of reciprocal disclosure between prosecution and defence is the pre-trial review adopted in selected cases at the Central Criminal Court and now at other Crown Court centres. A note provided by the Lord Chancellor's Department about these arrangements is at Appendix 27.

201. Existing practice on pre-trial disclosure in cases tried on indictment also varies considerably between different prosecuting solicitors' departments. Appendix 28 sets out the existing practice in this respect in the office of the Director of Public Prosecutions, in the Metropolitan Police Solicitor's Department and in one of the largest prosecuting solicitors' departments, that of Greater Manchester.

202. The rules set out above leave much to the discretion of the prosecution, both because of uncertainties about their precise requirements and because they depend to some extent on subjective judgment (for example as to what might be "material" to the defence case). In practice, this discretion is frequently left to prosecution counsel, who may be specifically asked to advise what material should be disclosed. Much material is in fact disclosed on a "counsel to counsel" basis, an arrangement which encourages the wide use of the prosecution's discretion because it enables a degree of confidentiality to be maintained. Partly for this reason, current practice on disclosure is often considerably more liberal than the formal rules set out above require. However, disclosure between counsel has the drawback that it often does not take place until, or shortly before, the trial when it becomes known who counsel is, though some kinds of material (for example the results of forensic examinations) are disclosed at an earlier stage.

b. *In cases tried summarily*

203. With one exception existing procedures for summary trial place no obligation on the prosecution to give the accused advance notice of the evidence on which it intends to rely at the trial. Prosecutors may, however, indicate informally to the defence solicitor the nature of the prosecution case if he asks for it. But there is an obligation on the prosecution to supply to the defence the name and address of any witness who they know can give material evidence but whom they do not intend to call (see the *Leyland Justices* case cited at paragraph 195). Section 48 of the Criminal Law Act 1977 (reproduced in Appendix 29) enables rules of court to be made which could provide for disclosure by the prosecution in summary or either way offences. No rules have been made and a working party convened by the Home Office is studying the relative merits and costs of various possible schemes of disclosure, concentrating initially on either way offences.

204. The exception is in cases where the procedure under the Magistrates' Courts Act 1957 for pleading guilty in absence is adopted. This procedure is

[1]Home Office Circular 158/1947.

limited to summary offences punishable on conviction by not more than three months imprisonment.[1] It allows the prosecutor to serve on the accused with the summons "a concise statement in the prescribed form of such facts relating to the charge as will be placed before the court by or on behalf of the prosecutor if the accused pleads guilty without appearing before the court". A statement of the effect of the 1957 Act is also sent with the summons and this tells the accused that he may, if he wishes, plead guilty in writing and have the case dealt with in his absence. If this procedure is adopted the prosecution may refer only to the facts contained in the statement together with any previous convictions notified.

205. There is at present no statutory provision in force requiring the prosecution to disclose particulars of its case to the defence before the defendant has to choose the mode of trial. Nor will the defence receive such information (except by informal arrangement between defence solicitor and prosecutor) if the offence is tried summarily. On the other hand, if the accused elects trial at the Crown Court, he will obtain disclosure of the prosecution case to the extent outlined in paragraphs 194 ff.

D. Disclosure by the defence

206. The preceding section has set out the various requirements for disclosure of evidence by the prosecution to the defence. In contrast, the defence is under no such obligation, apart from certain very limited exceptions which are set out in the following paragraphs. The defence is not required to disclose any statements or the names of the witnesses who will be called or the evidence they will give; nor does the defendant have to plead until the trial.

207. There are two exceptions to the rule that the defence may reserve the whole of its case until the trial. The first relates to defences of alibi in trials on indictment. The disclosure of the defence of alibi was recommended by the Criminal Law Revision Committee in its *Ninth Report on Evidence* in 1966.[2] That recommendation was implemented in s. 11 of the Criminal Justice Act 1967, which provides that in proceedings on indictment the defendant may not without the leave of the court adduce evidence in support of an alibi unless he has given notice of that evidence within seven days of the conclusion of the committal proceedings.

208. The second exception is a very few statutory offences of a specialised nature, such as breaches of regulatory requirements. An example is s. 2 of the Consumer Safety Act 1978. It is a statutory defence for offences under that Act against safety regulations for the defendant to prove that he took all reasonable steps and exercised all due diligence to avoid the commission of the offence. That section also provides that if in any case the defence involves the allegation that the commission of the offence was owing to the act or default of another, or to reliance on information supplied by another person, the defendant shall not, without the leave of the court, be entitled to rely on this defence unless he has served notice on the prosecution at least seven days

---

[1]Sentence of imprisonment or disqualification cannot be imposed until the defendant has been given the opportunity to make specific representations to the court (s. 24 Criminal Justice Act 1967).
[2]London HMSO Cmnd 3145.

beforehand, giving such information identifying or assisting in the identification
of the other person as was then in his possession.

Statutory police powers to stop and search persons

This list is restricted to stop and search of persons. Where there are linked powers to stop and search vehicles or vessels these have been mentioned, but these references are not a comprehensive list of such powers. It should also be noted that powers to stop persons which are not linked with powers to search them, for example section 4 of the Conservation of Seals Act 1970, are not included.

Table 1.1 Public general legislation

Statutory provision	Person on whom power conferred	Circumstances in which exercisable/person who may be searched
Airports Authority Act 1975, s. 11	Any constable appointed under the Act on any aerodrome owned or managed by the Authority	Any person employed by the Authority, or working on any aerodrome owned or managed by the Authority whom the constable has reasonable grounds to suspect of having in his possession or conveying in any manner anything stolen or unlawfully obtained on any such aerodrome (Note: there is a linked power to search any vehicle or aircraft in similar circumstances)
Badgers Act 1973, s. 10	Any constable	Where there are reasonable grounds for suspecting that a person is committing, or has committed, an offence under the Act, and that evidence of the commission of the offence is to be found on that person or any vehicle or article he may have with him (Note: power of search extends to any such vehicle or article)
Canals (Offences) Act 1840, s. 11	Any constable appointed under the Act in respect of a canal or river	Any person who may be reasonably suspected of having or conveying in any manner anything stolen or unlawfully obtained (Note: there is also a power to search any vessel, boat, cart or carriage in similar circumstances)
Conservation of Wild Creatures and Wild Plants Act 1975, s. 10	Any constable	Any person reasonably suspected of committing, or of having committed, an offence under the Act, if the constable reasonably suspects that he has evidence on his person of the commission of an offence under the Act (Note: there is an attached power to search any vehicle, boat or animal which the person is using at the time)

Appendix 1

Statutory provision	Person on whom power conferred	Circumstances in which exercisable/person who may be searched
Firearms Act 1968, s. 47(3)	Any constable	Where there is reasonable cause to suspect a person of having a firearm with him in a public place, or to be committing, or about to commit, elsewhere than in a public place, one of certain offences under the Act (Note: there is also a power in similar circumstances to search a vehicle)
S. 49 (1) & (2)	Any constable	A police officer may search for and seize any firearms or ammunition which he has reason to believe are being removed or have been removed in contravention of an order under s. 6 of the Act *etc.* Any person having the custody or control of firearms or ammunition in course of transit shall on demand by a constable allow him all reasonable facilities to inspect and examine them, and shall produce any documents relating thereto
Metropolitan Police Act 1839, s. 66	Any constable within the Metropolitan Police District (Note: by virtue of the Special Constables Act 1923 this power extends to constables of the Ministry of Defence Police, and, further, by virtue of the Atomic Energy Authority Act 1954 (Schedule 3) to constables of the Atomic Energy Authority Police, within their respective jurisdictions)	Any person who may be reasonably suspected of having or conveying in any manner anything stolen or unlawfully obtained (Note: there is a linked power to search any vessel, boat, cart or carriage in similar circumstances)
Misuse of Drugs Act 1971, s. 23(2)	Any constable	Any person reasonably suspected of being in unlawful possession of a controlled drug (Note: there is also a power to search any vehicle or vessel in which the constable suspects that the drug may be found)
Pedlars Act 1871, s. 19	Any constable or officer of police	Power to open and inspect any pack, box, bag, trunk or case in which a pedlar carries his goods

Statutory provision	Person on whom power conferred	Circumstances in which exercisable/person who may be searched
Poaching Prevention Act 1862, s. 2, as amended by the Games Laws (Amendment) Act 1960	Any constable	Any person in any public place whom the constable may have good cause to suspect of coming from any land where he shall have been unlawfully in search of or pursuit of game, or any person aiding or abetting such person, and having in his possession any game unlawfully obtained, or any gun or part of a gun or ammunition, nets, traps *etc* (Note: there is also a linked power to stop and search any cart or conveyance)
Policing of Airports Act 1974, s. 3	Any relevant constable (ie a constable for the area in which the airport is situated) within a designated airport	Any airport employee whom the constable has reasonable grounds to suspect of having in his possession or of conveying in any manner anything stolen or unlawfully obtained on the aerodrome (Note: there are also linked powers to search any vehicle or aircraft in similar circumstances, and to stop any person leaving a cargo area and inspect any goods carried by him)
Prevention of Terrorism (Temporary Provisions) Act 1976, s. 14 and Sch. 3, Part II, paragraph 6(1)	Any constable	In any circumstances in which a constable has power under s. 12 of the Act to arrest a person, he may also stop and search him for the purpose of ascertaining whether he has in his possession any document or article which may constitute evidence that he is a person liable to arrest
Protection of Aircraft Act 1973, s. 19(2)	Any constable (or other person specified in a direction by the Secretary of State under s. 10 of the Act)	Any person who is for the time being in any part of an aerodrome in respect of which a direction has been issued under s. 10 of the Act, and where there is reasonable cause to believe that a firearm, explosive *etc* is, or may be brought (Note: the power extends to any person who is in any part of the aerodrome at the relevant time, and is not restricted to persons suspected of carrying such firearm, explosive *etc*. There is also a power to search any part of the aerodrome, or any aircraft, vehicle, goods or other movable property of any description)
Protection of Birds Act 1954, s. 12	Any constable	Any person found committing an offence against the Act (Note: power of search extends to any vehicle, boat or animal which such person may then be using)

77

Statutory provision	Person on whom power conferred	Circumstances in which exercisable/person who may be searched
Protection of Birds Act 1967 s. 11	Any constable	Where there are reasonable grounds for suspecting that a person has taken or destroyed an egg of a protected bird (as specified in Sch. 1 to the Protection of Birds Act 1954) and that evidence of the commission of the offence is to be found on that person or on any vehicle, boat or animal which that person may be using (Note: power of search extends to any such vehicle, boat or animal)
Public Stores Act 1875, s. 6	Any constable of the Metropolitan Police within the limits for which he is constable, and any constable if deputed by a public department (Note: by virtue of the Special Constables Act 1923 this power extends to constables of the Ministry of Defence Police, and, further, by virtue of the Atomic Energy Authority Act 1954 (Schedule 3) to constables of the Atomic Energy Authority Police)	Any person reasonably suspected of having or conveying in any manner any of Her Majesty's stores, stolen or unlawfully obtained (Note: there is also a power to search any vessel, boat or vehicle in similar circumstances. By virtue of Sch. 3 to the Atomic Energy Authority Act 1954 "Her Majesty's stores" includes any goods or chattels belonging to or in the possession of the Authority)

Table 1. 2 Local legislation

The following provisions confer upon police in the relevant (pre–1974) local authority areas powers which are similar to those conferred on the Metropolitan Police by s. 66 of the Metropolitan Police Act 1839 (see above):

1. Birkenhead Corporation Act 1881, s. 99, as amended by the Birkenhead Corporation Act 1923, s. 104.

2. Birmingham Corporation (Consolidation) Act 1883, s. 137(2).

3. Burnley Borough Improvement Act 1871, s. 342.

4. City [of London] Police Act 1839, s. 48.

5. Hertfordshire County Couneil Act 1935, s. 130.

6. Liverpool Corporation Act 1921, s. 514.

7. Manchester Police Act 1844, s. 218.

8. Newcastle-upon-Tyne Improvement Act 1841, s. 39.

9. Oldham Borough Improvement Act 1865, s. 204.

10. Rochdale Corporation Act 1948, s. 115.

11. St Helens Borough Improvement Act 1869, s. 257.

12. Salford Improvement Act 1862, s. 242.

In addition, there are also the two following provisions:

13. British Transport Commission Act 1949, s. 54(1). This provision confers on any constable the power to stop and search any person employed by, or on the premises of, the former British Transport Commission—including the premises of the British Railways Board, the London Transport Executive and the British Transport Docks Board—whom there is reasonable cause to suspect of being in possession of anything stolen or unlawfully obtained from such premises.

14. Port of London Act 1968, s. 157. Under this provision a constable within the port police area has power to stop and search any person whom he reasonably suspects to be in possession of anything stolen or unlawfully obtained on or from the port premises, a vessel in dock or at a pier, or other specified premises.

Table 1. 3. Secondary legislation

The Mersey Docks and Harbour (Police) Order 1975 (SI 1975/1224), Article 4. This order, made under s. 14 of the Harbours Act 1964, gives constables a power in respect of the port of Liverpool similar to that conferred in respect of the port of London by the Port of London Act 1968.

Stops and searches for controlled drugs under the Misuse of Drugs Act 1971

Table 2.1 Stops and searches for controlled drugs in England and Wales (excluding Metropolitan Police District)

	1972	1973	1974	1975	1976	1977	1978
Numbers of occasions on which persons were stopped and searched	14046	12340[1]	9144[2]	9158	9912	10446	10023[3]
Numbers of occasions on which illegal possession of drugs was discovered	4481	4123[1]	2799[2]	2521	2515[4]	3135	3116[5]
Percentage of occasions on which illegal possession of drugs was discovered	31.9	33.4	30.6	27.5	25.4	30.0	31.1
Number of persons involved in searches	16953	18067	14831	14099	14859	15850	18107
Numbers of persons found in illegal possession of drugs	5095	5170	4115	3413	3503	4026	4051
Percentage of persons searched who were found in illegal possession of drugs	30.1	28.6	27.8	24.2	23.6	25.4	22.4
Number of formal complaints against police arising from stop-searches	46	41	33	37	38	65	35

[1] Does not include figures for Hertfordshire, Kent or Thames Valley.
[2] Does not include figures for Thames Valley.
[3] Including one pop festival in the course of which 1282 persons were stopped and searched.
[4] Does not include figures for Hertfordshire.
[5] Including one pop festival at which 75 persons were found in illegal possession of drugs.

Stops and searches for controlled drugs in the Metropolitan Police District.

New Scotland Yard have provided the following details in respect of the Metropolitan Police District:

In 1977, 5818 stop-searches were made under the Act and 2001 arrests made as a result. In 1978, 6412 stop-searches led to 2483 arrests. It is not known how many of those arrests were for illegal possession of drugs.

In 1978, 97 official complaints were registered as a result of all types of stop-searches but it is not known what proportion of those resulted from searches under this Act.

Stops of persons and vehicles under the Metropolitan Police Act 1839

Table 3.1 Statistics of stops by District and Division

District and Division	July 1978				January 1979			
	Total number of stops	Number of stops from road checks	Number of arrests from stops	Percentage of arrests from stops	Total number of stops	Number of stops from road checks	Number of arrests from stops	Percentage of arrests from stops
F								
Hammersmith	766	109	69		455	0	77	
Fulham	472	85	75		369	38	39	
Shepherds Bush	380	0	85		372	0	48	
Total	1618	194	229	14	1196	38	164	14
G								
City Road	341	32	59		201	0	21	
Hackney	645	312	80		309	61	42	
Stoke Newington	456	17	48		204	0	29	
Total	1442	361	187	13	714	61	92	13
H								
Leman Street	436	19	81		318	0	42	
Bethnal Green	320	129	60		441	0	46	
Limehouse	226	0	46		135	0	14	
Total	982	148	187	19	894	0	102	11
J								
Chingford	247	0	35		255	0	40	
Leyton	321	0	18		181	0	15	
Ilford	388	29	49		275	0	46	
Barkingside	299	0	46		241	0	45	
Total	1255	29	148	12	952	0	146	15

Table 3.1 (continued)

District and Division	July 1978				January 1979			
	Total number of stops	Number of stops from road checks	Number of arrests from stops	Percentage of arrests from stops	Total number of stops	Number of stops from road checks	Number of arrests from stops	Percentage of arrests from stops
K								
Romford	620	75	58		716	74	74	
East Ham	484	146	125		460	6	74	
Dagenham	321	0	66		363	0	51	
West Ham	546	0	77		446	0	62	
Total	1971	221	326	16	1985	80	261	13
L								
Brixton	423	0	98		880	0	166	
Kennington	237	0	31		593	0	50	
Clapham	137	0	50		277	0	65	
Streatham	186	0	31		526	0	131	
Total	983	0	210	21	2276	0	412	18
M								
Southwark	586	0	42		803	279	60	
Tower Bridge	396	138	50		388	24	60	
Carter Street	505	0	90		367	0	59	
Peckham	790	121	137		701	116	95	
Total	2277	259	319	14	2259	419	274	12
N								
Kings Cross Rd	317	0	25		217	0	28	
Holloway	636	58	106		364	20	54	
Islington	463	0	52		306	0	39	
Total	1416	58	183	13	887	29	121	14

Group	Area								
P	Catford	340	0	18		257	0	8	
	Lewisham	499	22	115		437	0	89	
	Bromley	320	27	47		264	47	45	
	St Mary Cray	375	0	57		327	0	45	
	Total	1534	49	237	15	285	47	187	15
Q	Wembley	382	0	46		435	0	26	
	Harlesden	896	42	127		674	0	81	
	Harrow	654	46	92		661	74	76	
	Total	1932	88	265	14	1770	74	183	10
R	Greenwich	417	0	60		876	338	73	
	Woolwich	501	44	43		433	65	43	
	Bexleyheath	650	85	66		496	50	45	
	Total	1568	129	169	11	805	455	161	9
S	Golders Green	475	130	56		625	310	23	
	West Hendon	679	0	56		470	98	42	
	Barnet	758	51	84		646	67	48	
	Total	1912	181	196	10	1741	475	113	6
T	Hounslow	440	0	56		534	0	94	
	Chiswick	621	0	48		365	0	31	
	Twickenham	423	0	22		321	0	22	
	Richmond	402	0	41		311	20	30	
	Total	1886	0	167	9	1531	20	177	12
V	Kingston	380	34	72		245	0	37	
	Esher	390	0	46		255	0	20	
	Wimbledon	615	131	64		512	0	80	
	Total	1385	165	182	13	1012	0	137	14

Table 3.1 (continued)

District and Division	July 1978				January 1979			
	Total number of stops	Number of stops from road checks	Number of arrests from stops	Percentage of arrests from stops	Total number of stops	Number of stops from road checks	Number of arrests from stops	Percentage of arrests from stops
W								
Tooting	440	35	60		492	0	59	
Battersea	685	60	62		517	40	28	
Putney	397	0	48		358	0	47	
Total	1522	95	170	11	367	40	134	10
X								
Ealing	740	88	125		664	13	45	
Southall	462	0	47		413	0	52	
Ruislip	367	0	41		352	0	59	
Total	1569	88	213	14	1429	13	156	11
Z								
Croydon	1381	346	126		665	86	91	
Norbury	1043	296	87		621	30	120	
Epsom	258	0	50		210	0	36	
Sutton	722	268	72		355	0	39	
Total	3404	910	335	10	1851	116	286	15
Airport								
Heathrow	1009	311	34		1084	126	30	
West Drayton	459	126	53		307	0	25	
Total	1468	437	87	6	1391	126	55	4
Grand Total	40477	3988	5110	13	35298	2293	4189	12

84

Powers of entry of public officials

Table 4.1 Entry to private premises

Department[1]	Statutory authority	Person(s) authorised	Form of authority	Place to which there is power of entry	Power and circumstances of use	Points of interest
1. Customs and Excise	Customs and Excise Act 1952 s. 71(3)	Any customs officer, constable, member of HM forces	Commission of appointment	House or place from which there are reasonable grounds to suspect signals or messages being transmitted to smugglers	Enter and take steps to stop sending of message	
	s. 106(6)	Any customs officer	Commission of appointment	Premises in N. Ireland where reason to believe there is anything liable to forfeiture under provisions relating to unlawfully manufactured spirits	Enter, if necessary by force, search and remove anything liable to forfeiture	
	s. 296(1) and (2)	Any customs officer (if at night, only if accompanied by a constable)	1. Writ of Assistance, or 2. Magistrate's warrant	Premises where reasonable grounds to suspect there is anything liable to forfeiture under C & E Acts	Enter, if necessary by force, and search, seize, detain or remove anything liable to forfeiture	

[1]Or local authority or other official body.

Table 4.1 (continued)

Department	Statutory authority	Person(s) authorised	Form of authority	Place to which there is power of entry	Power and circumstances of use	Points of interest
1. Customs and Excise (continued)	Finance Act 1972 s. 37(3)	Any authorised person	Magistrate's warrant	Premises where reasonable grounds to suspect offence in connection with VAT being committed (or has been or is about to be) or that there is evidence of an offence	Enter, if necessary by force, taking with him such other persons as appear to be necessary, search, seize and remove evidence and search any person or premises who with reasonable cause believed to have committed or to be about to commit an offence	Entry must be within 14 days of issue of warrant
	s. 37(2)	Any authorised person	Commissioners' authorisation	Premises where reasonable grounds to suspect goods liable to VAT to be found	Enter at all reasonable times and inspect premises and goods	
	Sch 7 para 21(3)	Any authorised person	Magistrate's warrant	Premises where reasonable grounds to suspect offence in connection with car tax being committed (or has been or is about to be) or that there is evidence of an offence	Enter, if necessary by force, taking with him such other persons as appear to be necessary, seize and remove evidence and search suspected persons	Entry must be within 14 days of issue of warrant

2. Energy	Electric Lighting Act 1882 s. 24 Electric Lighting Act 1909 s. 16	Any officer appointed by the undertakers	Electricity authority's authorisation	Any premises to which electricity is or has been supplied	Enter at all reasonable times to assess quantity of electricity consumed, or to remove fittings, lines etc	All these powers are restricted by the Rights of Entry (Gas and Electricity Boards) Act 1954, which provides that except in an emergency no right of entry is exercisable except with the occupier's consent or under the authority of a magistrate's warrant which may, in certain circumstances, authorise entry by force and which remains in force until the purpose for which it was granted has been satisfied
	Gas Act 1972 s. 31(2)	Any officer authorised by the corporation	Gas Board's authorisation	Any premises in which there is a service pipe connected with the gas mains	Enter to inspect the fittings *etc* and, if necessary for safety, to disconnect gas	
	Sch. 4 para 1(3)(b)	The Corporation	Gas Board's authorisation	Any premises in which there is a service pipe connected with the gas mains	Enter, after giving 7 days notice, to replace or repair the pipe	
	Sch. 4 para 24(1)	Any officer authorised by the Corporation	Gas Board's authorisation	Any premises in which there is a service pipe connected with the gas mains	Enter at all reasonable times to inspect meters, fittings and supply	

Table 4.1 (continued)

Department	Statutory authority	Person(s) authorised	Form of authority	Place to which there is power of entry	Power and circumstances of use	Points of interest
2. Energy (continued)	Sch. 4 para 25(1)	Any officer authorised by the Corporation	Gas Board's authorisation	Any premises in which there is a service pipe connected with the gas mains	Enter, after giving 24 hours notice, where requested or authorised to disconnect supply	All these powers are restricted by the Rights of Entry (Gas and Electricity Boards) Act 1954, which provides that except in an emergency no right of entry is exercisable except with the occupier's consent or under the authority of a magistrate's warrant which may, in certain circumstances, authorise entry by force and which remains in force until the purpose for which it was granted has been satisfied
	Sch. 4 para 25(3)	Any officer authorised by the Corporation	Gas Board's authorisation	Premises where reasonable cause to suspect gas escaping or may escape, or where gas which has escaped has entered	Enter, inspect and take steps to avert danger to life and property	

3. Environment	Housing Act 1957 s. 159, Housing Act 1969 Sch. 3, Housing Act 1974 ss. 48, 54	Any person authorised for a particular purpose by S of S or housing authority	Written departmental or local authority authorisation	Any house, premises or building which local authority entitled to purchase compulsorily or where entry necessary for certain purposes under Acts	Enter at all reasonable times, after giving 24 hours notice, for survey and examination for compulsory purchase, or in relation to repairs, maintenance and sanitary condition of houses, demolition orders, general improvement areas, housing action areas or priority neighbourhoods	
	Housing Act 1964 s. 68	Person employed by or acting under instructions of housing authority	Magistrate's warrant to be issued only after admission requested and refused	Premises to which provisions of Act governing multi-occupation apply	Enter, if necessary by force, taking with him other persons if necessary, for purposes of provisions governing multi-occupation	Warrant continues in force until purpose for which entry required has been satisfied
	Housing Act 1969 s. 61(5)	Any person authorised for a particular purpose by S of S or housing authority	Written authority. Magistrate's warrant authorising entry by force may be issued if admission requested and refused	Any house in respect of which a notice requiring work to be done has been issued	Enter to see whether requirement has been complied with	

Table 4.1 (continued)

Department	Statutory authority	Person(s) authorised	Form of authority	Place to which there is power of entry	Power and circumstances of use	Points of interest
4. Health and Social Security.	Food and Drugs Act 1955 s. 100	Authorised officer of Council	Local authority's authorisation: entry by force may be authorised by magistrate's warrant	Any premises, after 24 hours notice if private dwelling house	Enter at all reasonable times to see whether contravention of provisions of Act or of regulations and bye-laws made under it or for performance by the council of their functions under the Act	Warrant authorising entry by force continues in force for one month
	Public Health Act 1963 s. 287	Any authorised officer of a Council	Local authority's authorisation: entry by force may be authorised by magistrate's warrant	Any premises, with 24 hours' notice except where factory workshop or workplace	Enter to ascertain whether there is any contravention of provisions of Act	Warrant authorising entry by force remains in force until purpose for which entry necessary has been satisfied

Medicines Act 1968 ss. 111, 112	Any person duly authorised	Departmental authority. Entry by force may be authorised by magistrate's warrant	Any premises, with 24 hours notice if private dwelling	Enter at any reasonable time to ascertain whether any contravention of Act, inspect, seize goods and documents	Credentials must be produced if requested. Warrant authorising entry by force remains in force for one month
Children and Young Persons Act 1969 ss. 58, 59	Person authorised by S of S	Departmental authorisation	Children's houses, including premises where foster child or child to be adopted being accommodated or maintained	Enter, inspect house and children	Authority must be produced if requested
5. Home Office					
Fire Services Act 1947 s. 1(2)	Any member of a fire brigade	Written authorisation from fire authority: entry by force may be authorised by magistrate's warrant	Any premises, after giving 24 hours notice except where factory, shop or workshop	Enter to ascertain whether there is any contravention of Act	Warrant authorising entry by force remains in force until purpose for which entry necessary has been satisfied
s. 30	Any member of a fire brigade		Premises where fire has broken out or is reasonably believed to have broken out, or which necessary to enter for fire fighting	Enter, without consent of occupier	

Table 4.1(continued)

Department	Statutory authority	Person(s) authorised	Form of authority	Place to which there is power of entry	Power and circumstances of use	Points of interest
5. Home Office (continued)	Wireless Telegraphy Act 1949 s. 15(1)	Persons authorised by S of S	Magistrate's warrant	Premises where reasonable grounds for suspecting offence committed in connection with licensing and use other than in accordance with licence	Enter and search	Entry must be within one month of issue of warrant
	s. 15(2)	Persons authorised by S of S	Magistrate's warrant issued within 7 days of admission being demanded and refused	Premises where reasonable grounds for suspecting offence committed in connection with radio interference regulations	Enter to obtain information	
	Post Office Act 1969 s. 91(1)	Person authorised by S of S	Magistrate's warrant	Premises where reasonable grounds to suspect offence of unlicensed broadcasting committed and evidence of offence to be found there	Enter, search and test any apparatus	Entry must be within one month of date of warrant
	Fire Precautions Act 1971 s. 19	Fire Inspectors	Written authority	Premises in same building as premises requiring certificate	Enter and inspect, giving 24 hours notice to occupier	Evidence of authority must be produced if required
6. Inland Revenue	Finance Act 1894 s. 7(8)	Person authorised by Commissioners	Commissioners' authorisation	Property to be valued for estate duty	Inspect at such reasonable times as the Commissioners consider necessary	

	Person authorised	Authority	Premises	Powers	Notes
War Damage Act 1943 s. 35	Person authorised by Commissioners	Commissioners' authorisation	Any premises on which war damage has occurred	Enter, after 24 hours notice if premises occupied	
General Rate Act 1967 s. 86	Valuation officer and any person authorised by him in writing	Written authority	Any hereditament in valuation officer's area	Enter at all reasonable times, after giving 24 hours notice, survey and value	Person authorised by valuation officer must produce his authority on request
Taxes Management Act 1970 s. 61	Collection of taxes	General Commissioners' warrant	Any house or premises where distress to be levied for non-payment of tax	Break open, in the daytime, calling to his assistance any constable to levy distress	
7. Trade					
Merchant Shipping Act 1894 s. 537	Receiver of Wrecks	Magistrate's warrant	Any house or other place, on suspicion or information that wreck secreted there	Enter, search and seize	
Merchant Shipping Act 1970 s. 76(3)	Surveyor of Ships, superintendent or person appointed by Board of Trade	Certificate of appointment	Any premises where reasonable grounds for believing there is food and water for supply to a ship not in accordance with regulations	Enter and inspect	
8. Treasury					
Exchange Control Act 1947 Sch. 5 para 2	Constable, together with other persons named in warrant	Magistrate's warrant issued on information given by person authorised by Treasury	Premises where reasonable grounds to suspect offence against Act being committed (or has been or is about to be) or where documents held which should have been produced	Enter, search, seize evidence and search persons there and recently there	Entry must be within one month of date of entry of warrant

Table 4.2 Entry to Business Premises

(This table covers powers of entry which relate to business premises only: where there is power to enter both business and private premises, details have been given in Table 4.1.)

Department	Statutory authority	Person(s) authorised	Form of authority	Place to which there is power of entry	Power and circumstances of use	Points of interest
1. Customs and Excise	Customs and Excise Act 1952, s. 120	Any customs officer	Commission of appointment	Premises of person authorised to receive methylated spirits	Enter, in the daytime, and inspect	
	s. 131(5)	Any customs officer	Commission of appointment	Premises used for brewing by holder of a brewing licence	Enter at all reasonable times to examine vessels and utensils and take samples	
	s. 228	Any customs officer (but at night only if accompanied by a constable)	Commission of appointment	Premises of any person licensed to keep a still	Enter and examine any still or retort	
	s. 248(1)	Any customs officer (but at night only if accompanied by a constable)	Commission of appointment	Premises of excise trader	Enter and inspect	
	s. 248(2)	A customs officer and any person acting in his aid (with a constable if at night)	Commission of appointment	Premises of excise trader in glucose or saccharin or maker of sweets	Enter, by force if admission refused, and inspect	
	s. 249(1)	A customs officer (with a constable if at night)	Commission of appointment	Premises of excise trader where an officer has reasonable grounds to suspect there are concealed pipes etc	Enter, by force if necessary to search for pipes, vessels etc	

	Person authorised	Authority	Premises	Powers	Notes
Purchase Tax Act 1963 s. 34(5)	Person authorised by Commissioners	Commissioners' authorisation	Premises which there is reasonable cause to believe are used for a wholesale or manufacturing business	Enter at all reasonable times and inspect goods	Authority must be produced if required
Finance (No. 2) Act 1964 s. 9(4)	Any officer or person authorised by Commissioners	Commissioners' authorisation	Premises used in connection with manufacture *etc* of goods in respect of which export rebates applied for	Enter at all reasonable times and inspect	
Hydrocarbon Oil (Customs and Excise) Act 1971 s. 15(5)	A customs officer	Commission of appointment	Any premises or plant used for production of horticulture produce in which heavy oil is used	Enter and inspect if Commissioners require producer applying for relief under Act to permit this	
Finance Act 1972 s. 37(1)	An authorised person	Departmental authority	Premises used in connection with the carrying on of a business	Enter at all reasonable times to exercise powers under the Act, eg to assess tax, require documents, take samples	
Betting and Gaming Duties Act 1972 Sch. 1, para 6	Any officer authorised by the Commissioners	Commissioners' authorisation	Any premises used for general or pool betting business	Enter and remain when being used or likely to be used	

Table 4.2 (continued)

Department	Statutory authority	Person(s) authorised	Form of authority	Place to which there is power of entry	Power and circumstances of use	Points of interest
1. Customs and Excise (continued)	Sch. 1, para 10(1)	Any officer	Commission of appointment	Track or any other place where reason to believe bookmaking, pool betting or totalisator operation going on in connection with events taking place there	Be admitted without payment and obtain information	
	Sch. 1, para 10(2)	Any officer	Commission of appointment	Place where person not a bookmaker but liable to pay betting duty operating	Be admitted without payment and obtain information	
	Sch. 2, para 9	Any officer	Commission of appointment	Any premises in respect of which a gaming licence is in force	Enter without payment, inspect and require information	
	Sch. 3, para 12	Any officer	Commission of appointment	Premises where bingo played or where reasonable cause to suspect this	Enter without paying, inspect and require information	
	Sch. 3, para 20	Any officer	Magistrate's warrant	Premises where reasonable grounds to suspect offence concerned with evasion of bingo duty taking place	Enter, seize and remove evidence and search any person on premises where reasonable cause to believe connected with promotion or management of premises	Entry must be within 14 days of issue of warrant

Sch. 4, para 18	Any officer	Magistrate's warrant	Premises not licensed for the purpose where reasonable grounds to suspect there are gaming machines	Enter, seize and remove evidence and search any person on premises if reasonable cause to believe concerned with provision of machines or admission to premises	Entry must be within 14 days of issue of warrant
2. Health and Social Security	National Assistance Act 1948, s. 39	Person authorised by S of S	Departmental authority	Any premises used or reasonably believed to be used as disabled persons or old persons home	Enter at all reasonable times and inspect	
	National Insurance Act 1965, s. 90, Social Security Act 1971, s. 4(1)	Inspectors appointed by S of S	Departmental authority	Any premises where inspector has reasonable grounds for believing persons employed, or that used as employment agency (but not private dwelling house not used by or with consent of occupier for trade or business)	Enter at all reasonable times, make examination and inquiries for enforcement of Acts, and investigating entitlement to supplementary benefit	
	Nursing Homes Act 1975 s. 9	Person authorised by S of S	Departmental authority	Any premises used or with reasonable cause believed to be used as a mental nursing home	Enter, inspect records, interview patients	

Table 4.2 (continued)

Department	Statutory authority	Person(s) authorised	Form of authority	Place to which there is power of entry	Power and circumstances of use	Points of interest
2. Health and Social Security (continued)	Social Security Act 1975 s. 144	Inspector appointed under Act	Departmental authority	Any premises where reasonable grounds for suspecting persons employed or there is employment agency (but not private dwelling house not used by or with consent of occupier for trade or business)	Enter at all reasonable times to make examination and inquiries for enforcement of provisions of Act and for investigation of circumstances of industrial injury or disease	
3. Home Office	Gaming Act 1968 s. 43(2)	Any Gaming Board inspector	Warrant of appointment	Any premises licensed under the Act	Enter, inspect premises, machines, equipment, books, documents	
	Misuse of Drugs Act 1971 s. 23(1)	Person authorised by S of S	Departmental authority	Premises of person carrying on business as producer or supplier of controlled drugs	Enter, inspect books, documents and stocks	
	Fire Precautions Act 1971 s. 19	Fire inspectors	Written authority	Premises requiring fire certificate or where there are restrictions on use till fire risk reduced, or to which there is reasonable cause to believe this applies	Enter and inspect, after giving 24 hours notice	Evidence of authority must be produced if required

4. Prices and Consumer Protection	Counter Inflation Act 1973 Sch. 4(3)	Duly authorised officer of Minister or of local weights and measures authority	Departmental or local authority authorisation	Any premises other than those used only as a dwelling	Enter at all reasonable times to determine whether provisions of order or notice under Act being complied with
	Fair Trading Act 1973 s. 29	Authorised officer of local weights and measures authority or person authorised in writing by S of S	Written authority. Entry by force may be authorised by magistrate's warrant	Any premises other than those used only as a dwelling	Enter at all reasonable hours to see whether there has been any contravention of an order made under the Act	Warrant authorising entry by force remains in force for one month
	Fair Trading Act 1973 s. 123	Person authorised in writing by S of S	Written authority. Entry by force may be authorised by magistrate's warrant	Any premises other than those used only as a dwelling	At all reasonable hours enter to see whether any contravention of provisions of Act relating to trading agreements	Warrant authorising entry by force remains in force for one month

99

Table 4.3. Entry to land

Department	Statutory authority	Person(s) authorised	Form of authority	Place to which there is power of entry	Power and circumstances of use	Points of interest
1. Customs and Excise	Customs and Excise Act 1952 s. 69(2)	Any customs officer and any person acting in aid of an officer	Commission of appointment	Any part of coast or shore, or bank of any river or creek, any railway or aerodrome or land adjoining it	Patrol upon and pass freely along, for prevention of smuggling	
	Customs and Excise Act 1952 s. 71(3)	Any customs officer, constable, member of HM forces	Commission of appointment	Any place from which there are reasonable grounds to suspect messages being transmitted to smugglers	Enter and take steps to stop sending of message	
	Customs and Excise Act 1952 s. 106(6)	Any customs officer	Commission of appointment	Land in N. Ireland where reason to suspect there is anything liable to forfeiture under provisions relating to unlawful manufacture of spirits	Enter, if necessary by force, search and remove anything liable to forfeiture	
	Customs and Excise Act 1952 s. 296(1) and (2)	Any customs officer (at night only if accompanied by a constable)	Writ of assistance (Subs. 1) or magistrate's warrant (Subs. 2)	Any place where there is reason to suspect there is anything liable to forfeiture under the Custom and Excise Acts	Enter, if necessary by force, search, seize, detain or remove anything liable to forfeiture	

			Authorisation of electricity authority		
2. Energy	Electricity (Supply) Act 1919 s. 22	Any authorised undertaker		Any land where electric line runs	Enter to repair or alter the line
	Gas Act 1965 Sch. 6	Person authorised by gas authority	Written authorisation	Any land subject of Ministerial direction that it should be prospected for an underground storage site	Enter and survey, after giving 24 hours notice if land occupied
	Gas Act 1972, Sch. 4 para 1(3)(b)	The Gas Corporation	Gas Corporation's authorisation	Any land	Enter, after giving 7 days notice, to repair or replace gas pipe
3. Environment	Ancient Monuments Act 1931 s. 9	Any person specially authorised by the Commissioners of Ancient Monuments	Commissioners' authorisation	Any land which Commissioners have reason to believe contains an ancient monument. Houses, gardens *etc* not to be entered without consent of occupier	Enter, after giving 14 days notice, and make excavations for purpose of examination
	National Parks and Access to the Countryside Act 1949 s. 108	Any person authorised by the Minister or other authority having power to do so	Departmental or local authority authorisation	Any land	Enter, after giving 7 days notice, and survey in connection with acquisition of land, either voluntary or compulsorily, making of public path or access order, or claim for compensation. Evidence of authority to be produced if requested

Table 4.3 (continued)

Department	Statutory authority	Person(s) authorised	Form of authority	Place to which there is power of entry	Power and circumstances of use	Points of interest
3. Environment (continued)	Water Resources Act 1963 s. 111	Any person authorised by a river authority, or by the Minister	Written authorisation. Entry by force may be made under magistrate's warrant	Any land	Enter, taking with him such other persons as may be necessary, to perform any functions of river authority (or of Minister) in relation to pollution, land drainage *etc*, whether in relation to that land or not. 7 days notice must be given before entering land used for residential purposes	a. Evidence of authority to be produced if requested b. Where entry is under warrant, warrant continues in force until purpose for which entry required has been satisfied
	New Towns Act 1965 s. 49	Any official of valuation office or person authorised by authority having power to purchase land compulsorily	Written authorisation	Any land	Enter at any reasonable time (after 24 hours notice if land occupied) and survey and estimate value, in connection with compulsory purchase of land, or development proposals	Evidence of authority to be produced if requested

Town and Country Planning Act 1971 ss. 280, 281	Any person authorised in writing by S of S or local planning authority	Written authorisation	Any land	Enter at any reasonable time (24 hours notice if land occupied) and survey, in connection with structure or local plan, application for planning permission, unauthorised works, failure to carry out required works, applications for listed building consent, tree preservation orders, claims for compensation	Evidence of authority to be produced if requested
4. Home Office Civil Defence Act 1948 s. 4(3)	Any person authorised by S of S or local or police authority exercising functions under Act	Departmental or local authority authorisation	Any land	Enter at all reasonable hours (but 24 hours notice must be given before entering as of right), inspect to see whether anything ought to be constructed or done on land or use made of it for civil defence purposes	Evidence of authority to be produced if requested

Table 4.3 (continued)

Department	Statutory authority	Person(s) authorised	Form of authority	Place to which there is power of entry	Power and circumstances of use	Points of interest
5. Inland Revenue	Finance Act 1894 s. 7(8)	Person authorised by Commissioners of Inland Revenue	Commissioners' authority	Property to be valued for estate duty	Inspect at such reasonable times as the Commissioners consider necessary	
	General Rate Act 1967 s. 86	Valuation officer and any person authorised by him in writing	Written authority	Any hereditament in valuation officer's area	Enter at all reasonable times after giving 24 hours notice, survey and value	Person authorised by valuation officer must produce his authority on request
6. Prices and Consumer Protection	Counter-Inflation Act 1973 Sch. 4(3)	Any authorised official of the Minister or of local weights and measures authority	Departmental or local authority authorisation	Any land	Enter at all reasonable times to determine whether provisions of order or notice made under Act are being carried out	

Table 4.4 Entry to vessels, vehicles, aircraft etc

Department	Statutory authority	Person(s) authorised	Form of authority	Place to which there is power of entry	Power and circumstances of use	Points of interest
1. Customs and Excise	Customs and Excise Act 1952, s. 19	Any customs officer and any person engaged in the prevention of smuggling	Commission of appointment or departmental authority	Ship within limits of port, aircraft at a customs airport, vehicle on approved route	Board, rummage and search, to detect and prevent smuggling	
	Customs and Excise Act 1952 s. 7(3)	Any customs officer, constable, member of HM forces or coastguard	Commission of appointment	Any ship, aircraft or vehicle from which there are reasonable grounds to suspect signals or messages are being transmitted to smugglers	Enter and take steps to prevent or stop sending of messages	
	Customs and Excise Act 1952 s. 297	Customs officer, constable, member of HM forces or coastguard	Commission of appointment	Vehicle or vessel which there are reasonable grounds to suspect is carrying goods on which duty has not been paid, or which are being unlawfully removed or are liable to forfeiture	Stop and search	

Table 4.4 (continued)

Department	Statutory authority	Person(s) authorised	Form of authority	Place to which there is power of entry	Power and circumstances of use	Points of interest
2. Environment	Water Resources Act 1963 ss. 111(5), 112	Person duly authorised by Secretary of State	Written authorisation. Entry by force may be made under magistrate's warrant	Any vessel	Enter for purpose of performing functions under Act in connection with river pollution	Evidence of authority must be produced on request. If entry made under warrant, warrant continues in force until purpose for which entry was required is satisfied
3. Health and Social Security	Food and Drugs Act 1955 s. 111(1)(a) s. 111(1)(b)	Authorised officer of council	Written authority. Entry by force under magistrate's warrant	(a) Any ship or aircraft (b) any vehicle, still or home going ship	(a) Enter at all reasonable times to see whether there is any improperly imported food on board (b) Enter to ascertain whether there has been any contravention of the Act	If entry under warrant, warrant continues in force for one month
	Medicines Act 1967 ss. 111, 112	Person authorised by S of S	Departmental authority on entry by force under magistrate's warrant	Ship, aircraft, vehicle, hovercraft	Enter at any reasonable time, inspect, take samples and seize goods and documents, to ascertain whether there is any contravention of the Act's provisions	Credentials must be produced if requested. If entry under warrant, warrant continues in force for one month

106

Department	Act	Person	Authority	Premises/Circumstances	Powers	Notes
4. Home Office	Wireless Telegraphy Act 1949 s. 15(1)	Person authorised by S of S	Magistrate's warrant	Vehicle, vessel or aircraft where reasonable grounds for suspecting offence under Act relating to licence and use other than in accordance with licence	Enter and search	Entry must be within one month of date of issue of warrant
	Wireless Telegraphy Act 1949 s. 15(2)	Person authorised by S of S	Magistrate's warrant, issued within 7 days of admission being demanded and refused	Vehicle, vessel or aircraft where reasonable grounds for suspecting offence committed in connection with radio interference regulations	Enter to obtain information	
5. Trade	Merchant Shipping Act 1894 s. 537	Receiver of wrecks	Magistrates's warrant	Any vessel, on suspicion or information that any wreck is secreted there	Enter, search and seize	
6. Treasury	Exchange Control Act 1947, Sch. 5, para 2	Constable and other persons named in warrant	Magistrate's warrant issued on sworn information given by person authorised by Treasury	Vehicle, vessel or aircraft where reasonable grounds to suspect offence against Act committed or about to be committed, or where there are documents which should have been produced	Enter, search and seize evidence of evasion of exchange controls	Entry must be within one month of date of issue of warrant

Statutory police powers to enter and search premises under warrant or other written authority

The following list gives those powers to enter and search premises under warrant, Table 5.1, and under other written authority, Table 5.2, which are normally exercised by the police. There are other provisions which confer similar powers on officials—see Appendix 4. Some powers of entry and search may be exercised either by the police or by some other person; only those which usually fall to be exercised by the police are included in this list. The list is restricted to provisions in public general legislation. It should be noted that while in most cases the power of entry is connected with the search of premises for evidence relating to a criminal offence, in some cases the entry is to enable the police to search the premises for a person, or for some other purpose. In Table 5.1 the relevant powers to issue warrants are conferred on magistrates, except where otherwise mentioned.

Table 5.1. Powers of entry and search under warrant

Provision	Circumstances in which warrant can be issued	Power (brief details)	Notes
Betting, Gaming & Lotteries Act 1963, s. 51	Where there is reasonable ground for suspecting that an offence under the Act is being, has been or is about to be committed on any premises	To enter the premises, search them, seize and remove anything likely to be evidence of an offence under the Act, and arrest and search any person reasonably believed to be committing or to have committed an offence under the Act	The warrant is valid for 14 days after issue
Biological Weapons Act 1974, s. 4	Where there is reasonable ground for suspecting that an offence under s. 1 of the Act has been, or is about to be committed	To enter the premises, and to search them and any person found there; to inspect and copy or seize and detain any document found there or in possession of any person found there; and to inspect, seize and detain any equipment or substance so found, and to sample such substance	The constable executing the warrant must be named therein. The warrant is valid for one month

Table 5.1. (continued)

Provision	Circumstances in which warrant can be issued	Power (brief details)	Notes
Children Act 1975, s. 30(4)	Where there are reasonable grounds for believing that a child to whom an order under subs. (1) (concerning the removal of a child from the custody of a person in contravention of certain provisions of the Adoption Act 1958) relates is in the premises specified	To search the premises and return the child (if found) to the person from whom he was taken	
s. 42(4)	Where there are reasonable grounds for believing that a child to whom an order under subs. (1) (concerning the removal of a child from the custody of an applicant for a custodianship order) relates is in the premises specified	To search the premises and return the child (if found) to the person from whom he was taken	
Children & Young Persons Act 1933, s. 40 (as amended)	Where there is reasonable cause to suspect that a child or young person has been or is being assaulted, ill-treated or neglected in a manner likely to cause him unnecessary suffering or injury to health, or that one of certain offences has been or is being committed in respect of the child or young person	To enter any place named in the warrant to search for such child or young person and, if it is found that the ill-treatment *etc* is or has been occurring in the manner aforesaid, to remove him to a place of safety	Constable executing the warrant must be named therein. Warrant may include power to arrest any person accused of any offence in respect of the child or young person in question
Children and Young Persons Act 1969, s. 32(2A) (as added by Children Act 1975, s. 68)	Where there are reasonable grounds for believing that a child or young person is absent without proper authority from a place of safety, or a place where he is living in the care of a local authority, or a remand home, special reception centre *etc* and is in specified premises	To search the premises for the said person	

Table 5.1. (continued)

Provision	Circumstances in which warrant can be issued	Power (brief details)	Notes
Children & Young Persons (Harmful Publications) Act 1955, s. 3	Where a summons or warrant of arrest in respect of an offence under s. 2 of the Act has been issued, and there is reasonable ground for believing that a person has in his possession or under his control copies of a harmful publication within the meaning of the Act, or any plate or film prepared for the purpose of printing copies of such a publication	To enter and search premises named in the warrant; to seize any harmful publication within the meaning of the Act, and any plate or film prepared for printing such a publication	Constable executing the warrant must be named therein. Power of search and seizure can extend to any vehicle or stall used by the suspect for trade or business
Coinage Offences Act 1936, s. 11(3)	Where there is reasonable cause to suspect that any person has been concerned in counterfeiting any current coin; or has any counterfeit coin, or counterfeiting machine or material	To search the relevant premises and seize any counterfeit coin or counterfeiting instrument, machine or material	
Companies Act 1967, s. 110	Where there are reasonable grounds for suspecting that there are on any premises any books or papers of which production has been required by virtue of s. 109 of the Act, or s. 36 of the Insurance Companies Act 1974, and which have not been produced.	To enter and search the premises and take possession of any books or papers appearing to be those required; or to take any steps which may appear necessary for preserving them and preventing interference with them	Warrant valid for one month
Criminal Damage Act 1971, s. 6(1)	Where there is reasonable cause to believe that any person has anything which there is reasonable cause to believe has been used or is intended for use unlawfully to destroy or damage property belonging to another, or in such a way as to be likely to endanger the life of another	To enter and search the premises and to seize anything believed to have been so used or to be intended to be so used	
Cruelty to Animals Act 1876, s. 13	Where there is reasonable ground to believe that experiments in contravention of the Act are being performed by an unlicensed person in any place not registered under the Act	To enter and search such place, and to take the names and addresses of the persons found therein	

Table 5.1. (continued)

Provision	Circumstances in which warrant can be issued	Power (brief details)	Notes
Customs & Excise Act 1952, s. 296(3)	Where there are reasonable grounds to suspect that any still, vessel, utensil, spirits or materials for the manufacture of spirits is or are unlawfully kept or deposited in any building or place	To enter and search the building or place, and seize and detain or remove articles *etc*	
Emergency Laws (Re-enactments and Repeals) Act 1964, Sch. 1, para 2	Where there are reasonable grounds for suspecting that there are on any premises any documents of which production has been required by virtue of paragraph 1 of the Schedule, and which have not been produced	To enter and search premises and take possession of any documents appearing to be those required by virtue of paragraph 1 of the Schedule; or to take any steps which may appear necessary for preserving them and preventing interference with them	
Exchange Control Act 1947, Fifth Schedule, Part 1, para 2	Where there is reasonable ground for suspecting that an offence against the Act has been or is being committed, and that evidence of the offence is to be found at the premises specified, or in any vehicle, vessel or aircraft specified; or that documents which ought to have been produced under the previous paragraph of the Schedule and which have not been so produced are to be found in any premises, vehicle, vessel or aircraft as specified	To enter and search the premises, vehicle, vessel or aircraft specified, and to seize any article likely to be evidence of an offence under the Act, or any documents which have not been produced under the preceding paragraph of the Schedule	Warrant valid for one month
Explosives Act 1875, s. 73 (as extended by the Explosive Substances Act 1883, s. 8)	Where there is reasonable cause to believe that an offence has been or is being committed with respect to any explosive in any case, *etc*	To enter and search the relevant premises; and take samples of any explosive, or ingredient of explosive, or of any substance reasonably supposed to be an explosive or an ingredient of an explosive	As to entry in an emergency, see Table 5.2 of this Appendix
Firearms Act 1968, s. 46	Where there is reasonable ground for suspecting that an offence under the Act (with certain exceptions) has been, is being, or is about to be committed	To enter and search the premises or place, and to search every person found therein; to seize and detain any firearm or ammunition; and (if the premises are those of a registered firearms dealer) to examine any books relating to the business	Constable executing the warrant must be named therein

111

Table 5.1. (continued)

Provision	Circumstances in which warrant can be issued	Power (brief details)	Notes
Forgery Act 1913, s. 16	Where there is reasonable cause to believe that any person has in his custody or possession without lawful authority or excuse any bank note, any implement or material which might be used to forge bank notes, any forged document, seal or die, or any machinery *etc* or material used or intended to be used for the forgery of any document	To search for and seize any such article	
Gaming Act 1968, s. 43(4) & (5)	Where there are reasonable grounds for suspecting that an offence under the Act is being, has been or is about to be committed	To enter and search premises and remove anything which may be required as evidence for the purpose of proceedings under the Act; and to arrest and search any person found on the premises who is reasonably believed to be committing or to have committed an offence under the Act	Warrant valid 14 days
Hop (Prevention of Frauds) Act 1866, s. 10	Where there is good reason to believe that any hops, or bags or pockets in which they are contained are not marked as required in the Act and certain other Acts	To enter any premises where the relevant hops, bags or pockets may be, to search for them and any such article which is reasonably believed not to be marked as required	
Immigration Act 1971, Sch. 2, para 17	Where there is reasonable ground for suspecting that a person liable to be arrested (for the purpose of examination or removal) under a provision of the Act is to be found on any premises	To enter the premises for the purpose of searching for and arresting the person	Warrant may only be executed by a constable for the police area in which the premises are situated. Warrant valid for one month. Entry may be made at any time or times within that period

Table 5.1. (continued)

Provision	Circumstances in which warrant can be issued	Power (brief details)	Notes
Incitement to Disaffection Act 1934, s. 2	Where there is reasonable ground for suspecting an offence under the Act and that evidence of the commission of such an offence is to be found at any premises or place	To enter the premises or place, to search it and every person found therein, and to seize anything which is reasonably believed to be evidence of an offence under the Act	Warrant may only be issued by a judge of the High Court on application by a police officer of rank no lower than inspector. Warrant valid for one month
Licensing Act 1964, s. 54	Where there is reasonable ground for cancelling in whole or in part a registration certificate held by a club, and that evidence of it is to be obtained at the club premises; or that intoxicating liquor is sold, supplied or kept by a club in contravention of the provisions of the Act	To enter and search the club premises and to seize any documents relating to the business of the club	Warrant valid for one month. Entry may be made at any time or times within that period
s. 85	Where there is reasonable ground for believing that any premises are kept or habitually used for the holding of parties at which the provisions of s. 84(1) of the Act (relating to parties organised for gain through the sale of liquor) are contravened	To enter and search the premises and to seize and remove any intoxicting liquor reasonably believed to be connected with a contravention of s. 84(1) of the Act	As for s. 54
s. 187	Where there is reasonable ground to believe that any intoxicating liquor is sold by retail, or exposed or kept for sale by retail at any place	To enter and search the place for intoxicating liquor; and to seize and remove any liquor reasonably supposed to be there for the purpose of unlawful sale, and any vessels containing such liquor	As for s. 54
Lotteries & Amusements Act 1976, s. 19	Where there is reasonable ground for suspecting that an offence under the Act is being, has been or is about to be committed	To enter and search the premises and seize and remove any documents *etc* which may be required as evidence for the purpose of proceedings under the Act; and to arrest and search any person found on the premises who is reasonably believed to be committing or to have committed an offence under the Act	Warrant valid for 14 days

Appendix 5

Table 5.1. (continued)

Provision	Circumstances in which warrant can be issued	Power (brief details)	Notes
Mental Health Act 1959, s. 135(1)	Where there is reasonable cause to suspect that a person believed to be suffering from mental disorder has been or is being ill-treated, neglected or kept otherwise than under proper control, or, being unable to care for himself, is living alone	To enter the premises specified and, if thought fit, to remove the person to a place of safety	Information must be laid by a mental welfare officer. The warrant may only be executed by a constable named therein, and he must be accompanied by a mental welfare officer and a medical practitioner
Mental Health Act 1959, s. 135(2)	Where there is reasonable cause to believe that a patient in respect of whom there is authority to take to any place, or to take or re-take into custody, is to be found on premises, and that admission to such premises has been refused, or such refusal is apprehended	To enter the premises and remove the patient	Information must be laid by a constable or other person authorised under the Act. The warrant may only be executed by a constable named therein, who may be accompanied by a medical practitioner and/or an authorised person within the meaning of the Act
Misuse of Drugs Act 1971, s. 23(3)	Where there is reasonable ground for suspecting that any controlled drugs are unlawfully in the possession of a person on any premises, or that a document relating to a transaction which is or would be an offence under the Act is unlawfully in the possession of a person on any premises	To enter the premises, and search them and any persons found therein, and to seize and detain drugs or documents in respect of which or in connection with which there is reasonable ground for suspecting that an offence under the Act has been committed	Warrant valid for one month

Table 5.1. (continued)

Provision	Circumstances in which warrant can be issued	Power (brief details)	Notes
Obscene Publications Act 1959, s. 3	Where there is reasonable ground for suspecting that in any premises, stall or vehicle obscene articles are, or are from time to time, kept for publication for gain	To enter and search the premises, or to search the stall or vehicle and to seize and remove any articles which there is reason to believe are obscene and to be kept for publication for gain. If such articles are seized other trade or business documents may be seized too	Warrant valid for 14 days
Offences Against the Person Act 1861, s. 65	Where any gunpowder, other explosive, dangerous or noxious substance or thing or any machine, engine, instrument or thing is suspected to be made, kept, or carried for the purpose of being used for certain offences under the Act	To search any house, mill, magazine, storehouse, warehouse, shop, cellar, yard, wharf or other place, or any carriage, waggon, cart, ship, boat or vessel in which the gunpowder *etc* is suspected to be made, kept or carried and to seize and remove to a proper place the gunpowder *etc* and any receptacle in which it is contained	Warrant may only be executed in the daytime
Official Secrets Act 1911, s. 9(1)	Where there is reasonable ground for suspecting that an offence under the Act has been or is about to be committed	To enter the premises specified and to search them and any person found therein, and to seize any sketch, plan, model, article, note, document *etc*, which is evidence of an offence under the Act having been or being about to be committed and with regard to which there is reasonable ground for suspecting that such an offence has been or is about to be committed	Warrant may only be executed by a constable named therein. As to entry in an emergency, see Table 5.2 of this Appendix

115

Table 5.1. (continued)

Provision	Circumstances in which warrant can be issued	Power (brief details)	Notes
Pawnbrokers Act 1872, s. 36	Where linen or apparel or unfinished goods or materials have been entrusted to another person, and such goods have been unlawfully pawned, and there is good cause to suspect that a pawnbroker has taken in pawn the relevant goods without the privity or authority of the owner	To enter and search the pawnbroker's shop for the relevant article	Information may only be laid by the owner of the apparel *etc.* If the pawnbroker refuses to open his shop and permit it to be searched a constable authorised by the warrant may enter by force, but only in business hours. The whole of the 1872 Act is liable to repeal under the Consumer Credit Act 1974
Prevention of Fraud (Investments) Act 1958, s. 14(8)	Where there is reasonable ground for suspecting that a person has any documents in his possession in contravention of the section, at any premises	To enter the premises, and to search for, seize and remove any documents found there which he has reasonable ground for believing to be in the possession of a person in contravention of the section	Warrant valid for one month
Prevention of Terrorism (Temporary Provisions) Act 1976, Sch. 3, Part II para 4	Where there is reasonable ground for suspecting that evidence of an offence under certain sections of the Act, or evidence to justify an exclusion order or the proscription of any organisation is to be found at any premises or place	To enter the premises or place and search them and any person found therein, and to seize anything found on any such premises place or person which is reasonably suspected to be evidence of an offence under certain sections of the Act	Application for such warrant may only be made by a police officer of rank not lower than inspector. Warrant may be executed by the applicant and any other police officer. As to entry in an emergency, see Table 5.2 of this Appendix

Table 5.1. (continued)

Provision	Circumstances in which warrant can be issued	Power (brief details)	Notes
Protection of Birds Act 1954, s. 6	Where there is reasonable ground to suspect that an offence has been committed under the section, and that evidence thereof may be found on any premises	To enter and search the premises for the purpose of obtaining the evidence	
Protection of Depositors Act 1963, s. 19	Where there is reasonable ground for suspecting that there are on any premises any books or papers of which production has been required by virtue of s. 18 of the Act, and which have not been produced.	To enter and search the premises, and to take possession of any books or papers appearing to be those required, or to take such steps as may appear necessary for preserving them and preventing interference with them	Warrant valid for one month
Public Order Act 1936, s. 2(5)	Where there is reasonable ground for suspecting that an offence under the section (relating to the prohibition of quasi-military organisations) has been committed, and that evidence thereof is to be found at any place or premises	To enter and search the premises or place, and to search every person found there, and to seize anything which is reasonably suspected to be evidence of the commission of such an offence	Warrant may only be issued by a judge of the High Court on the application of a police officer of rank not lower than inspector. Warrant valid one month
Public Stores Act 1875, s. 12, as substituted by the Theft Act 1968, Sch. 2, Part III	Where there is reasonable cause to believe that any person has any stores in respect of which an offence under s. 5 of the Act has been committed	To search for and seize the stores	
Scrap Metal Dealers Act 1964, s. 6(3)	Where admission to the place specified is reasonably required in order to secure compliance with the provisions of the Act, or to ascertain whether those provisions are being complied with	To enter the place	Warrant valid for one month
Sexual Offences Act 1956, s. 42	Where there is reasonable cause to suspect that any house or part of a house is used by a woman for prostitution and that a man residing in or frequenting the house is living wholly or partly on her earnings	To enter and search the house, and to arrest the man	

Table 5.1. (continued)

Provision	Circumstances in which warrant can be issued	Power (brief details)	Notes
Sexual Offences Act 1956, s. 43	Where there is reasonable cause to suspect that a woman is detained in any place in order that she may have unlawful sexual intercourse, and that she is detained against her will, or is a defective, or is under 16, or if under 18 is detained against the will of her parent or guardian	To enter and search the premises specified and to remove the woman to a place of safety, and detain her there until she can be brought before a magistrate	Warrant may only be executed by a constable named therein
Theatres Act 1968, s. 15(1)	Where there are reasonable grounds for suspecting that a performance of a play is to be given at the specified premises and that an offence under ss. 2, 5 or 6 of the Act is likely to be committed in respect of that performance, or that an offence under s. 13 of the Act is being or will be committed in respect of the premises	If an offence under ss. 2, 5 or 6 is reasonably suspected, to enter and attend any relevant performance; if an offence under s. 13 is reasonably suspected, to inspect the premises	Warrant valid for 14 days
Theft Act 1968 s. 26(1) & (3)	Where there is reasonable cause to believe that any person has in his custody or possession or on his premises any stolen goods	To enter and search the specified premises, and seize any goods believed to be stolen goods	
Vagrancy Act 1824 s. 13	Where a person described in the Act to be an idle and disorderly person, or a rogue and vagabond, or an incorrigible rogue, is, or is reasonably suspected to be, harboured or concealed in any house kept for the lodging of travellers	To enter the house and apprehend such person	

Table 5.2 Powers of entry and search under other forms of written authority

Provision	Form of authority	Circumstances in which authority can be issued	Power
Children & Young Persons Act 1933, s. 28(1) (as extended by s. 59 of the Education Act 1944)	Magistrate's order	Where there is reasonable cause to believe that certain provisions of the Act (in regard to the employment of children, or their performance in entertainments) are being contravened with respect to any person	To enter any place where the person is, or is believed to be, employed, taking part in a performance, or being trained, and to make enquiries with respect to that person. (Order valid only at reasonable times within 48 hours of its making)
Criminal Libel Act 1819, s. 1	Order of a judge	Where a person is convicted of composing, printing or publishing a blasphemous or seditious libel	To enter and search any house, building or any place whatsoever belonging to the person convicted, and of any person named as keeping copies of the libel for the use of the convicted person; and to carry away and detain any copies of the libel which are found
Explosives Act 1875, s. 73 (as extended by the Explosive Substances Act 1883, s. 8)	Written order by a police officer of at least superintendent rank	Where there is reasonable cause to believe that an offence has been or is being committed with respect to any explosive in any case *etc* and the delay in obtaining a magistrate's warrant (as to which see Table 5.1 of this Appendix) would be likely to endanger life	To enter and search the relevant premises; and take samples of any explosive or ingredient of explosive, or of any substance reasonably supposed to be an explosive or an ingredient of an explosive
Licensing Act 1964, s. 45	Written authority of chief officer of police, or his designee	Where a club applies for the issue of a registration certificate in respect of any premises, and in the opinion of the chief officer of police there are special reasons making it necessary for the premises to be inspected for the proper discharge of his functions in relation to the registration of clubs	To enter and inspect the premises
Metropolitan Police Act 1839, s. 47	Written order of Commissioner to superintendent of Metropolitan Police, with such constables as he shall think necessary		To enter any place in the Metropolitan Police District kept or used for bear-baiting, cock-fighting *etc*, and take into custody all persons found therein without lawful excuse

Table 5.2 (continued)

Provision	Form of authority	Circumstances in which authority can be issued	Power
Official Secrets Act 1911, s. 9(2)	Written order of a superintendent of police	Where there is reasonable ground for suspecting that an offence under the Act has been or is about to be committed and the case is one of great emergency, and immediate action is necessary in the interests of the State. (As to entry under warrant, where the case is not one of great emergency, see Table 5.1 of this Appendix)	To enter the premises specified and to search them and any person found therein, and to seize any sketch, plan, model, article, note, document *etc*, which is evidence of an offence under the Act having been or being about to be committed and with regard to which there is reasonable ground for suspecting that such an offence has been or is about to be committed
Prevention of Terrorism (Temporary Provisions) Act 1976, Sch. 3, Part II para (4)	Written order by a police officer of at least superintendent rank	Where there is reasonable ground for suspecting that evidence of an offence under certain sections of the Act, or evidence to justify an exclusion order or the proscription of any organisation is to be found at any premises or place and the case is one of great emergency and immediate action is necessary in the interests of the State. (As to entry under warrant, where the case is not one of great emergency, see Table 5.1 of this Appendix)	To enter the premises or place and search them and any person found therein, and to seize anything found on any such premises, place or person which is reasonably suspected to be evidence of an offence under certain sections of the Act
Safety of Sports Grounds Act 1975, s. 11	Authority of a chief officer of police, the local authority, the building authority or the Secretary of State		On production, if required, of his authority, to enter a sports ground at any reasonable time, and make such inspection of it and such enquiries relating to it as he considers necessary for the purposes of this Act, and in particular to examine records of attendance and records relating to the maintenance of safety, and to copy such documents

Table 5.2 (continued)

Provision	Form of authority	Circumstances in which authority can be issued	Power
Theft Act 1968, s. 26(2)	Written authority of a police officer of at least superintendent rank	If the person in occupation of premises has been convicted within the preceding five years of handling stolen goods or of any offence involving dishonesty and punishable with imprisonment; or, where the premises have been occupied within the preceding twelve months by a person convicted within the preceding five years of handling stolen goods	To search the relevant premises for stolen goods

Statutory police powers to enter premises without warrant

The following list of provisions in public general legislation is in addition to those mentioned in Table 5.2 of Appendix 5. The list refers to premises and does not extend to powers to enter and search vehicles, ships *etc*, except where these are referred to in the same provision

Table 6.1 Police powers of entry without warrant

Provision	Power (brief details)	Restrictions on the power
Betting, Gaming and Lotteries Act 1963, s. 10(4)	To enter any licensed betting office for the purpose of ascertaining whether the provisions of subs. (1) of the section (relating to the conduct of licensed betting offices) are being complied with	
s. 23	To enter any race track for the purpose of ascertaining whether the provisions of the relevant part of the Act (relating to betting) are being complied with	Entry may be made only "at all reasonable times"
Children and Young Persons Act 1933, s. 12(4)	To enter any building in which the constable has reason to believe that an entertainment for children is being, or is about to be, provided, with a view to seeing whether the provisions of the section (relating to the safety of children at entertainments) are carried into effect	
s. 28(2)	To enter any place where a person (to whom a licence under ss. 22 or 24 of the Act relates) is authorised by the licence to take part in an entertainment, or to be trained, and to make enquiries therein with respect to that person	
Cinematograph Act 1909, s. 4	To enter any premises, whether licensed or not, in which the constable has reason to believe that a cinematograph exhibition is being or is about to be given, with a view to seeing whether the provisons of the Act, or any regulations made thereunder, and the conditions or restrictions attached to any licence have been complied with	Entry may be made only "at all reasonable times"

Table 6.1 (continued)

Provision	Power (brief details)	Restrictions on the power
Criminal Law Act 1967, s. 2(6)	For the purpose of arresting a person for an "arrestable offence" (ie one carrying a maximum penalty of five years imprisonment or more on first conviction), power to enter (if need be, by force) and search any place where the person is or the constable reasonably suspects him to be	
Criminal Law Act 1977, s. 11	To enter and search any premises where a person liable to arrest under certain powers conferred by that part of the Act (concerning offences relating to entering and remaining on property) is, or is reasonably suspected to be, for the purpose of arresting him	Power conferred only on constables in uniform. Entry may not be made to premises enjoying diplomatic immunity
Explosives Act 1875, s. 75	To enter, inspect and examine any wharf, ship *etc* of any carrier *etc* (where there is reasonable cause to suppose an explosive to be for the purpose of or in the course of conveyance) for the purpose of ascertaining whether the provisions of the Act relating to the conveyance of explosives are being complied with	Power exercisable by chief officer of police only; the work or business of the carrier *etc* should not be obstructed unnecessarily
Fire Services Act 1947, s. 30(1)	To enter any premises or place in which a fire has or is reasonably believed to have broken out, or any premises or place which it is necessary to enter in order to extinguish a fire, or to protect the premises from acts done for fire fighting purposes, and to do all such things as may be deemed necessary for extinguishing the fire, or protecting the premises or for rescuing any person or property found therein	
Game Laws (Amendment) Act 1960, s. 2	Where there are reasonable grounds for suspecting that a person is committing an offence on any land under s. 1 or s. 9 of the Night Poaching Act 1828 or under s. 30 or s. 33 of the Game Act 1831 to enter on the land for the purpose of exercising the powers conferred on the constable (ie the power of arrest under ss. 1 and 9 of the 1828 Act and the power under s. 31 of the 1831 Act to require the person to quit the land and give his name and address and, in the event of failure to do so, to apprehend him)	Power does not extend to land occupied by the Ministry of Defence *etc*
Gaming Act 1845, s. 14	To enter any house room or place where any public table or board is kept for playing at billiards, bagatelle, or any game of the like kind	

123

Table 6.1 (continued)

Provision	Power (brief details)	Restrictions on the power
Gaming Act 1968, s. 43(2)	To enter any premises in respect of which a licence under the Act is for the time being in force and to inspect the premises and any machine or other equipment and any book or document which the constable reasonably requires to inspect for the purpose of ascertaining whether a contravention of the Act, or the regulations made thereunder, is being, or has been committed. (Note: see also power of entry under warrant shown in Table 5.1 of Appendix 5)	Entry may be made only "at any reasonable times"
Hypnotism Act 1952, s. 4	To enter any premises where any entertainment is held if he has reasonable cause to believe that any act is being or may be done in contravention of the Act	
Late Night Refreshment Houses Act 1969, s. 10(1)	To enter a late night refreshment house licensed under the Act, and any premises belonging thereto	
Licensing Act 1964, s. 186 (as substituted by the Licensing (Amendment) Act 1977, s. 1)	To enter any licensed premises, a licensed canteen or premises for which a special hours certificate is in force, for the purpose of preventing or detecting the commission of an offence under the Act of 1964	The power may only be exercised within certain times as set out in the section
Misuse of Drugs Act 1971, s. 23(1)	For the purpose of the execution of the Act, to enter the premises of a person carrying on business as a producer or supplier of any controlled drugs, and to demand the production of, and to inspect, any books or documents relating to dealings in such drugs and to inspect stocks of such drugs	
Performing Animals (Regulation) Act 1925, s. 3	To enter and inspect any premises in which any performing animals are being trained or exhibited or kept for training or exhibition and any animals found thereon; and to require any person whom there is reason to believe to be a trainer or exhibitor of perfoming animals to produce his certificate	A constable exercising the power may not go on or behind the stage during a public performance. Entry may only be made "at all reasonable times"
Protection of Aircraft Act 1973, s. 19(2)	To enter and search any building, works or land in an aerodrome in respect of which a direction under s. 10 of the Act is in force, and where there is reasonable cause to suspect that a firearm, explosive *etc* is in, or may be brought into, any part of the aerodrome. (Note: power also extends to aircraft, vehicles, goods or movable property of any description)	

Table 6.1 (continued)

Provision	Power (brief details)	Restrictions on the power
Protection of Animals Act 1911, s. 5(2)	To enter any knackers yard for the purpose of examining whether there is or has been any contravention of or non-compliance with the Act	Entry may only be made "at any hour by day, or at any hour when business is or apparently is in progress or is usually carried on therein"
Scrap Metal Dealers Act 1964, s. 6(1)	To enter and inspect any place registered as a scrap metal store, or in connection with scrap metal dealings, and to require production of, and to inspect, any scrap metal kept there, and any book or receipt which the dealer is required to keep, and to take copies or extracts from any such book or receipt	Entry may only be made "at all reasonable times"
Theatres Act 1968, s. 15(3)	To enter any premises in respect of which a licence under the Act is in force at which he has reason to believe that a performance of a play is being or is about to be given and to inspect them with a view to seeing whether the terms or conditions of the licence are being complied with	Entry may only be made "at all reasonable times". (Officers shall not, if wearing uniform, be required to produce any authority)

Search of premises:
a survey

Ten police forces agreed at the Royal Commission's request to take part in a survey of searches of premises in selected divisions and sub-divisions within their force areas. The survey ran for a four week period from 1 September 1979 and was aimed at documenting the number, type and results of all the searches carried out by divisional officers and officers from specialist squads in the areas concerned. Officers were asked to complete a form on each occasion that they searched an address either on warrant, with consent before arrest, after arrest without a warrant or in order to effect an arrest under the power conferred by section 2(6) of the Criminal Law Act 1967.

2. The forces which took part in the survey were chosen to give a reasonable geographical spread, and the division or sub-divisions within them because they were thought to be busy ones. This was in order to collect a reasonably large sample within the shortest possible time. Officers recorded a total of 341 searches during the survey period. The Metropolitan Police District (MPD) contributed nearly one-third of these, with most of the other forces contributing between 20 and 30 searches. The participating forces (and divisions and sub-divisions) were:

Avon and Somerset:	Broadbury Road; Bishopsworth
Cleveland:	Middlesborough
Hampshire:	Southampton Central; Shirley; Portswood
Leicestershire:	Charles Street
Metropolitan Police District:	Bethnal Green; Catford; Dagenham; Hammersmith; Hounslow; Rochester Row; Stoke Newington; West Hendon
Staffordshire:	Hanley
Surrey:	Guildford
Thames Valley:	Reading; Woodley
West Yorkshire:	Chapeltown
Wiltshire:	Swindon

3. It must be stressed that the survey was not a random one and does not give a generalised picture of the numbers, type and success rate of searches of premises. First, it is heavily weighted towards the MPD. Second, only a small number of stations was involved in the survey. Third, several stations have

specialist squads based at them which has probably biased the survey towards certain kinds of activity, most notably drug searches. Six stations—Portswood (Hampshire), Charles Street (Leicestershire), Hanley (Staffordshire), Guildford (Surrey), Reading (Thames Valley) and Swindon (Wiltshire)—house a Drugs Squad and searches in connection with drugs were over represented in these areas. Other specialist squads contributed relatively little to the survey although Regional Crime Squads carried out several searches in one or two areas.

4. Most searches were carried out in connection with offences of theft and handling (44 per cent) or burglary (28 per cent). Twelve per cent were in relation to drugs offences. The remainder were for violent offences including robbery (6 per cent), sex offences (3 per cent), fraud or forgery (2 per cent), or miscellaneous other offences—pornography, firearms or criminal damage (4 per cent). The range of offences involved was considerable, from conspiracy to rob and murder, to low value theft.

5. Details of the authority for searches are shown in Table 7.1.

Table 7.1 The authority for searches

Force	Authority for search											
	Magistrate's warrant		Superin-tendent's warrant		With consent before arrest		After arrest without warrant		To effect arrest		Total	
	No	%	No	%	No	%	No	%	No	%	No	%
MPD	63	61	0	—	5	5	29	28	6	6	103	100
Provincial forces	56	24	7	3	38	16	117	49	20	8	238	100
All forces	119	35	7	2	43	13	146	43	26	8	341	100

6. Over half the searches in the sample were conducted before arrest with the consent (whether explicitly or otherwise) of the suspect or householder[1] or after arrest and without a warrant; in most of these cases the suspect was in fact already under arrest. About a third of the searches were backed by a warrant issued by a magistrate. This figure is considerably inflated by the survey's bias towards the MPD where the majority (61 per cent) of searches were backed by warrant. Although the numbers of returns made by the provincial forces are too small to provide reliable comparisons, they furnish some evidence that the practice over obtaining search warrants varies between forces; in Cleveland none of the 26 searches was on a warrant issued by a magistrate.

7. Superintendents' warrants were rarely used. Of the seven issued during the survey period, five were in Avon and Somerset.

8. Table 7.2 shows how the authority that was obtained for searches was related to the type of offence under investigation. As can be seen, magistrates'

---

[1] The two were usually synonymous. One or two searches were of houses where the police expected to find stolen property but did not suspect the householder of stealing or dishonestly obtaining it.

warrants were most frequently used in connection with drugs offences; over two-thirds of drugs searches were conducted on warrant. Forty per cent of searches in connection with burglary were conducted on warrant, as were a quarter of those in relation to theft, handling and fraud.

Table 7.2. Authority for search and principal offence suspected at the time the search was made

Authority for search	Offence											
	Violence /sex		Burglary		Theft/ handling/ fraud/ forgery		Drugs		Other/not specified		Total	
	No	%	No	%	No	%	No	%	No	%	No	%
Magistrate's warrant	9	31	39	40	40	25	27	68	4	24	119	35
Superin- tendent's warrant	0	—	3	3	4	3	0	—	0	—	7	2
With consent before arrest	3	10	10	10	22	14	4	10	4	24	43	13
After arrest, without warrant	11	38	42	43	81	51	8	20	4	24	146	43
To effect arrest	6	21	3	3	11	7	1	3	5	29	26	8
Total	29	100	97	100	158	100	40	100	17	100	341	100

9. Thirty nine per cent of searches uncovered evidence linking the suspect with the offences which were under investigation at the time the search was made. In most cases it was stolen property (in 60 per cent of successful searches) or drugs (in 20 per cent of them) that were found. Other incriminating articles included pornographic pictures, firearms and forged documents. In one in every ten searches, material evidence implicating the suspect in offences which were not suspected when the search was made came to light. This was mainly stolen property, or, occasionally, drugs. A small number of searches—31—provided material linking other persons with the offence under investigation or with other offences. Typical examples were the recovery of stolen property which the suspect was charged with receiving but which could then be traced to the person who had stolen it, or the recovery of drugs which were then traced to a supplier. In all, 43 per cent of the searches were successful on at least one of the above criteria.

10. Whether or not a search was carried out under warrant made very little difference to its success. Forty five per cent of the searches backed by either a magistrate's or a superintendent's warrant resulted in the discovery of evidence linking the suspect with the offence of which he was suspected; 40 per cent of the searches carried out with consent before arrest or after arrest without a warrant did so. (Searches carried out to effect an arrest very rarely led to the

discovery of material evidence but they were not usually aimed at doing so.) Details are shown in Table 7.3.

Table 7.3. Authority for search and whether evidence of suspected offence was recovered

Authority for search	Evidence of suspected offence recovered					
	Yes		No		Total	
	No	%	No	%	No	%
Magistrate's warrant	55	46	64	54	119	100
Superintendent's warrant	2	(29)[1]	5	(71)[1]	7	100
With consent before arrest	18	42	25	58	43	100
After arrest, without warrant	58	40	88	60	146	100
To effect arrest	1	4	25	96	26	100
Total	134	39	207	61	341	100

[1]Bracketed percentages indicate a base number of less than 16.

11. One-third (114) of the suspects were not charged after a search had been carried out. In a further four cases, the question of whether or not to charge remained at issue while further enquiries were made. It is clear that the police did not always require evidence from a search in order to charge suspects. There were 192 cases where a search failed to turn up any evidence; nonetheless, charges were preferred in 64 (exactly a third) of them and in a further 20 cases the decision whether or not to charge was still to be made.

13. In all, there were 108 cases where a search failed to produce any evidence and where the suspect was not charged (nor were charges pending). Forty two of these searches had the backing of a magistrate's warrant and five had the backing of a superintendent's warrant.

Statistics of summons and arrest and charge

Table 8. Persons proceeded against at magistrates' courts by offence group and how dealt with prior to first scheduled court appearance, 1978

Offence group	Percentage of total number proceeded against		Percentage of those arrested and charged	
	Summonsed	Arrested and charged	Released on bail	Held in custody
Indictable offences				
Violence against the person	23	77	80	20
Sexual offences	21	79	73	27
Burglary	25	75	70	30
Robbery	8	92	39	61
Theft and handling stolen goods	23	77	87	13
Fraud and forgery	18	82	79	21
Criminal damage	30	70	83	17
Other indictable offences	16	84	75	25
Total indictable offences	24	76	82	18
Non-indictable offences				
Assault on constable	13	87	86	14
Drunkenness	3	97	78	22
Motor vehicle licencing offences	100	—[1]	91	9
Wireless Telegraphy Act	100	—[1]	100	—[1]
Drug offences	7	93	83	17
Other non-indictable offences (excluding motoring)	68	32	90	10
Driving or in charge of motor vehicle while unfit through drink or drugs	87	13	86	14
Other motoring offences	100	—[1]	83	17
Total non-indictable offences	87	13	83	17

[1] less than 0.5 per cent.

Statutory police powers of arrest without warrant

This is a list of police powers of arrest without warrant in public general legislation. It is probably comprehensive though there may be a few omissions. The powers listed are in addition to section 2 of the Criminal Law Act 1967 (see paragraph 44 of text) which confers a power of arrest without a warrant in respect of all offences which carry a maximum penalty of 5 years' imprisonment on first conviction. For ease of reference the list has been divided into four groups, as follows:

Table 9.1 Powers of arrest exercisable only where a person is found, or seen, committing the offence specified.

Table 9.2 Powers exercisable where there is reasonable suspicion that a person has committed or is committing the offence specified.

Table 9.3 Powers exercisable only where the name and address of the person cannot be ascertained and/or he is likely to abscond etc. (These powers have been excluded from Tables 9.1 and 9.2.)

Table 9.4 Other miscellaneous powers.

Table 9.1 Powers of arrest exercisable only where a person is found, or seen, committing the offence specified

Provision	Offence (brief details)	Power of arrest (brief details)
Airports Authority Act 1975, s. 9(6)(b) and Policing of Airports Act 1974, s. 4(3)(b)	Person, in contravention of byelaw, does not leave aerodrome or a particular part of it after being requested to do so by a constable appointed under the 1975 Act (in the case of an offence under that Act) or by the relevant constable under the 1974 Act (in the case of an offence under that Act)	Upon such failure to leave
Betting, Gaming & Lotteries Act 1963, s. 8(2)	Street betting	Found committing
Coinage Offences Act 1936, s. 11	Any offence against the Act (eg import and export of counterfeit coin) except an offence against s. 8 (making, possessing and selling medals resembling gold or silver coins)	Found committing

Table 9.1 (continued)

Provision	Offence (brief details)	Power of arrest (brief details)
Criminal Justice Act 1967, s. 91	Being guilty, while drunk, of disorderly behaviour	Found committing
Diseases of Animals Act 1950, s. 71(3)	Obstructing or impeding a constable or other officer in the execution of the Act *etc*	Constable may arrest that person (see Table 9.3 of this Appendix for the power of arrest under s. 71(2))
Ecclesiastical Courts Jurisdiction Act 1860, s. 3	Riotous, violent or indecent behaviour or other misconduct in any church *etc*	Immediately after commission
Explosives Act 1875, s. 78	Any act which is an offence under the Act, and which tends to cause explosion or fire in or about any factory, magazine, store, railway, canal, ship *etc*	Found committing
Highways Act 1959, s. 121(2),	Wilful obstruction of highway	Seen committing
Indecent Advertisements Act 1889, s. 6	Any offence under the Act	Found committing
Licensing Act 1872, s. 12	Drunk in charge of any carriage, horse, cattle or steam engine in a public place, or drunk (anywhere) in possession of a loaded firearm	Found committing
Licensing Act 1902, s. 1	Drunk in a public place or licensed premises (offence under s. 12 of the Licensing Act 1872)	Any such person who is incapable of taking care of himself
Licensing Act 1902, s. 2(1)	Drunk in a public place or licensed premises in charge of a child under seven years old	Any person found drunk in a public place or licensed premises in charge of a child apparently under seven years old
London Hackney Carriages Act 1843, s. 27	Person acting as a taxi driver in the London area without a cab proprietor's consent	Any constable may take into custody any person unlawfully so acting
Metropolitan Police Act 1839, s. 47	Every person found in premises within the Metropolitan Police District kept or used for bear-baiting, cock-fighting *etc* without lawful excuse	Found when premises entered under the authority of an order in writing issued by the Commissioner of Police of the Metropolis (as to which see Table 5.2 of Appendix 5)
Metropolitan Police Act 1839, s. 54	Various street nuisances, including threatening behaviour, indecent language, and suffering to be at large an unmuzzled ferocious dog	Any person committing such an offence within view of a Metropolitan Police constable

Table 9.1 (continued)

Provision	Offence (brief details)	Power of arrest (brief details)
Metropolitan Police Act 1839, s. 66	Any offence under the Act	Found committing
Night Poaching Act 1828, s. 2	Poaching by night	Found committing. (Any such person may be apprehended by the owner or occupier of the land *etc* and delivered by him to a "peace officer" who is to convey the person before two justices of the peace)
Pedlars Act 1871, s. 18	Refusal to show certificate, or having none, or resisting inspection of his pack	When committing
Prevention of Offences Act 1851, s. 11	Any indictable offence at night	Found committing
Public Health Act 1925, s. 74(2)	Driving dangerously (outside the Metropolitan Police District)	Any constable "who witnesses"
Railway Clauses Consolidation Act 1845, s. 104	Refusal to leave carriage	Discovered "either in or after committing or attempting to commit"
Railway Regulation Act 1840, s. 16	Obstructing railway staff, trespassing on railway *etc*, and refusing to quit	Every person so offending may be detained by an officer of the railway, or his agent, or any person whom he may call to his assistance (which would usually be a constable)
Railway Regulation Act 1842, s. 17	Any engine-driver, guard, porter *etc* who is drunk while on duty, or commits an offence against railway byelaws *etc*, or does, or omits to do, any act by which the life or limb of passengers is or might be endangered *etc*	Every person so offending may be detained by an officer of the railway or his agent, or any special constable duly appointed, or any person whom he may call to his assistance (which would usually be a constable)
Representation of the People Act 1949, Sch. 2; para 34 of the Parliamentary Elections Rules and para 29 of the Local Elections Rules	Misconduct at polling stations	To remove the person by order of the presiding officer or other authorised person and, if the person is charged with the commission of an offence in the polling station, take him into custody
Road Traffic Act 1972, ss. 5(5) and 19(3)	Driving or attempting to drive, or being in charge of, a motor vehicle, or riding a cycle, while unfit through drink or drugs	When apparently committing
Sexual Offences Act 1956, s. 41	Solicitation by men	Found committing
Sexual Offences Act 1967, s. 5	Living on the earnings of male prostitution	Found committing

Table 9.1 (continued)

Provision	Offence (brief details)	Power of arrest (brief details)
Town Gardens Protection Act 1863, s. 5	Injuring public gardens (by trespass, depositing rubbish, stealing or damaging flowers *etc*)	Any constable who shall see
Town Police Clauses Act 1847, s. 15	Any offence under the Act or an offence under s. 52 of the Police Act 1964 (impersonating a police officer *etc*)	Found committing
Town Police Clauses Act 1847, s. 28	Various street nuisances	Any constable within whose view
Unlawful Drilling Act 1819, s. 2	Unlawful military training and exercise	Any person present at, or aiding, assisting or abetting any assembly or meeting for the purpose
Vagrancy Act 1824, s. 6	Any offence under the Act (begging, loitering with intent *etc*) other than the fortune-telling offence in s. 4 (as to which see Table 9.3 of this Appendix)	Found offending

Table 9.2 Powers exercisable where there is reasonable suspicion that a person has committed or is committing the offence specified

Provision	Offence (brief details)	Power of arrest (brief details)
Army Act 1955, s. 186, Air Forces Act 1955, s. 186 and Naval Discipline Act 1957, s. 105 (as amended by the Armed Forces Act 1971, s. 56)	Desertion or absence without leave	Reasonable cause to suspect. (Power to issue warrants also exists under all three sections. There are similar powers of arrest under s. 27 of the Auxiliary Forces Act 1953 in the event of embodiment, and under s. 13 of the Visiting Forces Act 1952 in the event of a request from the appropriate authority of the country to which the person belongs)
Army Act 1955, s. 195 and Air Force Act 1955, s. 195	Unlawful purchase of military or air force stores	Reasonable grounds to suspect of having committed the offence
Betting, Gaming & Lotteries Act 1963, s. 51(1)(b)	Any offence under the Act	Reasonable cause to believe to be committing or to have committed any such offence. (Power may only be used in respect of persons found on premises being searched under the authority of a search warrant issued under the section)
Children and Young Persons Act 1933, s. 10(2)	Vagrants preventing children from receiving education	Any constable who finds person wandering from place to place with a child, and has reasonable ground to believe that the person is guilty of the offence. (There is also a power to detain the child—see Table 9.4 below)
Criminal Law Act 1977, ss. 6(6), 7(11), 8(4), 9(7), 10(5)	Offences relating to entering and remaining on property	Anyone who is, or who there is reasonable cause to suspect to be, guilty of one of the relevant offences. (The power may only be exercised by a constable in uniform)
Customs & Excise Act 1952, s. 274(1) & (2)	Smuggling *etc*	Anyone who has committed or whom there are reasonable grounds to suspect of having committed an offence. (In certain circumstances power may only be exercised within three years of the offence)
Deer Act 1963, s. 5	Any offence against the Act	Suspects with reasonable cause of committing an offence
Firearms Act 1968, s. 50(1)	All offences under the Act except an offence under s. 22(3) or an offence relating specifically to air weapons	When searching premises under the authority of a warrant issued under s. 46 of the Act, and there is reason to believe that the person is guilty of a relevant offence

135

Table 9.2 (continued)

Provision	Offence (brief details)	Power of arrest (brief details)
Firearms Act 1968, (contd) s. 50(2)	Carrying firearms in a public place; trespassing with; possession by a previously convicted person or refusal to hand over firearm after stop and search	Reasonable cause to suspect to be committing an offence
Gaming Act 1968, s. 5(2)	Gaming in street *etc*	Suspects with reasonable cause to be taking part in gaming
s. 43(5)	Any offence under the Act	Constable entering the premises under authority of a search warrant issued under s. 43(4) may arrest any person found on the premises whom he has reasonable cause to believe to be committing or to have committed an offence under the Act
Immigration Act 1971, s. 24(2)	Illegal entry and similar offences	Reasonable cause to suspect to have committed or attempted to commit
s. 25(3)	Knowingly concerned in making or carrying out arrangements for securing or facilitating entry of illegal immigrant	Reasonable cause to suspect of committing an offence
Metropolitan Police Act 1839, s. 34	Any arrestable offence in or on board a ship *etc* lying in the River Thames *etc*	Where there is just cause to suspect that an offence has been or is about to be committed, power, on entry to the vessel, to take into custody all persons suspected of being concerned. (The power is restricted to superintendents, inspectors and sergeants of the Metropolitan Police)
Metropolitan Police Act 1839, s. 65	Any aggravated assault within the Metropolitan Police District	Where a person is charged by another person with such an assault, and the constable has good reason to believe that such assault has been committed, though not within his view, and that by reason of the recent commission of the offence, a warrant could not have been obtained. (The power is restricted to constables belonging to the Metropolitan Police)
Naval Discipline Act 1957, s. 106(1)	Unlawful purchase of naval stores and other offences under Part 3 of the Act punishable on summary conviction	Reasonable grounds for suspecting of having committed the offence

Table 9.2 (continued)

Provision	Offence (brief details)	Power of arrest (brief details)
Official Secrets Act 1911, s. 6	Wrongful communication of information	Found committing or reasonably suspected of having committed, or having attempted to commit, or being about to commit
Prevention of Terrorism (Temporary Provisions) Act 1976, ss. 2(2) & 12(1)(a)	Offences under ss. 1 & 2 (proscribed organisations), 9 (exclusion orders), 10 (contribution towards terrorism) and 11 (information about terrorism) of the Act	Reasonably suspects to be guilty of a relevant offence
Protection of Animals Act 1911, s. 12	Offences under the Act punishable by imprisonment without the option of a fine	Reason to believe person is guilty, whether upon the constable's own view or acting on the word of another if that other gives his name and address
Public Order Act 1936, s. 7(3)	Wearing uniform signifying association with any political organisation, carrying an offensive weapon at public meeting or procession, and offensive conduct in a public place	Reasonably suspected to be committing an offence
Public Stores Act 1875, s. 12 (as substituted by the Theft Act 1968, Sch. 2, Part II)	Offences against ss. 5 of the 1875 Act (obliterating marks denoting that property in stores is HM property) and 8 thereof (sweeping, dredging *etc* near docks, artillery ranges *etc*)	Reasonable cause to suspect to be in the act of committing, or attempting to commit, an offence
Rabies Act 1974, s. 5A (as inserted by the Criminal Law Act 1977, s. 55)	Contravention of the anti-rabies controls	Reasonable cause to suspect to be in the act of committing, or to have committed, an offence
Representation of the People Act 1949, Sch. 2; para 37 of the Parliamentary Elections Rules and para 32 of the Local Elections Rules	Personation by applicant for a ballot paper	If at time person applies for ballot paper, or after that but before he leaves polling station, candidate or agent tells presiding officer that he has reasonable cause to suspect personation, and undertakes to substantiate this in court, presiding officer may order constable to arrest applicant
Road Traffic Act 1972, s. 100	Driving while disqualified	Constable in uniform may arrest any person driving or attempting to drive a motor vehicle on a road whom he has reasonable cause to suspect of being disqualified
Road Traffic (Foreign Vehicles) Act 1972, s. 3(2)	Driving a foreign goods or public service vehicle after prohibition by examiner or other authorised person, and related offences under the Act	Constable in uniform may arrest on reasonable cause to suspect of having committed such offence

Table 9.2 (continued)

Provision	Offence (brief details)	Power of arrest (brief details)
Sexual Offences Act 1956, s. 40	Causing prostitution of women and procuration of girls under 21	Reasonable cause to suspect of having committed, or of attempting to commit
Street Offences Act 1959, s. 1(3)	Soliciting in a street *etc* for the purposes of prostitution	Suspects with reasonable cause to be committing an offence
Theft Act 1968, s. 12(3)	Taking motor vehicle or other conveyance other than a pedal cycle without authority	Deemed an arrestable offence for the purposes of s. 2 of the Criminal Law Act 1967 (and therefore attracts the power of arrest under that section)
s. 25(4)	Going equipped for theft, burglary or cheating	Reasonable cause to suspect to be committing an offence
Sch. 1, paras 1(2) and 2(4)	Unlawfully taking or killing deer and unlawfully taking or destroying fish	Reasonable cause to suspect to be committing an offence

Table 9.3 Powers exercisable only where the name and address of the person cannot be ascertained and/or he is likely to abscond

Provision	Offence (brief details)	Power exercisable (brief details)	Condition attached to power before arrest can be made
Airports Authority Act 1975, s. 9(6)(a) and the Policing of Airports Act 1974, s. 4(3)(a)	Offences under airport byelaws	Reasonable cause to believe that person has contravened byelaw. (Power conferred only on constables appointed under the 1975 Act in the case of offences against that Act, and on "relevant" constables—ie constables for the area in which the airport is situated—in the case of offences against the 1974 Act)	If the constable does not know and cannot ascertain the person's name and address
Badgers Act 1973, s. 10	Any offence under the Act (unlawfully taking badgers *etc*)	Reasonable grounds for suspecting that an offence is being committed, or that an offence has been committed and that evidence of that commission is on the suspect or his property	If he fails to give his full name and address to the constable's satisfaction
Children and Young Persons Act 1933, s. 13(1)(a)	Offences set out in first schedule to the Act being offences against children and young persons (including murder, manslaughter, various sexual offences *etc*)	Any person who commits a relevant offence within the constable's view	If the constable does not know and cannot ascertain his name and residence
s. 13(1)(b)	Offences set out in the first schedule to the Act (see above)	Any person who has committed, or whom there is reason to believe has committed, a relevant offence	If there is reasonable ground for believing that the person will abscond or the constable does not know and cannot ascertain his name and address
Conservation of Seals Act 1970, s. 4	Any offence under the Act (use of unlawful methods for killing seals *etc*)	Suspects with reasonable cause of committing an offence	If he fails to give his name and address to the constable's satisfaction
Conservation of Wild Creatures and Wild Plants Act 1975, s. 10	Any offence under the Act (restrictions on killing *etc* protected wild creatures and wild plants)	Suspects with reasonable cause of committing or of having committed an offence	If he fails to give his name and address to the constable's satisfaction

139

Table 9.3 (continued)

Provision	Offence (brief details)	Power exercisable (brief details)	Condition attached to power before arrest can be made
Diseases of Animals Act 1950, s. 71(2)	Any offence under the Act	Any person seen or found committing or reasonably suspected of being engaged in committing an offence. (For the further power of arrest under s. 71(3), see Table 9.1 of this Appendix)	If his name and address are not known to the constable and he fails to give them to the satisfaction of the constable
Firearms Act 1968, s. 50(3)	Refusal or failure to give name and address, when asked to do so in consequence of failure to produce a firearms certificate	Any person who refuses to give name and address, or who is suspected of giving a false name and address or of intending to abscond	See preceding column
Game Act 1831, s. 31 (as amended by Game Laws (Amendment) Act 1960, s. 1(2))	Trespassing in search or pursuit of game *etc* in the daytime	Committing. (To be conveyed before a justice within 12 hours, otherwise released and proceeded against by summons or warrant)	If the person does not give real name and address, or continues or returns on land when required to quit and give his name and address
Licensing Act 1964, s. 187(5)	Failure or refusal to give name and address or answer questions to verify these when liquor is seized under the authority of a justice's warrant	Any person suspected of having committed the offence	
Metropolitan Police Act 1839, s. 63	Any offence under the Act or s. 52 of the Police Act 1964 (impersonating a police officer *etc*)	Any person who, within view of a Metropolitan Police constable, so offends	If the person's name and address are unknown to, and cannot be ascertained by, the constable
Misuse of Drugs Act 1971, s. 24	Any offences under the Act	Any person who has committed or who is suspected with reasonable cause to have committed an offence. (This power is declared by s. 24(2) to be without prejudice to any other power of arrest)	If there is reasonable cause to believe that the person will abscond unless arrested, or his name and address are unknown to the constable and cannot be ascertained by him, or the constable is not satisfied that the name and address given are true
Parks Regulation Act 1872, ss. 5 and 8	Offences against regulations concerning conduct in Royal Parks	Offence committed within view of park constable or constable for the area in which the park is situated	If name or residence of the offender is unknown to, and cannot be ascertained by, such constable

Table 9.3 (continued)

Provision	Offence (brief details)	Power exercisable (brief details)	Condition attached to power before arrest can be made
Prevention of Crime Act 1953, s. 1(3)	Having an offensive weapon in a public place without lawful authority or excuse	Any person believed with reasonable cause to be committing an offence	If the constable is not satisfied as to the person's identity or place of residence or has reasonable cause to believe that it is necessary to arrest him in order to prevent an offence in the course of which an offensive weapon might be used
Protection of Birds Act 1954, s. 12(1)	Any offence against the Act	Any person found committing an offence	If the person fails to give his name and address to the constable's satisfaction
Protection of Birds Act 1967, s. 11	Taking or destroying an egg of a protected bird	Any person suspected with reasonable grounds of having committed an offence	If the person fails to give his name and address to the constable's satisfaction
Public Meeting Act 1908, s. 1(3) (as added by Public Order Act 1936, s. 6)	Acting in a disorderly manner in order to break up a meeting	Reasonably suspects of committing an offence	If on being required to give his name and address by a constable (if so requested by the chairman of the meeting) the person refuses or fails to give his name and address, or the constable reasonably suspects him of giving a false name and address
Public Service Vehicles (Arrest of Offenders) Act 1975, s. 1	Misconduct on a public service vehicle	Suspects with reasonable cause that an offence has been committed	If the person refuses to give his name and address, or does not answer to the satisfaction of the constable questions put to him for the purpose of ascertaining whether the name and address are correct
Regulation of Railways Act 1889, s. 5(2)	Failure to pay or show ticket	Committing	If the person refuses or fails to give his name and address when requested to do so (by an officer or servant of the railway company)

Table 9.3 (continued)

Provision	Offence (brief details)	Power exercisable (brief details)	Condition attached to power before arrest can be made
Representation of the People Act 1949, s. 84(3)	Disturbance at election meetings	Reasonably suspects of committing an offence	If on being required to give his name and address by a constable (if so requested by the chairman of the meeting) the person refuses or fails to give his name and address, or the constable reasonably suspects him of giving a false name and address
Road Traffic Act 1972, s. 164(2)(a)	Driving a motor vehicle recklessly, or carelessly, or without reasonable consideration	Any person who within the constable's view commits an offence	If the person neither gives his name and address, nor produces his driving licence
s. 164(2)(b)	Riding a cycle recklessly, or carelessly, or without reasonable consideration	Any person who within the constable's view commits an offence	If the person does not give his name and address
Vagrancy Act 1824, s. 6 as restricted by Criminal Justice Act 1948, s. 68	Telling fortunes contrary to s. 4 of the 1824 Act	Any person found committing an offence	If the constable has reason to believe that the person will abscond unless arrested, or is not satisfied as to the identity or place of residence of the person

Table 9.4 Other miscellaneous powers

Provision	Power (brief details)
Airports Authority Act 1975, s. 11(2)(a)	To arrest without warrant any person employed by or on one of the Authority's airports whom the constable has reasonable grounds to suspect of having in his possession or conveying in any manner anything stolen or unlawfully obtained on the aerodrome. (Power conferred only on constables appointed under the Act. For the power of stop and search under the same subsection see Appendix 1)
Army Act 1955, s. 190B and Air Force Act 1955, s.190B (as added by the Armed Forces Act 1971)	To arrest without warrant any person who, having been sentenced by the service authorities to imprisonment or detention, is unlawfully at large during the currency of the sentence. (There are similar powers under s. 27 of the Auxiliary Forces Act 1953 in the event of embodiment and under s. 13 of the Visiting Forces Act 1952 in the event of a request from the appropriate authority of the country to which the person belongs)
Bail Act 1976, s. 7(3)	To arrest without warrant a person released on bail and under a duty to surrender into the custody of a court if the constable has reasonable grounds for believing that the person is not likely so to surrender, or that the conditions attached to bail have been or are likely to be broken, or where a surety notifies a constable in writing that the person is unlikely to surrender to custody and that therefore the surety wishes to be relieved of his obligations
Canals (Offences) Act 1840, s. 10	To take into custody without a warrant any loose, idle or disorderly person whom the constable shall find disturbing the public peace, or whom he shall have good reason to suspect of having committed or being about to commit any offence or breach of the peace or other offence contrary to the Act, and any person found at nighttime loitering or lying in or on the tow-path, wharfs *etc* of a canal, and not giving a satisfactory account of himself. (Power conferred only on constables appointed under the Act)
Children and Young Persons Act 1969, s. 28(2)	To detain a child or young person whom the constable has reasonable cause to believe to be neglected or ill-treated, or exposed to moral danger, or beyond his parents' control, or whom the constable has reasonable cause to believe that an appropriate court would take the view that it is probable that the child will be ill-treated or neglected, and also to detain any child or young person whom the constable has reasonable cause to believe to be a child or young person in respect of whom an offence is being committed under s. 10 of the Children and Young Persons Act 1933 (which penalises a vagrant who takes a juvenile from place to place)
Children and Young Persons Act 1969 s. 32(1) (as amended by the Children Act 1975, s. 68)	To arrest without warrant any child or young person absent without proper authority from a place of safety, or a place where he is living in the care of the local authority, or a remand home, special reception centre *etc*, and to take him back there at the expense of the appropriate person or authority
Criminal Justice Act 1972, s. 34	To take to a treatment centre any person whom the constable has power to arrest for certain offences of drunkenness
Domestic Violence and Matrimonial Proceedings Act 1976, s. 2	To arrest without warrant any person whom the constable reasonably suspects of being in breach of an injunction (restraining a spouse from using violence or from entering or coming within a certain area of the matrimonial home) to which the judge has attached a power of arrest, and to bring that person before a judge within 24 hours

Table 9.4 (continued)

Provision	Power (brief details)
Immigration Act 1971, Sch. 2, para 17	To arrest without warrant a person liable to be detained under the Act for examination or removal from the United Kingdom
Immigration Act 1971, Sch. 2, paras 24 and 33	To arrest without warrant a person bailed under the Act if the constable has reasonable cause to believe that the person is not likely to appear at the time and place required or that any other condition of bail has been, is being, or is likely to be broken; or where a surety provides written notification that the person is unlikely to surrender to custody, and that therefore the surety wishes to be relieved of his obligations
Mental Health Act 1959, s. 40	Where a patient is compulsorily admitted to hospital or subject to guardianship *etc* constables are among those empowered to take him into custody and return him to the proper place. (There are time limits—six months or 28 days according to the circumstances—within which this power must be exercised)
s. 136(1)	To remove to a place of safety any person whom the constable finds in a place to which the public has access and who appears to him to be suffering from mental disorder, and to be in immediate need of care or control, where the constable considers such removal to be in the interests of that person or for the protection of other persons. (Person arrested may be detained for up to 72 hours while treatment, care *etc* are arranged)
s. 140	To retake any mentally disordered person who has escaped from legal custody
Metropolitan Police Act 1839, ss. 38 and 39, and Metropolitan Fairs Act 1868, s. 2	Fairs in the Metropolitan Police District may not operate between 11 pm and 6 am. If any booth, caravan *etc* be open for business or amusement at the fair within those hours a constable may take into custody the person having its care or management and any person who does not quit when so told (s. 38). Section 39 provides that the Commissioner has power to inquire into the lawfulness of a fair. If a fair is declared unlawful by a magistrate then, subject to certain formalities, the Commissioner may direct officers to remove certain fairground equipment and arrest persons who are trying to pitch the fair, run a booth *etc*. There are similar procedures and powers under s. 2 of the 1868 Act if the fair at a particular site was not held there for each of the last seven years
s. 62	To apprehend with or without warrant any person who, within the Metropolitan Police District, by committing any offence "herein forbidden" has caused hurt or damage to any person or property. (The person is to be taken before a magistrate if he does not make amends to the satisfaction of the person aggrieved)
s. 64	To take into custody without a warrant any loose, idle or disorderly person whom the constable shall find disturbing the public peace, or whom he shall have good cause to suspect of having committed or being about to commit any offence or breach of the peace, and any person found at night-time lying or loitering in any highway, yard or other place and not giving a satisfactory account of himself. (Power conferred only on Metropolitan Police constables)
Municipal Corporations Act 1882, s. 193	To apprehend any idle and disorderly person whom a borough constable finds disturbing the public peace

Table 9.4 (continued)

Provision	Power (brief details)
Naval Discipline Act 1957, s. 104(1)	To arrest without warrant any person who having been sentenced by the service authorities to imprisonment or detention is unlawfully at large during the currency of the sentence
Pawnbrokers Act 1872, ss. 34 and 49	In certain events (eg, person offering article for pawn cannot say where he got it from; trying to redeem pledge when not entitled; uttering pawn ticket which the pawnbroker reasonably suspects to be forged) the pawnbroker may seize and detain the person and/or the article and deliver him/it into the custody of a constable who shall convey the person, if detained, before a justice. (Note: the whole of the 1872 Act is liable to repeal under the Consumer Credit Act 1974, s. 192(3) and Sch. 5)
Policing of Airports Act 1974, s. 3(1)(a)	To arrest without warrant in any designated airport any airport employee whom the constable has reasonable grounds to suspect of having in his possession or conveying in any manner anything stolen or unlawfully obtained on the aerodrome. (Power conferred only on "relevant" constables—ie, constables of the force within whose area the airport is situated. For the power of stop and search under the same subsection see Appendix 1)
Prevention of Terrorism (Temporary Provisions) Act 1976, s. 12(1)(b) and (c)	To arrest without warrant any person whom the constable reasonably suspects to be a person who is or has been concerned in the commission, preparation or instigation of acts of terrorism, or a person subject to an exclusion order. (For the power of arrest under s. 12(1)(a) see Table 9.2 of this Appendix)
Prison Act 1952, s. 49(1)	To arrest without warrant any person who, having been sentenced to imprisonment or detention, is unlawfully at large, and return him to the place of detention
Protection of Aircraft Act 1973, s. 19(1)	Where a constable has reasonable cause to suspect that a person about to embark on an aircraft in the United Kingdom intends to commit in relation to the aircraft one of certain offences (relating to hijacking *etc*) he may prohibit him from travelling on the aircraft, and for that purpose may prevent him or remove him, and arrest him without warrant and detain him for so long as is necessary for the purpose
Road Traffic Act 1972, s. 8(4)	To arrest without warrant any person (except a hospital patient) in respect of whom a breath test indicates that the proportion of alcohol in the blood exceeds the prescribed limit. (Breath tests may only be required by a constable in uniform)
s. 8(5)	To arrest without warrant any person (except a hospital patient) who fails to provide a specimen of breath for a breath test, and who the constable has reasonable cause to suspect of having alcohol in his body. (Breath tests may only be required by a constable in uniform)

The use of equipment in police surveillance operations: extract from the general orders of one force.

1. *The use of equipment in police surveillance operations*

The use of certain equipment in police surveillance operations may involve encroachment on privacy. As a general principle, the primary purpose of using such equipment for aural or visual surveillance should be to help confirm or dispel a suspicion of serious crime, and not to collect evidence (except where, as in blackmail, the spoken word is the kernel of the offence). In each case officers should satisfy themselves that use of the particular equipment is:

    (a) operationally necessary;

    (b) operationally feasible; and

    (c) justified in all the circumstances.

2. *Aural and visual surveillance*

The covert use in operations of listening, recording and transmitting equipment, and the covert use of visual surveillance equipment, including cameras and closed circuit television, but excluding, for this purpose, ordinary binoculars, requires the permission of the chief constable. In certain circumstances, as listed at Appendix A,[1] this authority has been delegated.

3. *Binoculars*

The covert use of ordinary binoculars will be at the discretion of chief inspectors.

4. *Administration*

In normal circumstances equipment will be held within the Technical Support Unit at force headquarters. Where time permits, written applications for the supply and use of the equipment will be submitted through chief superintendents to the chief constable under confidential cover.

In cases of urgency, where time does not allow this procedure to be followed, a personal approach to the appropriate authorising officer should be made by an officer not below the rank of superintendent and a confirmatory report submitted as soon as possible.

When approval has been given for the use of equipment, the Technical Support Unit Liaison Inspector will be informed and he will make the necessary

[1]Not appended

arrangements. A record will be kept of each authority given for the use of equipment, as in paragraph 1.1 to 1.6 in Appendix A,[1] indicating the nature of the case and broadly how the criteria in paragraph 1(a), (b) and (c) were met.

[1]Not appended

Telephone calls (interception): Text of announcement in Parliament by the Home Secretary, House of Commons Official Report 1 April 1980, cols. 205–208.

Mr William Whitelaw: With permission, Mr Speaker, I shall make a statement on the interception of communications.

The House will recall that, following the Vice-Chancellor's judgment in *Malone v Commissioner of Police of the Metropolis*, my predecessor the right hon. Member for Leeds South (Mr Rees) informed the House on 8 March 1979 that he proposed to put in hand a study of the implications of that judgment. On 13 June 1979 I told the House that I had directed that this study should be continued to its completion, and would inform the House of my conclusions in due course.

Since that study began, a number of questions have been raised about the practice and extent of interception. The study has been completed. The Government have also made a thorough review of the procedures and conditions which, since the report of the Committee of Privy Councillors under the chairmanship of Lord Birkett in 1957, have been the basis of our arrangements in these matters. Over the years there have been minor changes of practice; but in all essentials the principles and procedures laid down by Birkett continue to be observed, including the fact that interception takes place only on the personal warrant of the Secretary of State. I have today published a Command Paper which sets out the Birkett principles and procedures as they operate today. It covers, as the Birkett report did, interception on behalf of the police, Her Majesty's Customs and Excise and the security service.

Information about interception in Northern Ireland is excluded from the command paper because the need to be able to combat terrorism there makes it undesirable to disclose any details. However, I can assure the House that the procedures, conditions and safeguards set out in the command paper are observed in Northern Ireland, subject only to the overriding requirements for dealing with terrorism. In particular, the personal authorisation of the Secretary of State for Northern Ireland has to be obtained for each individual interception.

The interception of communications, whether by the opening and reading of letters, or by recording and listening to telephone communications, is an interference with the freedom of the individual in a democratic society. None the less, when carried out by the properly constituted authorities it is justified if its aims and consequences help to protect the law abiding citizen from the threats of crime and violence and the fabric of democracy from the menaces of espionage, terrorism and subversion.

Allegations have been made that interception is now practised on a vastly wider scale than at the time of the Birkett inquiry. I hope that the figures quoted in the Command Paper, which bring up to date those in the Birkett report, will provide reassurance on this score. There has been a modest overall increase in the total number of warrants signed and a change in the balance between telephone and letter interception which reflects the greatly increased use of the telephone since 1957. But, given the very considerable growth in serious crime and in particular the development of the terrorist threat during the intervening years, I believe that the figures demonstrate that the use of interception continues to be tightly controlled.

In his judgment in *Malone v Commissioner of Police of the Metropolis*, the Vice-Chancellor, Sir Robert Megarry, found that interception undertaken on behalf of the police under the warrant of the Secretary of State was not illegal. There is, therefore, no need for legislation to make duly authorised interception lawful. He drew attention to the fact that the restrictions and safeguards under which interception is conducted are, in this country, matters of administrative practice and not, as in some other countries, of statute. He went on to suggest that it was for consideration whether the procedures and conditions governing the use of interception should be embodied in legislation.

In their review, the Government have considered this suggestion with great care. The interception of communications is, by definition, a practice that depends for its effectiveness and value upon being carried out in secret, and cannot therefore be subject to the normal processes of parliamentary control. Its acceptability in a democratic society depends on its being subject to ministerial control, and on the readiness of the public and their representatives in Parliament to repose their trust in the Ministers concerned to exercise that control responsibly and with a right sense of balance between the value of interception as a means of protecting order and security and the threat which it may present to the liberty of the subject.

Within the necessary limits of secrecy, I and my right hon. Friends who are concerned are responsible to Parliament for our stewardship in this sphere. There would be no more sense in making such secret matters justiciable than there would be in my being obliged to reveal them in the House. If the power to intercept were to be regulated by statute, then the courts would have power to inquire into the matter and to do so, if not publicly, then at least in the presence of the complainant. This must surely limit the use of interception as a tool of investigation. The Government have come to the clear conclusion that the procedures, conditions and safeguards described in the Command Paper ensure strict control of interception by Ministers, are a good and sufficient protection for the liberty of the subject, and would not be made significantly more effective for that purpose by being embodied in legislation. The Government have accordingly decided not to introduce legislation on these matters.

The Government have, however, decided that it would be desirable if there were a continuous independent check that interception was being carried out in accordance with the established purposes and procedures. We propose to invite a senior member of the judiciary to carry out this task. His terms of reference will be

"To review on a continuing basis the purposes, procedures, conditions and safeguards governing the interception of communications on behalf of the police, HM Customs and Excise and the security service as set out in Cmnd Paper 7873; and to report to the Prime Minister".

He will have the right of access to papers, and the right to request additional information from the Departments and organisations concerned. For the purpose of his first report, which will be published, he will examine all the arrangements set out in Cmnd Paper 7873. His subsequent reports on the detailed operation of the arrangements will not be published, but Parliament will be informed of any findings of a general nature and of any changes that are made in the arrangements.

The Government believe that these standing arrangements for monitoring the operation and control of interception will be a valuable, additional assurance to Parliament and the public that the powers of interception are exercised strictly, sparingly and responsibly.

Judges' Rules and Administrative Directions to the Police

HOME OFFICE CIRCULAR NO. 89/1978:

Judges' Rules and Administrative Directions to the Police

The Chief Officer of Police

Sir,

I am directed by the Secretary of State to say that he is anxious to ensure that the Judges' Rules and the related Administrative Directions to the police are known by all police officers and readily available to all members of the legal profession and others who may be concerned with them. He has accordingly decided, with the agreement of the Lord Chief Justice, to re-issue the Rules and Directions taking account of related Home Office circulars issued since new Rules were made in 1964.

2. The Rules which are reproduced in Appendix A to this circular are identical to those issued under cover of Home Office circular No. 31/1964. The Judges have made it clear that the Rules are concerned with the admissibility in evidence against a person of answers, oral or written, given by that person to questions asked by police officers and of statements made by that person. In giving evidence as to the circumstances in which any statement was made or taken down in writing, officers must be absolutely frank in describing to the court exactly what occurred, and it will then be for the Judge to decide whether or not the statement tendered should be admitted in evidence. The Rules should constantly be borne in mind, as should the general principles which the Judges have set out before the Rules. But in addition to complying with the Rules, interrogating officers should always try to be fair to the person who is being questioned, and scrupulously avoid any method which could be regarded as in any way unfair or oppressive.

3. Appendix B contains the Administrative Directions to the Police, which have been revised to take account of relevant Home Office circulars issued since 1964. Attention is drawn to the following points at which the Directions differ from those issued in 1964:

    (i) Home Office letter of May 31, 1968 on interviewing, fingerprinting and photographing children and young persons made it clear that the advice contained in the first sentence of paragraph 4 of the Directions should be taken as relating to all persons under 17 years of age. Paragraph 4 of the Directions has been amended accordingly.

(ii) Home Office circular No. 66/1976 clarified the second paragraph of Administrative Direction 7(*a*), by pointing out, for the avoidance of doubt, that the sending of telegrams and letters by persons in police custody should be subject to the same proviso as telephone communications with the person's solicitors and friends (covered by the first paragraph of Direction 7 (*a*)). Administrative Direction 7 (*a*) has now been recast accordingly.

(iii) Home Office circular No. 109/1976 gave guidance on the need for special care in the interrogation of mentally handicapped persons. A new paragraph, 4A, now incorporates that guidance. The reference to a "social worker" as an example of the sort of person who might be asked to be present should not be narrowly interpreted—any person with a professional interest in the mentally handicapped would be suitable. Chief officers of police may find that if the Director of Social Services is approached locally it may be possible to make suitable arrangements in advance.

In addition, the heading but not the sense of Administrative Direction 5 has been altered.

4. Home Office circular No. 148/1977 set out arrangements for obtaining the services of competent interpreters in cases where police enquiries involve the questioning of a deaf person. For convenience, the substance of this circular is set out in Appendix C attached.

5. Section 62 of the Criminal Law Act provides that where any person has been arrested and is being held in custody in a police station or other premises, he shall be entitled to have intimation of his arrest and of the place where he is being held sent to one person reasonably named by him without delay or, where some delay is necessary in the interest of the investigation or prevention of crime or the apprehension of offenders, with no more delay than is so necessary. Guidance to the police on section 62 is contained in Home Office circular No. 74/1978. Paragraph 1 of that circular makes it clear that the provision in section 62 in no way detracts from the Judges' Rules and Administrative Directions.

I am, Sir,

Your obedient Servant,

R. T. ARMSTRONG.

Appendix A

JUDGES' RULES

Note

The origin of the Judges' Rules is probably to be found in a letter dated October 26, 1906, which the then Lord Chief Justice, Lord Alverstone, wrote to the Chief Constable of Birmingham in answer to a request for advice in consequence of the fact that on the same Circuit one Judge had censured a member of his force for having cautioned a prisoner, whilst another Judge had censured a constable for having omitted to do so. The first four of the pre-1964 Rules were formulated and approved by the Judges of the King's Bench Division in 1912; the remaining five in 1918. They were much criticised, *inter alia* for lack of clarity and of efficacy for the protection of persons who were questioned by police officers; on the other hand it was maintained that their application unduly hampered the detection and punishment of crime. A Committee of Judges devoted considerable time and attention to producing, after consideration of representative views, a new set of Rules which was approved by a meeting of all the Queen's Bench Judges and issued in 1964.

The Judges control the conduct of trials and the admission of evidence against persons on trial before them; they do not control or in any way initiate or supervise police activities or conduct. As stated in paragraph (*e*) of the introduction to the present Rules, it is the law that answers and statements made are only admissible in evidence if they have been voluntary in the sense that they have not been obtained by fear of prejudice or hope of advantage, exercised or held out by a person in authority, or by oppression. The Rules do not purport to envisage or deal with the many varieties of conduct which might render answers and statements involuntary and therefore inadmissible. The Rules merely deal with particular aspects of the matter. Other matters such as affording reasonably comfortable conditions, adequate breaks for rest and refreshment, special procedures in the case of persons unfamiliar with the English language or of immature age or feeble understanding, are proper subjects for administrative directions to the police.

JUDGES' RULES

These Rules do not affect the principles

- (*a*) That citizens have a duty to help a police officer to discover and apprehend offenders;
- (*b*) That police officers, otherwise than by arrest, cannot compel any person against his will to come to or remain in any police station;
- (*c*) That every person at any stage of an investigation should be able to communicate and to consult privately with a solicitor. This is so even if he is in custody provided that in such a case no unreasonable delay or hindrance is caused to the processes of investigation or the administration of justice by his doing so;
- (*d*) That when a police officer who is making enquiries of any person about an offence has enough evidence to prefer a charge against that

person for the offence, he should without delay cause that person to be charged or informed that he may be prosecuted for the offence;

(e) That it is a fundamental condition of the admissibility in evidence against any person, equally of any oral answer given by that person to a question put by a police officer and of any statement made by that person, that it shall have been voluntary, in the sense that it has not been obtained from him by fear of prejudice or hope of advantage, exercised or held out by a person in authority, or by oppression.

The principle set out in paragraph *(e)* above is overriding and applicable in all cases. Within that principle the following Rules are put forward as a guide to police officers conducting investigations. Non-conformity with these Rules may render answers and statements liable to be excluded from evidence in subsequent criminal proceedings.

RULES

I. When a police officer is trying to discover whether, or by whom, an offence has been committed he is entitled to question any person, whether suspected or not, from whom he thinks that useful information may be obtained. This is so whether or not the person in question has been taken into custody so long as he has not been charged with the offence or informed that he may be prosecuted for it.

II. As soon as a police officer has evidence which would afford reasonable grounds for suspecting that a person has committed an offence, he shall caution that person or cause him to be cautioned before putting to him any questions, or further questions, relating to that offence.

The caution shall be in the following terms:

"You are not obliged to say anything unless you wish to do so but what you say may be put into writing and given in evidence."

When after being cautioned a person is being questioned, or elects to make a statement, a record shall be kept of the time and place at which any such questioning or statement began and ended and of the persons present.

III.*(a)* Where a person is charged with or informed that he may be prosecuted for an offence he shall be cautioned in the following terms:

"Do you wish to say anything? You are not obliged to say anything unless you wish to do so but whatever you say will be taken down in writing and may be given in evidence."

(b) It is only in exceptional cases that questions relating to the offence should be put to the accused person after he has been charged or informed that he may be prosecuted. Such questions may be put where they are necessary for the purpose of preventing or minimising harm or loss to some other person or the public or for clearing up an ambiguity in a previous answer or statement.

Before any such questions are put the accused should be cautioned in these terms:

"I wish to put some questions to you about the offence with which you have been charged (*or* about the offence for which you may be prosecuted). You are not obliged to answer any of these questions, but if you do the questions and answers will be taken down in writing and may be given in evidence."

Any questions put and answers given relating to the offence must be contemporaneously recorded in full and the record signed by that person or if he refuses by the interrogating officer.

(c) When such a person is being questioned, or elects to make a statement, a record shall be kept of the time and place at which any questioning or statement began and ended and of the persons present.

IV. All written statements made after caution shall be taken in the following manner:

(a) If a person says that he wants to make a statement he shall be told that it is intended to make a written record of what he said. He shall always be asked whether he wishes to write down himself what he wants to say; if he says that he cannot write or that he would like someone to write it for him, a police officer may offer to write the statement for him. If he accepts the offer the police officer shall, before starting, ask the person making the statement to sign, or make his mark to, the following:

"I,..., wish to make a statement. I want someone to write down what I say. I have been told that I need not say anything unless I wish to do so and that whatever I say may be given in evidence."

(b) Any person writing his own statement shall be allowed to do so without any prompting as distinct from indicating to him what matters are material.

(c) The person making the statement, if he is going to write it himself, shall be asked to write out and sign before writing what he wants to say, the following:

"I make this statement of my own free will. I have been told that I need not say anything unless I wish to do so and that whatever I say may be given in evidence."

(d) Whenever a police officer writes the statement, he shall take down the exact words spoken by the person making the statement, without putting any questions other than such as may be needed to make the statement coherent, intelligible and relevant to the material matters; he shall not prompt him.

(e) When the writing of a statement by a police officer is finished the person making it shall be asked to read it and to make any corrections, alterations or additions he wishes. When he has finished reading it he shall be asked to write and sign or make his mark on the following Certificate at the end of the statement:

"I have read the above statement and I have been told that I can correct, alter or add anything I wish. This statement is true. I have made it of my own free will."

(f) If the person who has made a statement refuses to read it or to write the above mentioned Certificate at the end of it or to sign it, the senior police officer present shall record on the statement itself and in the presence of the person making it, what has happened. If the person making the statement cannot read, or refuses to read it, the officer who has taken it down shall read it over to him and ask him whether he would like to correct, alter or add anything and to put his signature or make his mark at the end. The police officer shall then certify on the statement itself what he has done.

V. If at any time after a person has been charged with, or has been informed that he may be prosecuted for an offence a police officer wishes to bring to the notice of that person any written statement made by another person who in respect of the same offence has also been charged or informed that he may be prosecuted, he shall hand to that person a true copy of such written statement, but nothing shall be said or done to invite any reply or comment. If that person says that he would like to make a statement in reply, or starts to say something, he shall at once be cautioned or further cautioned as prescribed by Rule III(*a*).

VI. Persons other than police officers charged with the duty of investigating offences or charging offenders shall, so far as may be practicable, comply with these Rules.

Appendix B

ADMINISTRATIVE DIRECTIONS ON INTERROGATION AND THE TAKING OF STATEMENTS

1. *Procedure generally*

   (a) When possible statements of persons under caution should be written on the forms provided for the purpose. Police officers' notebooks should be used for taking statements only when no forms are available.

   (b) When a person is being questioned or elects to make a statement, a record should be kept of the time or times at which during the questioning or making of a statement there were intervals or refreshment was taken. The nature of the refreshment should be noted. In no circumstances should alcoholic drink be given.

   (c) In writing down a statement, the words used should not be translated into "official" vocabulary; this may give a misleading impression of the genuineness of the statement.

   (d) Care should be taken to avoid any suggestion that the person's answers can only be used in evidence against him, as this may prevent an innocent person making a statement which might help clear him of the charge.

2. *Record of interrogation*

   Rule II and Rule III(c) demand that a record should be kept of the following matters:

   (a) when, after being cautioned in accordance with Rule II, the person is being questioned or elects to make a statement—of the time and place at which any such questioning began and ended and of the persons present;

   (b) when, after being cautioned in accordance with Rule III(a) or (b) a person is being questioned or elects to make a statement—of the time and place at which any questioning and statement began and ended and of the persons present.

   In addition to the records required by these Rules full records of the following matters should additionally be kept:

   (a) of the time or times at which cautions were taken, and

   (b) of the time when a charge was made and/or the person was arrested, and

   (c) of the matters referred to in paragraph 1(b) above.

   If two or more police officers are present when the questions are being put or the statement made, the records made should be countersigned by the other officers present.

3. *Comfort and refreshment*

   Reasonable arrangements should be made for the comfort and refreshment of persons being questioned. Whenever practicable both the person being questioned or making a statement and the officers asking the questions or taking the statement should be seated.

4. *Interrogation of children and young persons*

As far as practicable children and young persons under the age of 17 years (whether suspected of crime or not) should only be interviewed in the presence of a parent or guardian, or in their absence, some person who is not a police officer and is of the same sex as the child. A child or young person should not be arrested, nor even interviewed, at school if such action can possibly be avoided. Where it is found essential to conduct the interview at school, this should be done only with the consent, and in the presence, of the head teacher, or his nominee.

4A. *Interrogation of mentally handicapped persons*

(a) If it appears to a police officer that a person (whether a witness or a suspect) whom he intends to interview has a mental handicap which raises a doubt as to whether the person can understand the questions put to him, or which makes the person likely to be especially open to suggestion, the officer should take particular care in putting questions and accepting the reliability of answers. As far as practicable, and where recognised as such by the police, a mentally handicapped adult (whether suspected of crime or not) should be interviewed only in the presence of a parent or other person in whose care, custody or control he is, or of some person who is not a police officer (for example a social worker).

(b) So far as mentally handicapped children and young persons are concerned, the conditions of interview and arrest by the police are governed by Administrative Direction 4 above.

(c) Any document arising from an interview with a mentally handicapped person of any age should be signed not only by the person who made the statement, but also by the parent or other person who was present during the interview. Since the reliability of any admission by a mentally handicapped person may even then be challenged, care will still be necessary to verify the facts admitted and to obtain corroboration where possible.

5. *Statements in languages other than English*

In the case of a person making a statement in a language other than English:

(a) The interpreter should take down the statement in the language in which it is made.

(b) An official English translation should be made in due course and be proved as an exhibit with the original statement.

(c) The person making the statement should sign that at *(a)*.

Apart from the question of apparent unfairness, to obtain the signature of a suspect to an English translation of what he said in another language can have little or no value as evidence if the suspect disputes the accuracy of this record of this statement.

6. *Supply to accused persons of written statement of charges*

(a) The following procedure should be adopted whenever a charge is preferred against a person arrested without warrant for any offence:

As soon as a charge has been accepted by the appropriate police officer the accused person should be given a written notice containing a copy of the entry in the charge sheet or book giving particulars of the offence with which he is charged. So far as possible the particulars of the charge should be stated in simple language so that the accused person may understand it, but they should also show clearly the precise offence in law with which he is charged. Where the offence charged is a statutory one, it should be sufficient for the latter purpose to quote the section of the statute which created the offence.

The written notice should include some statement on the lines of the caution given orally to the accused person in accordance with the Judges' Rules after a charge has been preferred. It is suggested that the form of notice should begin with the following words:

"You are charged with the offence(s) shown below. You are not obliged to say anything unless you wish to do so, but whatever you say will be taken down in writing and may be given in evidence."

(b) Once the accused person has appeared before the court it is not necessary to serve him with a written notice of any further charges which may be preferred. If, however, the police decide, before he has appeared before a court, to modify the charge or to prefer further charges, it is desirable that the person concerned should be formally charged with the further offence and given a written copy of the charge as soon as it is possible to do so having regard to the particular circumstances of the case. If the accused person has then been released on bail, it may not always be practicable or reasonable to prefer the new charge at once, and in cases where he is due to surrender to his bail within forty-eight hours or in other cases of difficulty it will be sufficient for him to be formally charged with the further offence and served with a written notice of the charge after he has surrendered to his bail and before he appears before the court.

7. *Facilities for defence*

(a) A person in custody should be supplied on request with writing materials.

Provided that no hindrance is reasonably likely to be caused to the processes of investigation or the administration of justice:

(i) he should be allowed to speak on the telephone to his solicitor or to his friends;

(ii) his letters should be sent by post or otherwise with the least possible delay;

(iii) telegrams should be sent at once, at his own expense.

(b) Persons in custody should not only be informed orally of the rights and facilities available to them, but in addition notices describing them should be displayed at convenient and conspicuous places at police stations and the attention of persons in custody should be drawn to these notices.

Appendix C

POLICE ENQUIRIES INVOLVING DEAF PERSONS

When, in the course of police inquiries, it becomes necessary to ask questions of a deaf person, there is sometimes difficulty in arranging for the proceedings to be interpreted with sufficient clarity, especially when such persons have no useful hearing and can only communicate manually by means of finger-spelling and signing. In these circumstances the services of competent interpreters for the deaf may be required. It has been agreed with the Association of Directors of Social Services and the Royal National Institute for the Deaf that Directors of Social Services will, on request, designate points of contact (which may, depending on local circumstances, be an office of the local authority or of a voluntary organisation) through which arrangements for securing the services of interpreters can be made. Chief officers of police are therefore requested to get in touch with Directors of Social Services locally so that arrangements for designating a point of contact can be made.

In cases of difficulty The Royal National Institute for the Deaf, 105 Gower Street, London WC1E 6AH (telephone number 01-387 8033) will be glad to advise.

Origin and history of the Judges' Rules

The implications of the law of evidence and its application by the courts for the investigation of crime were first defined for the police in an authoritative way by Lord Brampton (formerly Mr Justice Hawkins) in a Preface to Vincent's Police Code (1882), where he said of questioning:

"Much discussion has on various occasions arisen touching the conduct of the police in listening to, and repeating, statements of accused persons. I will try, therefore, to point out what I think is the proper course for a constable to take with regard to such statements.

Questioning; when Permissible: When a crime has been committed, and you are engaged in endeavouring to discover the author of it, there is no objection to you making enquiries of, or putting questions to, any person from whom you think you can obtain useful information. It is your duty to discover the criminal if you can, and to do this you must make such enquiries; and if in the course of them you should chance to interrogate and to receive answers from a man who turns out to be the criminal himself, and who inculpates himself by these answers, they are nevertheless admissible in evidence, and may be used against him.

When not Permissible: When, however, a constable has a warrant to arrest, or is about to arrest a person on his own authority, or has a person in custody for a crime, it is wrong to question such person touching the crime of which he is accused. Neither judge, magistrate, nor juryman, can interrogate an accused person—unless he tenders himself as a witness—or require him to answer questions tending to incriminate himself. Much less, then, ought a constable to do so, whose duty as regards that person is simply to arrest and detain him in safe custody. On arresting a man a constable ought simply to read his warrant, or tell the accused the nature of the charge upon which he is arrested, leaving it to the person so arrested to say anything or nothing as he pleases. For a constable to press any accused person to say anything with reference to the crime of which he is accused is very wrong. It is well also that it should be generally known that if a statement made by an accused person is made under, or in consequence of, any promise or threat, even though it amounts to an absolute confession, it cannot be used against the person making it. There is, however, no objection to a constable listening to any mere voluntary statement which a prisoner desires to make, and repeating such statement in evidence; nor is there any objection to his repeating in evidence any

162

conversation he may have heard between the prisoner and any other person. But he ought not, by anything he says or does, to invite or encourage an accused person to make any statement without first cautioning him that he is not bound to say anything tending to incriminate himself, and that anything he says may be used against him. Perhaps the best maxim for a constable to bear in mind with respect to an accused person is, 'Keep your eyes and your ears open, and your mouth shut'. By silent watchfulness you will hear all you ought to hear. Never act unfairly to a prisoner by coaxing him by word or conduct to divulge anything. If you do, you will assuredly be severely handled at the trial, and it is not unlikely your evidence will be disbelieved."

2. This clear and authoritative guidance issued by a judge in a police guide marks an important departure, and may be considered the forerunner of the present Judges' Rules. The origin of those rules as such however lies in a letter which the Chief Constable of Birmingham sent to the Lord Chief Justice in 1906 asking for advice following one case in which a judge disapproved of a caution and another in which a judge criticised its omission. In reply the Lord Chief Justice advised that the approved practice was that whenever a constable determined to made a charge against a man he should caution him before taking a statement from him. The Lord Chief Justice went on to suggest that the words "against you" should be omitted from the usual caution ("You are not obliged to say anything unless you wish to, but anything you say will be written down and may be used in evidence against you,") on the ground that the man might just as well say something in his favour as against him.

3. From this modest beginning the Judges' Rules have grown. Four rules were in existence by 1912. In 1918 there were nine. These rules remained in force until 1964. They were as follows:

"1. When a police officer is endeavouring to discover the author of a crime, there is no objection to his putting questions in respect thereof to any person or persons, whether suspected or not, from whom he thinks that useful information can be obtained.

2. Whenever a police officer has made up his mind to charge a person with a crime, he should first caution such person before asking any questions, or any further questions, as the case may be.

3. Persons in custody should not be questioned without the usual caution being first administered,

4. If the prisoner wishes to volunteer any statement the usual caution should be administered.

It is desirable that the last two words of the usual caution should be omitted, and that the caution should end with the words 'be given in evidence'.

5. The caution to be administered to a prisoner, when he is formally charged, should therefore be in the following words: 'Do you wish to say anything in answer to the charge? You are not obliged to say anything unless you wish to do so, but whatever you say will be taken down in writing and may be given in evidence.'

Care should be taken to avoid any suggestions that his answers can only be used in evidence against him, as they may prevent an innocent person making a statement which might assist to clear him of the charge.

6. A statement made by a prisoner before there is time to caution him is not rendered inadmissible in evidence merely by reason of no caution having been given, but in such a case he should be cautioned as soon as possible.

7. A prisoner making a voluntary statement must not be cross-examined, and no questions should be put to him about it except for the purpose of removing ambiguity in what he has actually said. For instance, if he has mentioned an hour without saying whether it was morning or evening, or has given a day of the week and day of the month which do not agree, or has not made it clear to what individual or what place he intended to refer in some part of his statement, he may be questioned sufficiently to clear up the point.

8. When two or more persons are charged with the same offence, and statements are taken separately from the persons charged, the police should not read these statements to the other persons charged, but each of such persons should be furnished by the police with a copy of such statements and nothing should be said or done by the police to invite a reply. If the person charged desires to make a statement in reply, the usual caution should be administered.

9. Any statement made in accordance with the above rules should, whenever possible, be taken down in writing and signed by the person making it after it has been read to him and he has been invited to make any corrections he may wish."

4. These rules were confirmed in 1930 when the Home Office issued a circular of guidance to the police (following consultations with the Judges) to deal with some points raised by the Royal Commission on Police Powers and Procedure, which had reported the previous year (Cmd 3297). Subsequently further guidance was issued by the Home Office on the use of interpreters, taking written statements, and administrative matters of that kind.

5. Matters remained in this form until the early 1960s when the Rules and attendant circulars were reviewed. In 1964 the revision was issued to the police under cover of Home Office Circular 31/1964, which was subsequently published.

6. The published document falls into a number of parts. First there is the Home Office circular, which explains the main changes made, and sets out the underlying basis of the rules. Secondly, there is a note which sets out briefly the origin of the Rules, and explains the nature of the rules. In the second part of this preamble there is a statement of certain fundamental principles which are not affected by the rules. Thirdly, there are the Rules proper. These had been revised by a Committee of Judges and approved by a meeting of all the Queen's Bench Judges. And, fourthly, there are some administrative directions drawn up by the Home Office and approved by the judges.

7. These Rules remain in force today. They were supplemented, so far as the police are concerned, by the issue of two Home Office circulars in 1968 and 1976 giving further guidance on particular points of doubt which had arisen in connection with the administrative directions, and in 1976 a circular was also issued on the interrogation of mentally handicapped persons. In June 1978 a revised edition of the Judges' Rules and Administrative Directions incorporating the guidance given in these circulars was published.

Text of Home Office circular No 74/1978 to chief officers of police concerning section 62 of the Criminal Law Act 1977, dated 28 April 1978.

The Criminal Law Act 1977 (Commencement No 5) Order 1977 will bring section 62 of the Criminal Law Act 1977 into force on 19 June 1978. Section 62 provides that—

> "Where any person has been arrested and is being held in custody in a police station or other premises, he shall be entitled to have intimation of his arrest and of the place where he is being held sent to one person reasonably named by him, without delay or, where some delay is necessary in the interest of the investigation or prevention of crime or the apprehension of offenders, with no more delay than is so necessary."

This circular, which contains guidance on the implementation of the section, has been drawn up in consultation with the Association of Chief Police Officers and others concerned. There has also been consultation with the Lord Chief Justice. Section 62 in no way detracts from the provisions of the Judges' Rules and the Administrative Directions to the Police. It is recognised that much of what follows already takes place as a standard procedure within police forces.

Information to the arrested person

2. When a person is arrested (with or without warrant) after the section has come into force, and is taken into custody, the terms of the section should be drawn to his attention. This should be done on arrival at the police station by the station officer and/or duty officer receiving the arrested person into custody. It will be for chief officers to decide the precise way in which this should be done. One possibility is for a notice outlining the provisions of section 62 to be displayed in conspicuous places at police stations to which the attention of arrested persons can be drawn. Alternatively, chief officers may wish to arrange to have leaflets available explaining the provisions of section 62 which can be handed to arrested persons. Where, exceptionally, an arrested person is held in custody in premises other than a police station, or it is clear that there will be some delay before he is taken to a police station, he should be told of the terms of the section by the senior police officer present. (See also paragraph 22 below.)

Initial steps on receiving a request

3. In some cases it is the responsibility of the police to initiate action to notify a parent, relative or other person of an arrest, even if the arrested

person does not himself make a request for this to be done. This is especially important in the case of mentally handicapped persons, children and young persons (see also paragraph 16 below) and nationals of certain foreign or Commonwealth states (see also paragraph 19 below). In these cases, and wherever there may be some doubt as to the capacity of the arrested person to understand his entitlement under section 62, the police should follow their normal practice of automatically seeking to notify a responsible person or the appropriate authorities of the arrest of the person concerned. In the majority of cases, however, it will be for the arrested person to decide whether he wishes to make use of the entitlement given to him by section 62. In most cases where he wishes to do so he will no doubt inform the officer who draws his attention to the terms of the section. However, if he makes no immediate request, it will nonetheless remain open to him to do so at any time while he is in custody. Similarly a request within the terms of section 62 which is made *before* the arrested person has been informed formally of his entitlement (for example one made in the police car on the way to the police station) will be a valid request for the purposes of section 62, and should be treated accordingly.

4. If a person in custody asks for a person to be informed of his arrest and of the place where he is being held, the effect of the Act is to require intimation to be sent to the person named without delay unless:

(i) the choice of person is not reasonable, or

(ii) some delay is necessary in the interest of the investigation or prevention of crime or the apprehension of offenders (in which case there is to be no more delay in sending the intimation than is necessary).

Reasonably named person

5. When a request is made the police should therefore first consider whether the person to be notified is a "reasonably named" person. In most cases a person in custody will name a member of his family or a solicitor as the person whom he wishes to be informed of his detention, and such a person should normally be considered "reasonably named". Where some other individual is named, and it is clear that he is known personally to the person in custody (eg a flat-mate or neighbour) he should normally be considered a reasonably named person. So should an individual not personally known to the arrested person if he is likely to take an interest in his welfare (eg a community worker or an official of an organisation likely to take such an interest). If the person names an organisation, but does not know the name of an official within it, the police should take account both of the likelihood of that organisation being concerned with the welfare of the arrested person, and also of the readiness with which they may be able to contact an official at the relevant time. If, however, the person in custody names someone who is not personally acquainted with him and cannot be expected to take an immediate interest in his welfare (eg famous pop star, football player or Government Minister not being the person's own Member of Parliament) then the arrested person should be informed that that person is not "reasonably named". If the person in custody then names a "reasonably named" person his request should be met without delay, provided that it is otherwise within the terms of the section. If the arrested person nominates a person who is not in the United Kingdom, the

Channel Islands or the Isle of Man he should be informed that that person is not "reasonably named".

Use of the proviso

6. When a request is made consideration will also need to be given to the possible application of that part of section 62 which provides that intimation may be delayed in the interest of the investigation or prevention of crime or the apprehension of offenders for so long as this is so necessary (but no longer). It will be for the station officer and/or duty officer, in consultation with the officer in charge of the case, to decide when this qualification applies (see also paragraph 21 below). The qualification will no doubt be particularly relevant where the arrested person is, or may be, associated with others involved in crime, or where the family of the arrested person, or a person living at the same address, may be aware of his criminal activities and there is a risk, for example, that stolen property will be disposed of, or evidence destroyed. In such cases immediate intimation may lead to the escape of other offenders, the destruction of evidence or the commission of other offences. It will therefore be appropriate to delay the intimation until such considerations have ceased to apply. Where the police decide that the qualification is to apply the arrested person should be informed that his request for an intimation to be conveyed is being delayed.

7. The following are some examples of situations when it may be considered necessary to delay an intimation—

(i) The police have arrested one member of a terrorist gang, and consider that immediate intimation of his arrest carries the risk that other members will escape and be able to continue their activities.

(ii) They have arrested a man in the act of conveying stolen goods to a receiver, and wish to conduct a search of the area for the receiver; immediate notification may lead to his escape.

(iii) A person suspected of being a persistent shoplifter is arrested and there is reason to believe that the family, if notified, will move or destroy the proceeds of previous thefts.

(iv) The police have arrested a member of a bank robbery gang and immediate intimation may lead to the destruction of evidence or threats to witnesses.

The Secretary of State recognises however that no list of possible situations in which the qualification may be appropriately exercised can be comprehensive. Equally, however serious the offence under investigation, the qualification set out in the latter part of section 62 should never be applied as a matter of routine, but only after a careful review of the considerations which apply in that particular case.

Conveying an intimation

8. Section 62 entitles the arrested person only to have intimation *sent* to a reasonably named person. Nevertheless the Secretary of State is sure that chief officers will take such steps as are reasonably practicable to ensure that an intimation is received by the person to whom it is addressed within a reasonable

period. He recognises however that there will be some cases where there can be no absolute assurance that the intimation has reached the person named.

9. Where the named person can be reached by telephone the intimation should be so conveyed. Alternatively, the arrested person may wish to name someone else with whom a telephone message can be left. In some cases it may be necessary to send a police officer to notify the named person personally; if so, it may be possible to combine this task with the perfomance of other duties in connection with the same, or some other enquiry. In cases where a person is arrested at his home in the presence of his relatives or of someone who is likely to be named as the person to whom intimation is to be conveyed, it is suggested that the arresting officer should wherever practicable inform the latter person of the police station to which the arrested person is being taken. It will then be clear, when the arrested person is informed of his entitlement on arrival at the police station, that the provisions of the section have already been complied with and that no further action by the police is required.

10. The Secretary of State fully recognises the burdens that the police are already carrying in dealing with crime, and in the course of their other duties. He is concerned therefore to ensure that the additional duties placed on the police by section 62 of the Criminal Law Act 1977 are kept to a minimum, commensurate with the proper observance of the section. It is for that reason among others that he suggests that the intimation should wherever possible be conveyed by telephone rather than by a police officer in person. Nevertheless he recognises that in some circumstances the duty of informing a named person will impose considerable extra duties on the police, and that the question of priorities will arise, particularly in busy urban police stations at peak periods.

He recognises that there may be periods when officers engaged on other urgent duties (for example, dealing with a large number of youths arrested during an outbreak of football hooliganism) cannot justifiably be spared to undertake a series of telephone calls or to pay a personal visit to the named person. In such cases, the police will no doubt follow their normal practice of giving priority to those cases where intimation is particularly pressing on humanitarian grounds (eg where the intimation affects the welfare of children). It is, however, important in all cases that a request for intimation should not be lost sight of, and that it should be attended to as soon as the other urgent duties permit. Chief officers will no doubt take steps to ensure that this is clearly understood, and that the importance of conveying an early intimation is appreciated, within their forces.

Persons about to be released

11. Another set of considerations arises where the arrested person is likely to be released on bail after only a short period in custody. Where such a person wishes to exercise his entitlement under section 62 it is open to the police to inform him that he will soon be released, and he may then decide to withdraw his request. If it becomes clear in the course of attempting to fulfil a request that this will materially add to the time before the person in custody can be released (by reason of preoccupying the time of the officers who would otherwise be dealing with him) the arrested person should be informed of this.

However, if, in either event, the person in custody persists with his request, his wishes should be observed.

12. If it has not proved possible to convey an intimation to the named person by the time the person in custody is released by either the police or a magistrates' court the request should be regarded as having lapsed. It may occasionally happen that a person appears in court and is remanded in custody before it has proved possible to convey an intimation to the named person. In these circumstances, the request should not be regarded as having lapsed and the police should try to ensure that an intimation is conveyed, even though the arrested person is no longer detained at a police station.

Intimation in other police areas

13. In some cases the arrested person will name a person in the area of another force as the person to whom the intimation is to be conveyed. If so the force carrying out the arrest should itself attempt to convey the intimation to the person named by telephone. In some cases it may be necessary however to ask the force for the area where the named person is to convey the intimation, but it is hoped that such cases will be few.

14. It is open to the person in custody to name a person living in Scotland, Northern Ireland, the Channel Islands or Isle of Man as the person to be notified. In such a case the procedure set out in the preceding paragraphs should be adopted. Police forces in other parts of the United Kingdom and in the Channel Islands and Isle of Man have agreed to assist in the implementation of section 62 by conveying the intimation, if this should be necessary. (The procedure for getting in touch with the Royal Ulster Constabulary is set out in the Annex to the circular.) Police forces in England and Wales are asked to reciprocate by conveying a similar intimation received from those police forces.

15. No charge should be made for telephone calls, *etc* in the course of meeting a request to police under section 62.

Children and young persons

16. Section 62 applies to juveniles, ie, children and young persons under 17 years of age, as well as to adults. Juveniles who have been arrested and are being held in custody should therefore be informed of the terms of section 62 in accordance with paragraph 2 of this circular. Where a juvenile is living with one or both of his parents, the existing legal requirement[1] that the person who arrests a juvenile shall take such steps as may be practicable to inform at least one of his parents or guardians will also satisfy the entitlement under section 62. This is because a child or young person, when informed of the terms of section 62, will almost invariably ask for his parents to be informed. But there may be occasions when a juvenile (eg a 16 year old living away from home) will nominate someone other than a parent, perhaps an employer, youth leader,

[1] See section 34(2) of the Children and Young Persons Act 1933 (as substituted by section 25(1) of the Children and Young Persons Act 1963 and amended by para. 3 of schedule 5 to the Children and Young Persons Act 1969). See also para. 9.14 of the Consolidated Circular on Crime and Kindred Matters, 1977 Edition.

probation officer or another relative or person living at the same address. The fact that the police have a statutory duty to inform the parent or guardian under section 34(2) of the 1933 Act should not prevent the juvenile's request from being considered within the terms of section 62. In some cases the police may wish to consult the parent or guardian; if the latter object to such a person being informed, the police should take this into account in considering whether or not that person is reasonably named for the purpose of section 62.

17. Since many juveniles who are arrested are held for only short periods, normally until their parents collect them, the advice in paragraphs 11 and 12 above is particularly relevant to juveniles. Normally, for instance, it would be unreasonable to spend police time on a personal visit to a named person other than a parent or guardian, when the juvenile is shortly to be released from custody.

18. The provisions of paragraph 4 of the Administrative Directions appended to the Judges' Rules will continue to apply to the interviewing of children and young persons.

Commonwealth citizens or foreign nationals in custody

19. Chief officers are reminded of the importance attached to the arrangements for notifying High Commissions, Embassies or consulates when citizens of other Commonwealth countries or foreign nationals are held in custody. In particular there is a requirement to notify the appropriate consular officer automatically in cases involving the arrest of a national of a foreign state with which the United Kingdom has entered into a bilateral Consular Convention. The entitlement under section 62 should be regarded as being additional to the need to notify the appropriate authorities in cases of this kind. The relevant guidance is being included in amendments to the Consolidated Circular on Crime and Kindred Matters.

Prevention of terrorism legislation

20. The provisions of the section apply to persons arrested under the Prevention of Terrorism (Temporary Provisions) Act 1976, in the same way as to persons arrested under other statutory and common law powers.

Arrest by persons other than police officers[1]

21. There will be occasions when a person is arrested by someone other than an officer from a "regular" police force (for example, by an officer of the British Transport Police or other "private" police force or of a Government Department such as Customs and Excise or by a store detective); and in the majority of such cases, the arrested person is likely to be taken to the police station of a regular police force. The section imposes a duty on those who for the time being have the custody of the arrested person unless those who had custody of him earlier have already sent the intimation required by the section. It will accordingly be for the station officer and/or duty officer to ensure that the arrested person is made aware of his entitlement under section 62, and that

[1]In this and the following para. a "regular" police force means one maintained under the Police Act 1964.

171

appropriate action is taken with regard to a request made in consequence. If the arresting officer (being an officer from a private police force or of a Government Department) objects to the person named or considers it right to apply the proviso that the intimation should be delayed in the interest of investigation or prevention of crime or the apprehension of offenders, the station officer and/or duty officer should give due regard to the views of the arresting officer and request a recommendation in writing to this effect.

22. Where an arrested person is held in custody at premises other than the police station of a regular police force or it is clear that there will be some delay before he is taken to such a police station, it is the responsibility of the senior officer present to inform him of the terms of section 62.

Notifications under s. 62: extract from Home Office Statistical Bulletin Issue 5/80 (mimeo)

Table 15.1 Persons arrested in England and Wales by time before action taken to notify person nominated under section 62 of the Criminal Law Act 1977

Period	Number of persons not dealt with within 4 hours		Number of persons not dealt with within 24 hours (included also in previous column)		Number of persons arrested
	Number	Per 10000 arrests	Number	Per 10000 arrests	Thousands
1978					
June 19–30	156	31	9	1.8	50.3
July	200	19	26	2.4	106.7
August	132	12	16	1.5	107.3
September	138	13	15	1.4	107.6
October	117	10	13	1.2	111.7
November	107	10	11	1.0	110.0
December	109	11	12	1.2	98.3
1979					
January	91	9	12	1.2	96.7
February	107	11	12	1.2	100.0
March	99	9	8	1.0	116.1
April	89	8	12	1.0	115.4
May	90	8	15	1.3	119.9
June	70	6	8	1.0	119.3
July	96	8	14	1.2	121.1
August	112	10	28	2.4	117.7
September	88	8	17	1.5	114.6
October	96	8	18	1.5	119.7
November	107	9	26	2.2	116.9
December	72	7	9	0.8	108.6
Total 19 June 1978– 31 December 1979	2076	10	281	1.4	2058.0

Table 15.2 Persons arrested by time before action taken to notify person nominated under section 62 of the Criminal Law Act 1977 by police force area

Police force area	Number of persons not dealt with within 4 hours		Number of persons not dealt with within 24 hours (included also in previous column)		Number of persons arrested	
	Number	Per 10000 arrests	Number	Per 10000 arrests	Thousands	Per 1000[1] population
Avon and Somerset	11	4	—	—	29.5	22
Bedfordshire	10	7	1	0.7	14.5	29
Cambridgeshire	15	10	2	1.3	14.9	26
Cheshire	9	5	—	—	17.4	19
Cleveland	13	6	—	—	22.7	40
Cumbria	6	6	—	—	10.7	23
Derbyshire	4	2	—	—	16.4	18
Devon and Cornwall	16	8	4	2.1	19.4	14
Dorset	18	17	—	—	10.8	18
Durham	4	3	—	—	13.6	22
Essex	42	16	6	2.3	26.5	19
Gloucestershire	1	1	—	—	9.7	20
Greater Manchester	8	1	—	—	88.3	33
Hampshire	42	10	11	2.7	40.9	26
Hertfordshire	7	4	1	0.6	16.1	20
Humberside	14	5	2	0.7	27.2	32
Kent	23	7	4	1.2	33.7	23
Lancashire	—	—	—	—	33.9	25
Leicestershire	20	10	2	1.0	19.8	24
Lincolnshire	22	19	2	1.7	11.5	22
London, City of	47	134	2	5.7	3.5	628
Merseyside	2	—	1	0.2	59.4	38
Metropolitan Police District	486	15	116	3.5	330.4	45
Norfolk	17	21	—	—	8.1	12
Northamptonshire	7	5	—	—	12.9	25
Northumbria	20	3	3	0.5	59.1	41
North Yorkshire	9	9	2	2.0	10.0	15
Nottinghamshire	—	—	—	—	27.7	28
South Yorkshire	—	—	—	—	38.5	30
Staffordshire	14	6	1	0.4	24.0	24
Suffolk	11	10	1	0.9	11.5	19
Surrey	12	7	—	—	16.7	23
Sussex	39	12	1	0.3	32.1	25
Thames Valley	50	13	5	1.3	37.3	21
Warwickshire	6	11	4	7.4	5.4	12
West Mercia	40	20	5	2.5	19.9	20
West Midlands	2	—	—	—	73.4	27
West Yorkshire	4	1	—	—	52.7	25
Wiltshire	4	6	—	—	7.0	14
Total England	1055	8	176	1.3	1307.1	28

[1]Persons arrested may not reside in the area in which they were arrested. This particularly applies to city areas.

Table 15.2 (continued)

Police force area	Number of persons not dealt with within 4 hours		Number of persons not dealt with within 24 hours (included also in previous column)		Number of persons arrested	
	Number	Per 10000 arrests	Number	Per 10000 arrests	Thousands	Per 1000[1] population
Dyfed-Powys	6	9	1	1.5	6.5	15
Gwent	43	30	2	1.4	14.2	32
North Wales	8	9	—	—	9.4	15
South Wales	5	2	—	—	28.9	22
Total Wales	62	11	3	0.5	59.0	21
Total England and Wales	1117	8	179	1.3	1336.1	28

[1]Persons arrested may not reside in the area in which they were arrested. This particularly applies to city areas.

Extract from the Home Office consolidated circular to the police on crime and kindred matters (1977 edition) dealing with medical examinations

Medical Examinations

Prisoner arrested on a charge of a sexual offence

4.22 When a prisoner has been arrested on a charge of rape, indecent assault or some other sexual offence, it is often desirable in the interest of justice that he should submit to a medical examination: and it is important that the examination should be so conducted as to protect the doctor from risk of an action being subsequently brought against him by the prisoner. If an examination is carefully made an innocent man is not likely to suffer, but cogent evidence may be obtained against the guilty.

4.23 The examination can be made only with the prisoner's consent; in the absence of consent any examination would be an assault. The police officer in charge of the station should inform the prisoner that it is proposed to examine him, and that he has the right to object if he desires. He should be told that if he desires the attendance of a qualified medical practitioner on his behalf, in addition to the police surgeon, an opportunity for this will be given. The officer should record (a) the fact of the prisoner's consent or refusal, and (b) the offer made to allow a doctor to attend on his behalf and the acceptance or refusal or the offer. The record should be read to the prisoner, and the officer should attend the trial in the event of a committal in order to prove the consent if necessary.

4.24 When consent is given, the examination should be made as soon as practicable after the prisoner is in custody and has been removed to the police station, and before he is taken before a magistrate. The police surgeon should record in writing the result of any examination, and he should be informed of the time and place where his attendance will be required to give evidence before the magistrate.

Prisoners who ask for medical examination

4.25 When a prisoner is in custody on any other charge and desires a medical examination, the examination should be made either by the police surgeon or by a doctor attending on behalf of the prisoner. The officer in charge of the station should record the prisoner's request and the compliance with it. It is important that medical examination of the prisoner should not be delayed owing to the non-arrival either of the police surgeon or of the private doctor, and the examination by either doctor should therefore take place as soon as possible after his arrival at the station. An examination by a private doctor will usually be conducted in the presence of the police surgeon, but if he is not in attendance at the time it should be conducted in the presence of the station officer. A police surgeon who completes his examination before the arrival of the private doctor should be requested to await the examination by the latter. A private doctor who completes his examination before the arrival of the police surgeon should be informed of the impending examination by the latter, in order that he may, if he so desires, be present.

Persons in police custody who appear to be ill or drunk

4.26 There is often difficulty in deciding whether a defendant's condition at the time of arrest can properly be ascribed to alcohol; and so the police should not bring a charge involving drunkenness if there is any probability of the fact being disputed, without first getting the best evidence they can obtain on the subject. This applies with special force when a defendant's character and antecedents are generally good, and he is therefore likely to use every means open to him to escape a conviction involving drunkenness. The evidence of a doctor called in to a police station immediately after the arrest of the alleged offender may often be desirable. The examination must be subject to the precautions mentioned in paragraph 4.13 above. If drunkenness is denied by a defendant and is proved by the prosecution, the court may properly be asked to order the defendant to pay the costs involved in calling evidence on the point, in addition to any penalty that may be imposed.

4.27 Special care should be taken over the treatment of persons suffering from illness, the arrangements for their care at the police station and during proceedings in court, and the manner in which they are taken from the police station to the court. A person who appears to be drunk may be suffering from illness (eg multiple sclerosis, or a diabetic's hypoglycaemia); or may have sustained an injury which is not apparent. A doctor should be called if there is the slightest suspicion that a person detained may be ill, particularly if there appear to be symptoms of drunkenness without the smell of alcohol. If a doctor has attended and certified that the prisoner is fit to be detained, the station officer should seek his advice on how frequently to visit the prisoner and should not hesitate to recall the doctor if that seems necessary or if the prisoner's condition does not appear to be improving. The following measures are suggested for dealing with persons thought to be drunk—

(1) A person who is found unconscious should be taken to hospital even if he smells of drink or there are other grounds for suspecting that he is in a drunken stupor.

(ii) If a person arrested for an offence involving drunkenness is unconscious on arrival at the police station, a doctor should be summoned. If a doctor cannot attend quickly, the patient should be transferred to hospital by ambulance.

(iii) If a prisoner, although not unconscious, is incapable of understanding the meaning of the charge, charging him should be delayed until he has sufficiently recovered to appreciate the nature of the proceedings.

If he has not recovered to that extent within four hours, a doctor should be summoned.

(iv) A prisoner who is drunk should be visited every half-hour, and aroused and spoken to on each visit. If he fails to respond, or if there is any noticeable evidence of deterioration in his condition, a doctor should be summoned.

(v) A prisoner who is drunk and drowsy should be placed flat in a three-quarters prone position with his head turned to one side so that he will not inhale his vomit.

4.28 Care should also be taken to prevent the unnecessary committal to prison of persons physically unfit for prison treatment (eg pregnant women and persons suffering from illness likely soon to end fatally); and for this purpose a prisoner's examination by the police surgeon or other doctor may be desirable. If the prisoner is found to be suffering from serious illness, a full report on his state of health should be submitted to the court before which he is brought.

4.29 A person coming into the hands of the police may carry documentary evidence of his medical condition. In particular—

(a) an identification card (coloured blue) is issued to patients receiving steroid therapy. A patient undergoing treatment with steroids may be endangered if the treatment is interrupted; and if any person coming into the hands of the police has such an identification card in his possession medical advice should be sought as soon as possible;

(b) identification cards are issued by the British Diabetic Association and by the Multiple Sclerosis Society to sufferers from those diseases;

(c) the Medic-Alert Foundation, 9 Hanover Street, London W1R 9HF supplies, on payment, a metal wrist bracelet indicating a medical condition or allergy. The bracelet is a stainless steel chain with a stainless disc bearing on one side in red a medical emblem incorporated a rod and a serpent flanked by the words "MEDIC-ALERT". On the reverse of the disc is engraved the appropriate medical warning (eg "Allergic to penicillin" or "Epilepsy"), the serial number allotted by the Foundation to the person, and the emergency telephone enquiry number of the Foundation (01-407 2818). Additional information about the medical condition of the wearer can be obtained by telephoning that number and quoting the serial number engraved on the disc.

When a person who is ill or injured comes to the notice of the police and is found to be carrying one of these (or any other) evidence of a medical condition, this should be brought to the attention of any member of the medical services (including the ambulance service) who comes into contact with him, so that the appropriate treatment may be given.

The use of complaints, disciplinary and criminal proceedings

1. This Appendix presents statistics on the use of complaints procedures, the type and results of complaints and the number of disciplinary and criminal proceedings brought against police officers.

2. Table 17.1 shows the number of complaints completed and the outcome of those complaints for the first two full years since the Police Complaints Board began its work in June 1977.

Table 17.1. Complaints completed in 1978 and 1979 and their outcome

Year	Result of complaint						Total
	substantiated		unsubstantiated[1]		withdrawn or not proceeded with		
	No.	%	No.	%	No.	%	No.
1978	1559	5.5	13720	48.6	12955	45.9	28234
1979	1338	4.6	14104	48.0	13941	47.5	29383

[1] Includes complaints in respect of which the Police Complaints Board granted dispensation from the normal requirements, under the Police (Withdrawn, Anonymous etc Complaints) Regulations 1977. A complaint is defined as unsubstantiated if there turns out to be no substance in it or if for some other reason disciplinary action is not possible or is inappropriate.

3. In both years, slightly fewer than 30,000 individual matters of complaint were completed. A little under half of these were withdrawn or not proceeded with. In 1979 48 per cent of complaints were found to be unsubstantiated (48.6 per cent in 1978) and 4.6 per cent were substantiated (5.5 per cent in 1978).

4. Table 17.2 shows, for complaints completed in 1979, the kinds of incidents which were alleged to have occurred in relation to complaints that were proceeded with. The table also shows whether or not these complaints were substantiated.

Table 17.2. Type of complaints and outcome in relation to complaints that were proceeded with in 1979

Type of complaint	Outcome				Total No.
	unsubstantiated		substantiated		
	No.	%	No.	%	
Incivility	1816	92.0	158	8.0	1974
Assault	2887	96.7	98	3.3	2985
Irregularity in procedure	2722	90.7	279	9.3	3001
Traffic irregularity	476	86.4	75	13.6	551
Neglect of duty	1114	75.8	356	24.2	1470
Corrupt practice	116	95.9	5	4.1	121
Mishandling of property	201	78.5	55	21.5	256
Irregularity in relation to evidence/perjury	688	97.3	19	2.7	707
Oppressive conduct or harassment	1170	84.7	65	5.3	1235
Other crime	599	94.2	37	5.8	636
Other	1537	88.9	191	11.1	1728
Total	13326	90.9	1338	9.1	14664

5. As can be seen, the three most frequently cited allegations involved incivility, assault and irregularity in procedure. Incivility, irregularity in procedure and neglect of duty featured most prominently amongst substantiated complaints, accounting for six out of ten of them.

6. Table 17.3 shows the type of proceedings that followed from substantiated complaints. Formal disciplinary proceedings were not thought to be necessary in respect of most substantiated complaints and 82.2 per cent of them were dealt with without recourse either to disciplinary or criminal proceedings, for example by a word of warning or advice from a senior officer. Formal disciplinary action was taken in 10.9 per cent of substantiated complaints, and criminal proceedings other than for traffic offences in respect of 4.4 per cent of them.

Table 17.3. Substantiated complaints by type of proceedings that resulted

Type of proceedings	number of complaints
Disciplinary proceedings	146
Criminal proceedings (other than for traffic offences)	59
Proceedings for traffic offences	45
Dealt with by other means	1096
Total substantiated complaints[1]	1338

[1]As a complaint may result in proceedings of more than one type, the figures do not add up to the total number of substantiated complaints.

Cases referred to the DPP

7. Section 49 of the Police Act 1964 provides that, unless the chief constable is satisfied from the report of the investigation into a complaint that no criminal offence has been committed, he must send the report to the Director

of Public Prosecutions for his independent scrutiny and advice on whether criminal proceedings should be instituted. In 1979, 3,992 criminal (other than traffic) cases were so referred and the Director recommended proceedings in respect of 63 (1.6 per cent) of them. In addition, 469 cases relating to traffic offences were referred to the Director, who recommended proceedings in 59 (12.6 per cent) of them. (It should be noted that these figures relate to *cases* which may contain more than one individual matter of complaint.)

Police officers convicted of criminal offences

8. The number of officers in England and Wales convicted of criminal offences (including traffic offences) in 1979 was 908. The majority of these, 781, were convicted of traffic offences and 42 were disqualified from driving. Of the 127 officers convicted of offences other than traffic offences, 38 were sentenced to imprisonment. The number of officers dismissed or required to resign as a result of disciplinary action following conviction was 59. In addition, 57 officers resigned after criminal charges had been preferred against them but before such proceedings were completed.

Discipline

9. Tables 17.4 and 17.5 give information about disciplinary proceedings and their outcome. Charges were brought and completed against 736 officers and one or more charges were proved against 691 (94 per cent) of them. It will be seen that only 157 (21 per cent) of the 736 proceedings arose directly out of complaints by members of the public.

Table 17.4. Police officers against whom disciplinary charges were brought and completed

Result of disciplinary proceedings	Reasons for investigation		
	Complaint	Other circumstances	Total
One or more charges were found proved	139	552	691
No charges were proved	18	27	45
Total number of officers	157	549	736

Details of punishments awarded as a result of disciplinary proceedings are given in Table 17.5. Where an officer received more than one punishment only the most serious is shown. In most cases officers were fined; 22 were dismissed and 46 were required to resign. In addition, during the year 28 officers resigned after disciplinary charges had been preferred against them but before the proceedings were completed.

Table 17.5. Police officers punished as a result of disciplinary proceedings

Most serious punishment awarded by the chief officer	number of officers
Dismissal	22
Requirement to resign	46
Reduction in rank	27
Reduction in pay	33
Fine	339
Reprimand	169
Caution	55
Total	691

The police discipline code (extracted from the Police (Discipline) Regulations 1977—SI 1977 No 580)

Disciplinary offences

5. A member of a police force commits an offence against discipline if he commits an offence set out in the discipline code contained in Schedule 2.

SCHEDULE 2   Regulation 5

Discipline Code

1. *Discreditable conduct,* which offence is committed where a member of a police force acts in a disorderly manner or any manner prejudicial to discipline or reasonably likely to bring discredit on the reputation of the force or of the police service.

2. *Misconduct towards a member of a police force,* which offence is committed where—

    (a) the conduct of a member of a police force towards another such member is oppressive or abusive, or

    (b) a member of a police force assaults another such member.

3. *Disobedience to orders,* which offence is committed where a member of a police force, without good and sufficient cause, disobeys or omits or neglects to carry out any lawful order, written or otherwise, or contravenes any provision of the Police Regulations containing restrictions on the private lives of members of police forces, or requiring him to notify the chief officer of police that he, or a relation included in his family, has a business interest, within the meaning of those Regulations.

4. *Neglect of duty,* which offence is committed where a member of a police force, without good and sufficient cause—

    (a) neglects or omits to attend to or carry out with due promptitude and diligence anything which it is his duty as a member of a police force to attend to or carry out, or

    (b) fails to work his beat in accordance with orders, or leaves the place of duty to which he has been ordered, or having left his place of duty for an authorised purpose fails to return thereto without undue delay, or

    (c) is absent without leave from, or is late for, any duty, or

    (d) fails properly to account for, or to make a prompt and true return of, any money or property received by him in the course of his duty.

5. *Falsehood or prevarication,* which offence is committed where a member of a police force—

    (a) knowingly or through neglect makes any false, misleading or inaccurate oral or written statement or entry in any record or document made, kept or required for police purposes, or

    (b) either wilfully and without proper authority or through lack of due care destroys or mutilates any record or document made, kept or required for police purposes, or

    (c) without good and sufficient cause alters or erases or adds to any entry in such a record or document, or

    (d) has knowingly or through neglect made any false, misleading or inaccurate statement in connection with his appointment to the police force.

6. *Improper disclosure of information,* which offence is committed where a member of a police force—

    (a) without proper authority communicates to any person, any information which he has in his possession as a member of a police force, or

    (b) makes any anonymous communication to any police authority, or any member of a police force, or

    (c) without proper authority, makes representations to the police authority or the council of any county comprised in the police area with regard to any matter concerning the force, or

    (d) canvasses any member of that authority or of such a council with regard to any such matter.

For the purposes of this paragraph the Isles of Scilly shall be treated as if they were a county.

7. *Corrupt or improper practice,* which offence is committed where a member of a police force—

    (a) in his capacity as a member of the force and without the consent of the chief officer of police or the police authority, directly or indirectly solicits or accepts any gratuity, present or subscription, or

    (b) places himself under a pecuniary obligation to any person in such a manner as might affect his properly carrying out his duties as a member of the force, or

    (c) improperly uses, or attempts to use, his position as a member of the force for his private advantage, or

    (d) in his capacity as a member of the force and without the consent of the chief officer of police, writes, signs or gives a testimonial of character or other recommendation with the object of obtaining employment for any person or of supporting an application for the grant of a licence of any kind.

8. *Abuse of authority,* which offence is committed where a member of a police force—

(a) without good and sufficient cause makes an arrest, or

(b) uses any unnecessary violence towards any prisoner or other person with whom he may be brought into contact in the execution of his duty, or

(c) is uncivil to any member of the public.

9. *Neglect of health,* which offence is committed where a member of a police force, without good and sufficient cause, neglects to carry out any instructions of a medical officer appointed by the police authority or, while absent from duty on account of sickness, commits any act or adopts any conduct calculated to retard his return to duty.

10. *Improper dress or untidiness,* which offence is committed where without good and sufficient cause a member of a police force while on duty, or while off duty but wearing uniform in a public place, is improperly dressed or is untidy in his appearance.

11. *Damage to police property,* which offence is committed where a member of a police force—

(a) wilfully or through lack of due care causes any waste, loss or damage to any police property, or

(b) fails to report as soon as is reasonably practicable any loss of or damage to any such property issued to, or used by him, or entrusted to his care.

12. *Drunkenness,* which offence is committed where a member of a police force renders himself unfit through drink for duties which he is or will be required to perform or which he may reasonably foresee having to perform.

13. *Drinking on duty or soliciting drink,* which offence is committed where a member of a police force, while on duty—

(a) without proper authority, drinks, or receives from any other person, any intoxicating liquor, or

(b) demands, or endeavours to persuade any other person to give him, or to purchase or obtain for him, any intoxicating liquor.

14. *Entering licensed premises,* which offence is committed where a member of a police force—

(a) while on duty, or

(b) while off duty but wearing uniform,

without good and sufficient cause, enters any premises in respect of which a licence or permit has been granted in pursuance of the law relating to liquor licensing or betting and gaming or regulating places of entertainment.

15. *Criminal conduct,* which offence is committed where a member of a police force has been found guilty by a court of law of a criminal offence.

16. *Being an accessory to a disciplinary offence,* which offence is committed where a member of a police force connives at or is knowingly an accessory to any offence against discipline.

Extracts from Home Office circular 63/1977: police complaints and discipline procedures

B. Recording and counting of complaints

Definition of a complaint

5. The requirement to record a complaint under section 49 of the Police Act 1964 does not extend to complaints about the general administration, efficiency or procedures of the force which do not amount to a complaint about the conduct of an individual officer. If, after initial inquiries, a complaint recorded as a section 49 complaint is found not to be a section 49 complaint, the record should be marked accordingly.

6. All section 49 complaints must be referred in due course to the Complaints Board unless they fall within one of the exclusions set out in section 2(2) of the 1976 Act, namely:

   (a) where the complaint concerns an officer covered by the Police (Discipline) (Senior Officers) Regulations 1977;

   (b) where the complaint has been withdrawn or the complainant has indicated that he does not wish any further steps to be taken—see paragraphs 24 to 27 below[1];

   (c) where disciplinary charges have been preferred in respect of the matter or matters complained of and the officer has admitted the charges—see paragraph 103[1];

or unless the Board have dispensed with the relevant statutory requirements under Regulation 4 of the Police (Withdrawn, Anonymous etc Complaints) Regulations 1977 . . .

C. Responsibility for handling of complaints and disciplinary matters

17. It is clearly desirable that in the great majority of cases in which disciplinary charges are eventually brought, the chief constable should have no prior knowledge of the case until it comes before him at a formal hearing under the Discipline Regulations. The Discipline Regulations and the Police (Complaints) (General) Regulations accordingly provide that all the functions exercised by a chief officer under section 49 of the Police Act 1964, sections 2, 3, 4(5) or 5(2) and (3) of the Police Act 1976 or under the Regulations, with the exception of those concerned with the actual hearing, are capable of delegation to the deputy chief constable. In accordance with established

---

[1]Not cited.

practice, therefore, the deputy chief constable should normally be responsible for the recording and investigation of complaints and other allegations of disciplinary offences, take any decision on the report of the investigating officer and conduct any subsequent dealings with the Complaints Board. Accordingly this circular refers to the chief constable and the deputy chief constable (by which should also be understood an assistant chief constable acting in his place) in relation to the duties which as a rule they respectively perform. In the City of London police the duties in question may be delegated by the commissioner to an assistant commissioner (or to a commander acting in his place); in the Metropolitan Police, they may be delegated by the commissioner to an assistant commissioner or deputy assistant commissioner (or, in the case of duties under the Discipline Regulations only, to a commander where the case arises out of a complaint by a member of the public and to a commander or chief superintendent in any other case) . . .

Timing of investigations

(a) Criminal proceedings

39. Special considerations arise in regard to the timing of the investigation of a complaint under section 49 of the 1964 Act against a police officer where the complaint is related in some aspect to pending criminal proceedings against a member of the public, for example against the complainant or his friends. There may also be difficulty in investigating a complaint where the related trial has been completed but an appeal is pending. It appears to the Secretary of State appropriate that chief officers should adhere to the practices set out in Annex F to this circular, which have the agreement of the Director of Public Prosecutions. The Registrar of Criminal Appeals has also been consulted where appropriate and is of the opinion that the proposed practices will be of value to the Court of Appeal. The practice of consultation by chief officers with the Director of Public Prosecutions on any matter concerning the handling of investigations in cases of special difficulty is unaffected by what is said in the Annex . . .

(b) Civil proceedings

40. It would not be right to refrain from a thorough investigation of a complaint or from bringing disciplinary charges, if that seems appropriate, merely because a complainant might decide to pursue a civil action. The chief constable is not relieved of his disciplinary responsibility simply because of the possibility that a complainant might decide to pursue the matter in a civil court. If, however, a complainant has actually begun a civil action, or has given positive indication that he intends to do so, there may well be difficulties in pursuing matters as far as a disciplinary hearing, although some form of investigation of the complaint is likely to be necessary, eg, in order to prepare for the civil action. Where, therefore, a complainant indicates that he proposes to take civil action it would be right to make it clear to the complainant that his complaint will be investigated to the extent possible, but that any disciplinary action (if appropriate) will not normally be taken until the proceedings in the civil courts have been finished. In deciding whether to defer disciplinary action, the deputy chief constable will, however, need to consider,

not only the likelihood of civil proceedings, but the effect of deferment on the maintenance of force discipline and the interests of the officer concerned . . .

E. Consideration of and action on investigation report

Action by the deputy chief constable

44. When the deputy chief constable receives the report of the investigating officer in a case arising out of a complaint he will need first to consider whether to send the report to the Director of Public Prosecutions in compliance with section 49(3) of the 1964 Act. Thereafter he will consider the disciplinary aspects *either* immediately if it is unnecessary to refer the case to the Director *or* upon receiving the Director's decision as to criminal proceedings where the case is referred.

45. *(a)* Where the case does not arise out of a complaint, the deputy chief constable will decide whether it would be appropriate to bring a disciplinary charge or charges under Regulation 8 of the Discipline Regulations against the officer concerned and, if he does not bring such charges, whether any other action is appropriate to deal with the matter. He may proceed with the preferring and arrangements for the hearing of any charges that he wishes to bring. The Complaints Board are not involved.

(b) Where the case does arise out of a complaint, the deputy chief constable will consider whether it would be appropriate to bring a disciplinary charge or charges against the officer concerned, and if he thinks not, whether any action other than the bringing of disciplinary charges is appropriate. Where he does not propose to bring disciplinary charges he will need to refer the case to the Complaints Board for their consideration. Where he does propose to bring a disciplinary charge he may refer it but if the charge is not admitted, the chief constable may not proceed to a hearing since the Complaints Board have to decide whether the case justifies a tribunal hearing . . .

The role of the Director of Public Prosecutions

47. Section 49(3) of the 1964 Act requires that, unless a chief officer is satisfied that no criminal offence has been committed, he must send to the Director of Public Prosecutions the report of the investigation into a complaint made by a member of the public against a police officer. This provision extends to all types of criminal offences, including traffic and minor offences, and allows no discretion to the deputy chief constable to decide to refer to the Director only those cases where the alleged criminal offence appears to be serious. Nor is the requirement met by referring only those cases where, in the deputy chief constable's view, there is sufficient evidence to show that a criminal offence has been committed: he must be positively satisfied from the report that no such offence has been committed before he can decide not to refer the case.

48. The possibility that a police officer should be charged with a criminal offence may come to notice without anyone making a formal complaint, for example, where a possible offence has been reported by another police officer. Such cases, unless they are of a trivial nature, should be referred to the

Director for advice, even though the circumstances of the offence have required a charge to be preferred forthwith.

49. When a case has been referred to the Director, it is his responsibility to consider whether further inquiries should be made or additional statements taken; and it is open to him to suggest that further inquiries should be undertaken by an officer from another force.

50. The Director will himself inform a complainant direct of his decision whether or not a police officer complained of should be prosecuted. The Director does not give reasons for his decision, but where the decision is against prosecution, the replies sent to the complainant and the deputy chief constable will normally indicate whether he considers that the evidence is insufficient to justify criminal proceedings or that criminal proceedings are not necessary in the public interest. The Director may sometimes indicate to the deputy chief constable that, although criminal proceedings are not appropriate, it is still open to him to consider disposing of the matter by means of disciplinary action.

The relationship between criminal and disciplinary proceedings

51. Section 11 of the 1976 Act states the principle that no officer who has been charged with and either acquitted or convicted of a criminal offence should be charged with a disciplinary offence which is in substance the same as that criminal offence. Apart from this it is not practicable to lay down absolute rules but there are a number of other considerations which may be relevant to the avoidance of double jeopardy in a case which has both criminal and disciplinary aspects.

52. Where it seems that a police officer has committed a criminal offence, the fact that he is a police officer subject to a discipline code is no sufficient reason to refrain from prosecuting him, particularly if the case is one in which proceedings would be taken against a member of the public. It therefore follows that misconduct which amounts to a criminal offence should not be dealt with under the discipline code as an alternative to criminal proceedings when the latter are clearly justified. Nor would it be proper to appear to have recourse to disciplinary proceedings simply because it was thought impossible to establish a criminal charge to the satisfaction of a court of law.

53. In some cases the alleged criminal offence is in itself unimportant and not serious enough to justify prosecution, but it would be entirely proper in the public interest that the misconduct should be dealt with as a matter of internal discipline. An instance of such misconduct might be a technical assault upon another member of the force (which is particularly specified as an offence against discipline in the discipline code).

54. There are cases in which, in addition to the circumstances pointing to a criminal offence, there are other elements which involve a breach or breaches of discipline. For example, a constable may have left his beat or other place of duty without authority or good cause, in circumstances which suggest that he was responsible for breaking into adjoining property. The evidence may be insufficient to justify prosecution for the criminal offence of say, burglary, but

there is no reason why the officer should not be dealt with for disobedience to orders, or neglect of duty in respect of his action in leaving his beat. Again, a man may be suspected of having misappropriated money or property entrusted to him, but evidence which is essential to support a criminal charge may be lacking. There may, however, be evidence that he has failed to account properly for the money or property, and in such circumstances it would be right to deal with the matter as a disciplinary charge. It is important in such cases that the charge is not framed in such a way as to suggest that the disciplinary authority is purporting to decide whether or not a criminal offence has been committed.

55. In some cases, the decision (of the Director or of the deputy chief constable) whether to bring proceedings may turn on the willingness of a complainant to give evidence in a criminal court. Generally speaking, disciplinary proceedings should not be brought in cases where a finding of guilt would depend upon the evidence of a complainant who was unwilling to give it in criminal proceedings; but where other evidence to prove a disciplinary offence is available proceedings should not be ruled out solely because the complainant's attitude prevents the possibility of criminal prosecution.

56. Where an allegation against a police officer has first been the subject of criminal investigation and it has been decided after reference to the Director (or otherwise) that criminal proceedings should *not* be taken, there should normally be no disciplinary proceedings if the evidence required to substantiate a disciplinary charge is the same as that required to substantiate the criminal charge. There will be cases, however, in which disciplinary proceedings would be appropriate as in the circumstances described in paragraphs 53 and 54 above. It must not be assumed that when the Director has decided not to institute criminal proceedings this must automatically mean that there should be no disciplinary proceedings.

57. Where a disciplinary charge is brought in a case in which the Director has decided that there should be no prosecution, the accused officer should be supplied with a copy of the Director's letter notifying his decision, unless the deputy chief constable, after such consultation with the Director as may be necessary, considers that there are special reasons against doing so in a particular case.

F. Complaints cases: functions of the Complaints Board

Summary of procedures

64. ... It should be noted that where a case has been referred to the Director under section 49(3) of the 1964 Act there is no reference to the Complaints Board until the Director has reached his decision on the case (section 5(1) of the 1976 Act) and that the Board are concerned only with the disciplinary aspect of the matter or matters complained of.

65. If on consideration of the investigating officer's report the deputy chief constable decides not to bring formal disciplinary proceedings he will refer the case to the Complaints Board. If the Complaints Board accept that no disciplinary charges are called for they will notify the deputy chief constable

accordingly, who will tell the officer concerned, and themselves notify the complainant, sending a copy of their notification to the deputy chief constable. If the Complaints Board are not satisfied they may ask the police for further information, and may discuss the matter with the deputy chief constable either before or after this is provided. In the last resort they may direct that disciplinary charges be brought.

66. Disciplinary charges may be brought by the deputy chief constable in three circumstances:

> (a) when he first considers the investigating officer's report and without reference to the Board. There is no requirement in the 1976 Act that he should obtain authority from the Board to prefer charges ...

> (b) after discussion with the Complaints Board as a result of which he has accepted their recommendation that charges should be brought ...

> (c) on the direction of the Complaints Board, failing agreement under (b).

If the officer, when notified of the charge(s), states that he admits the charge(s) the Complaints Board have no concern (or further concern) in the case, although they will be notified of the outcome of the case and the punishment awarded by the chief officer in due course ... If the officer, when notified of the charge(s), indicates that he intends to deny the charge(s), and the charge was brought in the circumstances described in (a) or (b) above the case may be heard either by the chief constable sitting alone or by a disciplinary tribunal comprising the chief constable as chairman and two members of the Board. (In either case, where the case has been remitted under Regulation 14 of the Discipline Regulations, the chief constable's place will be taken by another chief constable.) Where a charge is brought in the circumstances described in (c), a disciplinary tribunal will always be held if the officer states that he denies the charge(s).

67. The Complaints Board will decide in each case after considering a recommendation from the deputy chief constable whether there are exceptional circumstances justifying a hearing before a disciplinary tribunal. At a disciplinary tribunal the finding will be reached by all three members, if necessary by a majority although the fact will not be disclosed. If the officer is found guilty the chief constable will decide punishment after consultation with other members of the tribunal ...

(a) Recommendation by the Complaints Board

77. Where the Complaints Board consider that a disciplinary charge should be preferred against an officer in respect of a matter complained of which has not already been the subject of disciplinary charges, they will recommend to the deputy chief constable the charge which they consider should be preferred, giving reasons for their recommendation. The Complaints Board must be specific as to the charge which they regard as appropriate. The deputy chief constable will inform the Complaints Board whether he accepts their recommendation and if he does, proceed to prefer the charges. (The Complaints Board will normally indicate at the same time whether they consider that the charge should be heard by a disciplinary tribunal ...)

(b) Direction by the Complaints Board

78. Where the deputy chief constable disagrees with the Complaints Board's recommendation to prefer a disciplinary charge, he should inform them, giving his reasons. The Complaints Board may accept this; or they may enter into further discussion; or they may direct that specified charges be brought, again giving reasons for their direction in writing. If a direction is made, the deputy chief constable should prefer the charge forthwith and inform the officer concerned and the complainant that the charge has been brought at the direction of the Board. If the officer denies a charge brought on the direction of the Board the charge will automatically be heard by a disciplinary tribunal. The Secretary of State made clear to Parliament that he expected that the power to direct the preferring of charges would not be used very often and then only as a last resort . . .

Evidence and burden of proof

106A. The Royal Commission on the Police thought it of great importance that disciplinary proceedings should be fair and made as uniform as possible throughout the service, but they did not consider that it followed that every feature of a criminal trial should be faithfully copied in the hearing of a disciplinary charge. In particular, they recommended that a disciplinary tribunal should not be bound by technical rules of evidence (see paragraphs 459–461 of the Commission's Final Report). The Secretary of State commends these recommendations to chief officers.

106B. Occasionally an appeal to the Secretary of State has raised the issue of the standard of proof required in police disciplinary hearings; in particular it has been argued that it would not be enough for a disciplinary offence to be found proved on a mere balance of probabilities. It may be helpful to chief officers to note that where this issue has arisen on an appeal it has been decided on the basis that the offence must be proved beyond reasonable doubt.

Annex F

Timing of a complaint where there are pending criminal proceedings

Investigations before the trial

1. A common type of case where problems of timing may arise is one in which the complaint and allegations involved in it are directly or closely associated with criminal proceedings which are pending. In such a case, save in exceptional circumstances of the kind mentioned in paragraph 6, it is suggested that the complaint should be regarded as being in effect *sub judice* and that investigation should ordinarily be deferred until the conclusion of the trial. The desirability of identifying all possible witnesses as soon as possible and taking from them statements relevant to·the complaint is appreciated but in the normal case it is outweighed by the other considerations mentioned in paragraphs 2 to 5 below.

2. First, the investigation usually begins with the complainant being interviewed and questioned as to the details of his complaint and a statement being taken from him, provided he desires to make one. An inquiry of this nature of necessity involves a probing examination of the complainant on

matters touching upon offences with which he has been charged and which are still subject to determination by the court.

3. Such an inquiry is open to criticism in that it facilitates the obtaining of incriminating statements from the complainant, and the exposing of his defence to the pending proceedings. The undesirability of such a course is underlined by the terms of Rule III(b) of the Judges' Rules, which provides:

"It is only in exceptional cases that questions relating to the offence should be put to the accused person after he has been charged or informed that he may be prosecuted. Such questions may be put where they are necessary for the purpose of preventing or minimising harm or loss to some other person or to the public or for clearing up an ambiguity in a previous answer or statement."

4. Secondly, the interview might well involve the identification of witnesses whom the defence propose to call. If the investigation is pursued the investigating officer will need to interview these witnesses with a view to taking statements from them.

5. Thirdly, the complainant would require to be cautioned before being questioned, certainly if any statements made by him and indeed by any possible witnesses are to be made available to the prosecuting solicitor for use by the prosecution. To caution the complainant in these circumstances could well inhibit him from supplying any information and could be regarded as having the effect of discouraging him from pursuing his complaint.

6. There may, however, be exceptional circumstances where it is proper to proceed with the investigation of the complaint provided that the complainant is legally represented and that it is clear that the solicitor representing him, while fully appreciating the prejudice which could result to his client were he to be interviewed prior to the determination of the proceedings, indicates that he nonetheless desires that the complaint should be investigated immediately. One such example might be if the complaint appears so cogent that it makes the deputy chief constable doubtful after taking legal advice (see paragraph 8 below), whether it is proper to continue with the prosecution at all.

7. Where a complaint is investigated before trial the report of the investigation would, where this is necessary by virtue of section 49(3) of the 1964 Act, be sent to the Director of Public Prosecutions. It may be that the Director would not feel it right to give any decision as to proceedings being taken against the police officer or officers concerned until the pending proceedings had been disposed of but, dependent on the nature of the complaint and of the evidence available in support of it, the Director might think it right to give advice as to the desirability of continuing with the pending proceedings against the complainant.

8. The Secretary of State suggests that the prosecuting solicitor or counsel should in all cases be informed at an early stage of any relevant complaint and of its nature. The deputy chief constable may care to seek their advice as to when the investigation should take place, seeking further advice from the Director in cases of difficulty.

9. To sum up, it is suggested that in the type of case mentioned in paragraph 1:

(a) if the complainant is not legally represented, he should not, save in exceptional circumstances, be interviewed, but should be told that the investigation of the complaint will be suspended until after the trial;

(b) if the complainant is legally represented, his solicitors should be told that it is proposed to suspend the investigation until the pending proceedings have been disposed of since it would involve interviewing their client and questioning him on matters touching upon the charges preferred against him and might well necessitate interviewing any witnesses whom it might be possible he intended to call on his behalf. The solicitors should also be informed that if the investigation were to proceed any statements made by the complainant or by the relevant witnesses would be made available to the prosecution;

(c) if notwithstanding this warning, the solicitors still stated that the complainant wished that enquiries be not delayed pending his trial, then the deputy chief constable may think it proper for the investigation to proceed. The complainant might so wish if he thought it might bring to light evidence which would result in the prosecution being withdrawn. The complainant should be cautioned before any question were put to him or any statement taken from him;

(d) the solicitors should in such circumstances be asked to state in writing that they agree to the complaint being investigated and realise that the result may be given in evidence;

(e) the police legal advisers should be informed at an early stage of any relevant complaint and of its nature.

Police investigations in complaints and other matters affecting conviction after trial but before an appeal

10. If a person who has been convicted at a magistrates' court appeals to the crown court, his appeal is heard by way of a rehearing of the case. The considerations set out in the previous paragraphs regarding the investigation of a complaint before trial apply equally where an appeal against conviction has been made to the crown court.

11. The same objections do not apply, however, to investigation preceding an appeal from conviction at the crown court because the hearing of an appeal by the Court of Appeal does not constitute a retrial, the appellant rarely appears and fresh evidence is involved in only a very few cases. For the most part the question before the Court of Appeal is whether there was anything wrong with the conduct of the trial at the crown court. It is considered desirable that any material relevant to an appeal, including any such material which arises in the context of a complaint, should be before the Court of Appeal at the time of the hearing. Where this has not happened, it has sometimes been necessary for the case to be referred back to the court by the Secretary of State under section 17 of the Criminal Appeal Act 1968 for reconsideration in the light of fresh evidence arising from subsequent police investigations.

12. The Secretary of State therefore wishes to commend to chief officers the practice of rather greater flexibility as regards investigations following conviction in the crown court but before an appeal may have been heard. It is an essential element in such greater flexibility of practice that the defence should agree in writing to provide access to the defendant and their witnesses for the purpose of the investigation under section 49 of the 1964 Act. Investigations might for instance be appropriate in the following circumstances:

(a) at the request of the trial judge or the Court of Appeal;

(b) when information about documents in the possession of the police or the examination of exhibits has been requested by the appellant, either direct or through the Registrar of the Court of Appeal;

(c) because matters come to the attention of the police which throw doubt on the validity of the conviction.

There may be other cases.

13. It is not suggested that the investigation of a complaint should proceed automatically at this stage but that the deputy chief constable should consider seeking the advice, where necessary, of his legal advisers and/or the Director whether it would be appropriate to proceed with enquiries (see paragraph 8 above). Where, after such consultation, there are still doubts about whether it is proper to begin or to continue with enquiries before the hearing of an appeal, it is suggested that the deputy chief constable should inform the Registrar of the Court of Appeal what is proposed and why, so that the Court may, if they think it appropriate, indicate that they would see objection to enquiries proceeding. It would also help the Court of Appeal if the deputy chief constable informed the Registrar of any case where enquiries were proceeding before appeal at the beginning of those enquiries, if he considered that the outcome of the investigation might substantially affect the appeal.

14. When it is decided to proceed with an investigation pending appeal, the deputy chief constable should keep his legal advisers informed of progress, and notify them especially of any developments that may bear upon the conviction under appeal. In cases where it is not possible to assess the authenticity of information coming to light until all enquiries have been completed the deputy chief constable should apprise them of that situation. The prosecuting solicitor and, where appropriate, counsel will be able to advise whether any new material is relevant, and, if so, how it should be assembled so that it will be admissible in evidence, if necessary. They will also arrange for any such evidence to be made available to the Court of Appeal and, in accordance with the usual procedure, for copies to be supplied to the defence.

15. There should be no alteration in the normal rule that the report of the investigating officer is a confidential document that should not itself be disclosed.

Text of the leaflet "Police and Public" about complaints against the police under the Police Acts 1964 and 1976

This leaflet explains the procedure for members of the public who consider they have grounds for complaint against the conduct of a member of a police force in England and Wales. It also explains the way in which complaints are investigated and what action may be taken on them.[1]

The procedure described in this leaflet applies only to complaints about incidents occurring after 31 May 1977.

The handling of complaints

The law requires the chief officer of each police force to see that complaints against members of his force are promptly recorded, and are investigated. The deputy chief constable of a force outside London, or a senior officer in the Metropolitan or City of London Police, is responsible for considering what action to take as a result of each investigation. There is also an independent element in the procedure. This is provided by the Director of Public Prosecutions where a complaint suggests that a police officer may have broken the criminal law, and by the Police Complaints Board where there may have been an offence against police discipline. The records of complaints are regularly inspected by HM Inspectors of Constabulary and police authorities are required by law to keep themselves informed about the manner in which complaints are dealt with.

Making a complaint

Any complaint about the conduct of a police officer should be made in writing to the chief officer of the police force concerned (who is the Chief Constable of a force outside London and in London the Commissioner of Police of the Metropolis or of the City of London Police), or by calling at any police station. Only the police have the authority to investigate complaints against police officers. If a complainant writes to the Police Complaints Board, or to anyone other than the appropriate chief officer, his complaint has to be sent on to that chief officer; otherwise it cannot be investigated.

[1]The relevant statutory provisions in England and Wales are sections 49 and 50 of the Police Act 1964, the Police Act 1976, the Police (Discipline) Regulations 1977, the Police (Complaints) (General) Regulations 1977, the Police (Copies of Complaints) Regulations 1977 and the Police (Withdrawn, Anonymous etc Complaints) Regulations 1977. Under these provisions the chief officer can delegate his responsibilities for investigating and considering a complaint to his deputy or, in the Metropolitan or City of London Police, to another senior officer.

The investigation of a complaint

The investigation of a complaint against a police officer is carried out by a senior officer who may come from a different police force. It will normally start at once. If, however, the complaint is closely associated with criminal proceedings against the complainant or someone else and those charges are to be heard in court, the investigation will not as a rule begin until after the court proceedings are completed. The complainant will be asked to make a full statement, and the police will also seek information from anyone else who can help to establish the facts. The police officer who is complained about will also have an opportunity to make a statement. At the end of the investigation, a report will be sent to the deputy chief constable.

Criminal proceedings

Police officers, like everyone else, are subject to the law of the land. When a deputy chief constable receives the report of an investigation into a complaint he must first send it to the Director of Public Prosecutions unless he is satisfied that no criminal offence has been committed. The Director will consider whether or not criminal proceedings should be brought and he will inform both the deputy chief constable and the complainant whether or not he proposes to prosecute. If there is a prosecution, the complainant can be called upon to give evidence before the court.

Disciplinary proceedings

Police officers are also subject to a strict discipline code. The deputy chief constable will therefore consider (after any reference has been made to the Director of Public Prosecutions) whether as a result of the investigation of a complaint the evidence is such as to justify bringing a disciplinary charge. If the deputy chief constable decides that a disciplinary charge would not be justified he must send a report to the Police Complaints Board. If the Board accept that no disciplinary charges should be brought, they will inform the deputy chief constable and the complainant. If, however, the Board disagree with the deputy chief constable, they may recommend, and in the absence of agreement direct, that disciplinary charges should be brought. Where charges are to be brought the police will inform the complainant. (Even if a complaint proves to have some substance, it may not be necessary to deal with it by formal disciplinary charges; for example, advice to the officer concerned may be more appropriate.)

Hearing of disciplinary charges

Where disciplinary charges are brought against a police officer, there is a formal hearing. This will normally be before the chief officer alone but, in exceptional circumstances, the Police Complaints Board may direct that the charges should be heard by a tribunal consisting of the chief officer and two members of the Board. The hearing is in private, but, unless the accused officer has admitted the charges, the complainant has a right to attend and will normally be expected to give evidence.

Civil proceedings

A complainant may have a remedy at civil law. The police cannot give advice as to whether there is cause for a civil action: this is a matter for a solicitor. A Citizens Advice Bureau will be able to provide a list of solicitors practising in the area who can advise on this matter and give information about legal aid and advice schemes. If a complainant wishes to bring a civil action, the investigation of the complaint may sometimes be deferred until the civil action has been completed.

The rights of the officer

A police officer against whom a complaint has been made will normally receive a copy of the original complaint or of an account of it if the complaint was not made in writing. He is given a copy automatically if he is charged with any disciplinary offence as a result of the complaint; if he is not charged he can ask for a copy when the case is closed. A false and malicious complaint against a police officer may lead to his bringing legal proceedings for defamation.

Reminder

This leaflet explains what happens if you make a complaint about the conduct of a police officer. Inquiries into complaints are thorough and take a lot of police time. Before you complain please think carefully whether your complaint is against the police; it might, for example, be against some part of the law that the police have to enforce.

Remember that the police do a difficult and dangerous job on behalf of us all.

Arrangements for inspecting the Metropolitan Police: Announcement in Parliament by the Home Secretary, House of Commons Official Report, 12 December 1978, cols 99–100

With my agreement, the Commissioner has decided to strengthen arrangements for the inspection of the Metropolitan Police with effect from 1 January 1979.

The following details of the arrangements are being promulgated in Police Orders today:

"A Deputy Assistant Commissioner has been appointed Inspector of the Metropolitan Police. He will operate under the control and direction of the Deputy Commissioner, to whom he will report direct. He will be assisted by two Commanders as Deputy Inspectors. Together with three Chief Superintendents, who will act as staff officers, and a small clerical staff, these officers will comprise a new Force Inspectorate.

The duties of the Inspectorate will be to provide a continuing assessment of the efficiency and effectiveness of the Force, including headquarters branches but excluding those branches responsible to the Receiver, and to visit branches and divisions to ensure that: the policies laid down for the Force are understood and properly implemented; the functions of the branch or division are being carried out correctly and in the most efficient manner; the branch or division is adequately manned and equipped; and new developments and schemes are being considered or introduced as appropriate. It is anticipated that each branch and division will be inspected at regular intervals, and the Inspectorate will examine carefully the use of manpower and methods of work. To assist them in their work the Inspectors will be able to call on the services of specialist support units such as Management Services Department and the costing and audit branches of Finance Department. In the course of inspections particular attention will be paid to the procedures and methods of handling complaints against police and matters of police discipline.

It will be open to an officer of any rank to approach a member of the Inspectorate at any time to make representation or to discuss any matter."

The following are additional features of the arrangements:

"My Department will be consulted about the inspection programme, will be able to call for particular matters to be examined by the Inspectorate, and will receive copies of all inspection reports for my information.

If the Deputy Commissioner, in the exercise of his responsibility for controlling the operation of the Inspectorate, considers that a matter should be, and has not been, brought to my notice he will have the right and duty to submit a formal memorandum to the Commissioner with the request that it should be forwarded to me.

The Deputy Commissioner, accompanied by the Inspector, will attend regular meetings of HM Chief Inspector of Constabulary and HM Inspectors, and there will be close cooperation at staff officer level between HM Inspectorate and the Metropolitan Police Inspectorate. This cooperation is expected to enhance the development of common standards and procedures in areas where consistency or compatibility is desirable."

Prosecuting solicitors' departments

Table 22.1. Forces with prosecuting solicitors' departments (excluding Metropolitan and City of London[1] police forces)

Police force	Strength of legally qualified staff as at 1 January 1980[2]
Avon and Somerset	6
Cambridgeshire	8
Cheshire	10
Cleveland	10
Cumbria	6
Derbyshire	18
Devon and Cornwall	10
Dorset	9
Durham	8
Dyfed-Powys	8
Essex	17
Gloucestershire	5
Greater Manchester	59
Gwent	6
Hampshire	29
Humberside	8
Kent	21
Lancashire	27
Lincolnshire	8
Merseyside	37
Norfolk	7
Northamptonshire	9
Northumbria	24
Nottinghamshire	33
South Wales	29
South Yorkshire	32
Suffolk	10
Sussex	27
Thames Valley	25
West Midlands	56
West Yorkshire	40

[1]City of London Police use the City of London Solicitor's Department (the legal department of the Common Council).
[2]These figures include only qualified lawyers.

Table 22.2. Metropolitan Police Solicitor's Department

Grade	Legally qualified staff in post 31 August 1980[1]
Solicitor	1
Deputy Solicitor	1
Assistant Solicitors	10
Senior Legal Assistants	18
Legal Assistants	32
Total	62

[1]These figures include only qualified lawyers.

Statistics of cautioning

Table 23.1. Persons cautioned as a percentage of persons found guilty or cautioned in England and Wales by sex and age, 1957–1977.[1]

Year	Males[2]		Females	
	Aged 10 and under 17	Aged 17 and over	Aged 10 and under 17	Aged 17 and over
1957	22	4	31	9
1958	21	3	31	9
1959	21	4	32	10
1960	21	4	33	9
1961	20	4	30	8
1962	20	3	29	7
1963	20	3	31	8
1964	22	4	31	9
1965	22	4	35	9
1966	23	3	36	9
1967	24	4	35	10
1968	26	3	39	10
1969	32	3	46	10
1970	35	3	52	10
1971	44	4	65	10
1972	45	4	70	10
1973	46	4	70	10
1974	46	4	70	9
1975	45	3	69	9
1976	44	3	66	9
1977	47	3	70	9

[1]Adjusted for changes in legislation.
[2]Other offenders ie companies, public bodies etc are included with males because separate figures are not available before 1976.

Appendix 23

Table 23.2. Persons cautioned as a percentage of persons found guilty or cautioned in England and Wales in 1977 by police force area, type of offence, sex and age.

Police force area	Indictable offences				Non-indictable offences (excluding motoring offences)			
	Males		Females		Males		Females	
	Aged 10 and under 17	Aged 17 and over	Aged 10 and under 17	Aged 17 and over	Aged 10 and under 17	Aged 17 and over	Aged 10 and under 17	Aged 17 and over
Avon and Somerset	40	2	69	10	44	7	54	11
Bedfordshire	48	4	73	10	45	7	42	7
Cambridgeshire	47	3	65	7	52	9	42	12
Cheshire	42	1	75	7	31	9	46	6
Cleveland	27	1	57	2	37	6	41	9
Cumbria	43	2	60	12	28	4	41	6
Derbyshire	43	6	69	23	20	7	15	12
Devon and Cornwall	70	11	84	29	44	11	65	9
Dorset	55	8	83	20	49	12	60	12
Durham	40	2	62	4	2	4	7	4
Essex	55	6	78	18	57	5	44	3
Gloucestershire	50	3	64	6	57	14	52	5
Greater Manchester	40	1	70	3	23	6	28	13
Hampshire	50	3	76	10	45	4	39	6
Hertfordshire	45	1	75	5	21	5	33	9
Humberside	31	3	44	6	39	7	47	8
Kent	43	2	70	9	34	5	39	4
Lancashire	52	3	80	14	49	7	47	10
Leicestershire	50	3	64	9	71	10	69	25
Lincolnshire	62	11	72	14	52	14	65	8
London, City of	41	—[1]	83	1	9	1	20	—
Merseyside	40	—[1]	72	1	52	2	65	8
Metropolitan Police District	49	—[1]	68	—[1]	53	—[1]	52	22
Norfolk	54	6	74	12	1	—[1]	7	—
Northamptonshire	47	7	70	22	2	5	22	1
Northumbria	47	2	78	6	29	3	28	7
North Yorkshire	51	5	74	15	27	6	16	3
Nottinghamshire	56	9	78	17	31	7	55	7
South Yorkshire	44	7	65	17	36	8	17	19
Staffordshire	46	5	71	17	23	5	13	9
Suffolk	64	15	76	36	55	8	50	11
Surrey	58	6	81	11	47	10	59	22
Sussex	60	5	73	13	50	6	58	5
Thames Valley	49	4	67	11	43	7	49	10
Warwickshire	42	8	61	23	44	8	37	7
West Mercia	61	4	80	11	41	10	56	8
West Midlands	44	3	69	13	33	3	29	13
West Yorkshire	44	3	67	7	38	5	34	10
Wiltshire	67	12	80	33	25	4	—	5
Total England	47	3	71	9	42	4	40	12
Dyfed Powys	75	4	83	8	65	9	56	2
Gwent	46	4	60	5	52	4	32	5
North Wales	43	8	74	18	42	21	57	16
South Wales	29	2	60	11	17	2	15	7
Total Wales	40	4	65	11	35	6	31	7
Grand total England and Wales	47	3	71	9	42	4	39	12

[1]Less than ½ per cent.

Table 23.3. Persons cautioned as a percentage of persons found guilty or cautioned in England and Wales in 1977 by type of offence sex and age.

Type of offence	Males					Females				
	All ages	Aged 10 and under 14	Aged 14 and under 17	Aged 17 and under 21	Aged 21 and over	All ages	Aged 10 and under 14	Aged 14 and under 17	Aged 17 and under 21	Aged 21 and over
Violence against the person	8	56	24	2	4	20	61	35	7	11
Sexual offences	33	73	64	54	13	56[1]	83[1]	100[1]	60[1]	46[1]
Burglary	15	47	18	1	1	29	63	31	3	4
Robbery	3	23	6	—[2]	—[2]	6	25	11	—	—
Theft and handling stolen goods	24	76	43	3	4	34	87	63	5	11
Fraud and robbery	6	70	38	3	2	11	79	52	5	6
Criminal damage	16	60	29	2	2	19	69	38	5	6
Other indictable offences	3	69	30	3	2	7	95	53	5	3
Total indictable offences	19	67	34	3	3	31	85	58	5	10
Non-indictable offences (excluding motoring offences)	7	64	36	4	4	13	71	33	28	9

[1] These percentages are subject to wider fluctuations owing to the small number of persons involved.
[2] Less than ½ per cent.

205

Table 23.4. Persons cautioned as a percentage of persons found guilty or cautioned for indictable offences in England and Wales in 1978 by police force area and age.

Police force area	Aged 10 and under 17	Aged 17 and over
Avon and Somerset	44	4
Bedfordshire	53	8
Cambridgeshire	44	4
Cheshire	46	1
Cleveland	42	2
Cumbria	44	3
Derbyshire	43	10
Devon and Cornwall	69	15
Dorset	67	10
Durham	42	2
Essex	57	8
Gloucestershire	51	6
Greater Manchester	41	1
Hampshire	58	4
Hertfordshire	51	2
Humberside	38	4
Kent	54	5
Lancashire	51	4
Leicestershire	33	4
Lincolnshire	64	10
London, City of	21	1
Merseyside	46	1
Metropolitan Police District	46	—[1]
Norfolk	57	6
Northamptonshire	45	13
Northumbria	52	3
North Yorkshire	47	6
Nottinghamshire	58	9
South Yorkshire	47	9
Staffordshire	47	8
Suffolk	64	22
Surrey	57	8
Sussex	53	5
Thames Valley	49	3
Warwickshire	43	6
West Mercia	62	4
West Midlands	50	6
West Yorkshire	46	4
Wiltshire	59	14
ENGLAND	49	4
Dyfed-Powys	67	3
Gwent	45	4
North Wales	49	7
South Wales	34	3
WALES	43	4
ENGLAND AND WALES	49	4

[1]Less than ½ per cent.

Consents to prosecution: Note by the Director of Public Prosecutions

1. The Commission has asked me to provide information on the numbers of cases, classified by type of offence, referred to me and the Attorney General where consent to prosecution is required, the number of cases in which consent is withheld and, if possible, the grounds, by broad classification, for withholding consent. I now set out [in Table 24.1] the number of cases referred to me in 1977 in which my consent was required and, out of such cases, the number in which I withheld consent. [In Table 24.2] I similarly set out cases concerning the consent of the Attorney General; in some of these cases the Attorney General (or the Solicitor General) refused consent, and in some I decided that no action was justified and therefore did not seek his consent.

2. The figures in the columns showing "No Action" cases indicate only those cases in which no action was advised for any offence. In some cases, although no action was advised in respect of the offence requiring my consent or the Attorney's consent, proceedings were advised for other offences. For example, in some allegations of gross indecency proceedings were advised only for the offence of indecent assault and no consent was granted. The result of such classification is that the "withheld consents" figure may in fact be higher than is shown.

3. It has not been possible to classify the grounds on which consent was withheld in the cases enumerated [in Tables 24.1 and 24.2]. In some cases consent is withheld because the evidence is insufficient to justify proceedings. In others, although the evidence is sufficient, it may be that in the public interest proceedings are not merited. I have already mentioned in paragraphs 103–127 of my first Memorandum[1] the varied factors which, in my view, can properly be taken into consideration for this purpose.

---

[1]Written evidence of the Director of Public Prosecutions to the Royal Commission on Criminal Procedure.

Appendix 24

Table 24.1. Cases submitted in 1977 requiring the consent of the Director of Public Prosecutions.

Statute	Number of applications (cases) submitted	Number of applications when "No action" advised ie where consent not granted
BANKRUPTCY ACT 1914	31	15
CRIMINAL LAW ACT 1967, s. 4(1) (assisting an offender)	82	28
CRIMINAL LAW ACT 1967, s. 5(2) (wasting police time)	375	130
EXCHANGE CONTROL ACT 1947 (Fifth Schedule, Part II)	32	14
HEALTH & SAFETY AT WORK ACT 1974	5	4
INSURANCE COMPANIES ACT 1974	1	1
LOCAL GOVERNMENT ACT 1972, s. 94 (failing to declare pecuniary interest)	28	25
MARINE ETC BROADCASTING (OFFENCES) ACT 1967	1	—
MENTAL HEALTH ACT 1959, ss. 126 and 128 (ill-treatment of/sexual intercourse with patients)	45	30
PROTECTION OF DEPOSITORS ACT 1963	6	3
REHABILITATION OF OFFENDERS ACT 1964, s. 9(2) (unauthorised disclosure of spent convictions)	9	9
SEXUAL OFFENCES ACT 1956 (incest cases)	270	63
SEXUAL OFFENCES ACT 1967 (buggery; gross indecency etc)	609	117
SOUTHERN RHODESIA ACT 1965 (breach of S. Rhodesia sanctions order)	3	3
SUICIDE ACT 1961, s. 2(1) (aid/abet suicide)	13	9
THEFT ACT 1968, s. 30 (theft of/damage to property of spouse)	161	68
	1671	519

Table 24.2. Cases submitted in 1977 requiring the *fiat* of a Law Officer

	Number of applications (cases) submitted	Number of applications where "No action" advised, ie where *fiat* not granted
CHILDREN & YOUNG PERSONS (HARMFUL PUBLICATIONS) ACT 1955 ("horror comics")	4	4
COINAGE OFFENCES ACT 1936, s. 4(3)	3	3
COUNTER INFLATION ACT 1973	3	2
CRIMINAL JUSTICE ACT 1967, s. 3	3	2
EXPLOSIVE SUBSTANCES ACT 1883	20	4
NEWSPAPERS, PRINTERS READING ROOMS REPEAL ACT 1869	5	5
OFFICIAL SECRETS ACTS 1911–1939	33	31
PREVENTION OF TERRORISM (TEMPORARY PROVISIONS) ACT 1976	5	1
PREVENTION OF CORRUPTION ACT 1906	317	215
PUBLIC BODIES (CORRUPT PRACTICES) ACT 1889	18	12
PUBLIC ORDER ACT 1936, ss. 1 and 2	3	3
PUBLIC ORDER ACT 1936, s. 5A (as amended)	29	27
SEXUAL OFFENCES (AMENDMENT) ACT 1976	1	1
THEATRES ACT 1968	3	3
	447	313

The criteria for prosecution:
Note by the Director of Public Prosecutions

Of all the decisions which have to be made by those with responsibility for the conduct of criminal cases, by far the most important is the initial one as to whether or not a charge should be preferred. Naturally the degree of importance depends to some extent on the gravity of the offence but a wrong decision either way can have disastrous consequences affecting not only the suspect but, in certain circumstances, the whole community. If a guilty man is not prosecuted, he may go on to cause untold further harm; yet if an innocent man is prosecuted, he and his family may be seriously affected even if the offence is comparatively minor and he is ultimately acquitted.

Hence whenever there is some room for doubt as to whether the evidence is sufficient, every effort is made to ensure that the decision is reached dispassionately after due deliberation and by a person experienced in weighing the available evidence.

Sometimes, of course, a degree of haste is inevitable if there is a danger that the suspect will disappear, commit further offences, interfere with vital witnesses or otherwise impede the investigation.

There is, however, a tendency for some police officers to charge a man when none of these circumstances apply and where there is no reason why he should not be bailed under section 38(2) of the Magistrates' Courts Act, 1952, or merely told that the circumstances will be reported. The result is that my Department from time to time has to advise that a charge should be withdrawn or to refuse consent to prosecution where this is required by statute.

The test normally used in the Department in deciding whether evidence is sufficient to justify proceedings is whether or not there is a reasonable prospect of a conviction; whether, in other words, it seems rather more likely that there will be a conviction than an acquittal.

We set an even higher standard if an acquittal would or might produce unfortunate consequences. For example, if a man who has been convicted of some offence is subsequently acquitted of having given perjured evidence at his trial, that acquittal may cast doubt on the original conviction. Likewise an unsuccessful prosecution of an allegedly obscene book will, if the trial has attracted publicity, lead to a considerable increase in sales.

In such cases we are hesitant to prosecute unless we think the prospects of a conviction are high. We also tend to adopt a somewhat higher standard if the trial is likely to be abnormally long and expensive and the offence is not especially grave.

There are some who maintain that it is right to prosecute whenever there is a bare *prima facie* case as, it is said, to raise the minimum standard above this level is to usurp the proper function of the courts. In my view, however, the universal adoption of a "bare *prima facie* case" standard would not only clog up our already over-burdened courts but inevitably result in an undue proportion of innocent men facing criminal charges.

It is not of course easy in borderline cases to decide whether or not there is a reasonable prospect of a conviction, and this difficulty remains whatever the standard may be.

The prosecutor certainly cannot, or should not, base his decision merely on the number of people who have made statements implicating the accused but should, in evaluating the evidence, ask himself (and where necessary ask the police officer who has interviewed the witnesses) questions along the following lines:

1. Does it appear that the witness is exaggerating, or that his memory is faulty, or that he is hostile to the accused, or is otherwise unreliable?

2. Has he a motive for telling less than the whole truth?

3. Has he previous convictions, or are there other matters which might properly be put to him by the defence to attack his credibility?

4. What sort of impression is he likely to make as a witness? How is he likely to stand up to cross-examination? Does he suffer from any physical or mental disability?

5. If there is conflict between eye-witnesses, does it go beyond what one would expect and hence materially weaken the case?

6. If there is a lack of conflict between eye witnesses, is there anything which causes suspicion that a false story may have been concocted?

7. Are all the necessary witnesses available to give evidence, including any who may be abroad?

8. If identity is likely to be an issue, how cogent and reliable is the evidence of those who purport to identify the accused?

9. If the case depends in part on confessions by the accused, are there any grounds for fearing that the evidence may not be admitted or that they are of doubtful reliability having regard to the age and intelligence of the accused?

10. Are the facts of the case such that the jury is likely to be sympathetic towards the accused?

This list is not of course exhaustive, and the questions to be asked depend upon the circumstances of each individual case, but it is introduced to indicate that, particularly in borderline cases, the prosecutor must always delve beneath the surface of the statements. He must also draw, so far as is possible, on his own experience of how evidence of the type under consideration is likely to "stand-up" in court and commend itself to a jury before reaching a conclusion as to the likelihood of a conviction.

Having ultimately decided that the evidence is sufficient to justify proceedings, the prosecutor must then go on to consider whether the provable facts and the whole of the surrounding circumstances are such that it is incumbent upon him in the public interest to institute a prosecution. In many cases the answer will be an unhesitating "Yes" but in some it may be as difficult as the question of evidential sufficiency.

Again, there are some who maintain that if the evidence is sufficient, a prosecution must necessarily follow as, it is said, mitigating circumstances should always be left to the court to weigh before passing sentence.

I, however, strongly prefer to adopt the point of view expressed by Lord Shawcross who, when he was Attorney General, said in a House of Commons debate:

> "It has never been the rule in this country—I hope it never will be—that suspected criminal offences must automatically be the subject of prosecution. Indeed the very first Regulations under which the Director of Public Prosecutions worked provided that he should ... prosecute ... 'wherever it appears that the offence or the circumstances of its commission is or are of such a character that a prosecution in respect thereof is required in the public interest'. That is still the dominant consideration".[1]

He then went on to say that, in deciding whether or not to authorise a prosecution, we must have regard to "the effect which the prosecution, successful or unsuccessful as the case may be, would have upon public morale and order, and with any other considerations affecting public policy". Hence my overall aim is to try not only to be fair to the victim of a crime and to the offender himself, but to try to satisfy responsible public opinion that the criminal law is being administered impartially in the interests of the whole community.

The factors which can properly be taken into consideration on public policy grounds are many and varied. They will naturally depend on the special facts of each particular case but in general it can be said that the more minor the offence, the greater the attention that should be paid to mitigating circumstances.

It would not, for instance, normally be in the public interest to prosecute for an offence which can only be tried on indictment (particularly if the expense would be high) if it seems probable that the sentence would be no more than a conditional or absolute discharge.

The most common factors, and my attitude towards them, are as follows:

a. Staleness

One must have regard not merely to the date of the last known offence at the time the file is considered but the probable time interval when the case comes to trial, as up to eighteen months—and sometimes even longer—may elapse between the decision to prosecute and the eventual verdict.

Broadly speaking I am hesitant to prosecute if the last offence was committed three or more years before the probable date of trial unless the offences are of

---

[1] HC Debates Vol 483, Col 681 (29 January 1951)

such gravity that, despite the staleness, a custodial sentence of some length is likely to be imposed. Hence the less serious the offence, the greater the weight to be attached to the date of its commission.

I do, however, pay less regard to staleness if the complexity of a case has necessitated prolonged police enquiries or if the accused has caused or contributed to the staleness by disappearing or covering his tracks.

b. Youth

The younger the offender, the more one should consider whether a caution will suffice, particularly if he is of previously good character, has a good home background and is in steady employment.

I frequently consult the police officer in charge of the case as to the likelihood of a repetition of the offence if I am in doubt, and will take into account the attitude of the accused's parents and the extent to which the matter has caused concern in the neighbourhood.

c. Old age and infirmity

The older or more infirm the offender, the more I am reluctant to prosecute unless there is a real possibility of repetition or the offence is of such gravity that it is impossible to overlook. In general, it seems right not to prosecute whenever a court is likely to pay such regard to the age or infirmity of the offender as to induce it to impose only a nominal penalty, although there may be exceptional circumstances (such as if the accused still holds a position of some importance) when proceedings are required in the public interest regardless of what penalty may be imposed.

One must of course also consider whether the accused is likely to be fit enough to stand his trial. For this purpose I sometimes obtain from the defence solicitor any medical reports which have been made on his client and may arrange, through him, for an independent medical examination.

d. Mental illness or stress

The defence solicitor, knowing that the police are investigating his client's conduct, may sometimes send me a psychiatric report to the effect that the accused is suffering from some form of mental illness and that the strain of criminal proceedings will lead to a considerable and permanent worsening of his condition. This is nearly as worrying as, say, a report that the accused has a weak heart and that the shock of prosecution may be fatal.

Once again, I will normally try to arrange for an independent examination and will in any event give anxious consideration to such reports as I may receive. This is a difficult field because in some instances the accused may have become mentally disturbed or depressed by the mere fact that his misconduct has been discovered and I am sometimes dubious about a prognosis that criminal proceedings will adversely affect his condition to a significant extent.

I do not normally think it is right to pay much regard to evidence of mental instability which is not coupled with a prognosis as to the adverse effect of proceedings (unless it is of such a nature as to effect any issue of *mens rea*) as such instability may increase the likelihood that the offence will be repeated.

213

e. Sexual offences

My decisions are often strongly influenced by the relative ages of the offender and the "victim" if there is no element of corruption by the former and the latter was a fully consenting party.

Hence I do not normally prosecute, say, a youth of 17 for unlawful sexual intercourse with a girl of 15 but the larger the gap between their ages, the more I am likely to take proceedings.

Similarly I do not normally prosecute a man of 22 for a homosexual offence against a man of 19 although if, for instance, the elder went into a public toilet intent on finding a partner and the younger was or might become a male prostitute, I would probably decide to prosecute both.

I sometimes get cases in which it is abundantly clear that a girl of 15 has persistently seduced a number of men considerably older than herself. In such circumstances I may either take no proceedings or prosecute only those men who are of such maturity that it can reasonably be said that they should have resisted the temptation. I may at the same time suggest that the authorities should consider whether the girl is in need of care and protection.

f. Perjury

This is often difficult to prove but, if there is sufficient corroboration as required by section 13 of the Perjury Act 1911 and a reasonable prospect of a conviction, I will unhesitatingly take proceedings against a prosecution witness if his perjured evidence goes to the heart of the issue before the court. Sometimes, however, his perjury, although technically material, may be on a somewhat peripheral issue and it may then be proper to advise a caution if he lied to protect his own interests rather than with an intent to pervert the course of justice.

It is, however, necessary to apply somewhat different considerations when perjury is committed by a defendant although it has never been my view that he can in all circumstances lie with complete immunity, particularly if he conspires with or suborns other witnesses.

When perjury by a defendant has been unsuccessful, it is necessary to have regard to the punishment inflicted by the court and to assess whether a subsequent prosecution for perjury would be likely to result in any substantial increase of his sentence. It is also essential that the evidence should be so exceptionally strong that a conviction is virtually certain, because of the doubts which an acquittal would cast upon the verdict of guilty in the original case. Usually, although not necessarily, it is the emergence of some additional and compelling evidence after the original trial which removes the last trace of doubt.

Even, however, where there is abundant evidence against a defendant who has unsuccessfully lied without involving others, I would not normally think it right to prosecute unless there are aggravating factors.

One cannot of course lay down any hard and fast rules about such factors but in general I will consider whether the lies necessarily involved an attack on the truthfulness (as opposed to recollection or ability to identify) of one or more prosecution witnesses; whether the lie was clearly planned before the hearing or arose on the spur of the moment during cross-examination; and the degree of persistence in maintaining the lie.

g. *Miscellaneous offences*

There are other offences (such as bigamy) in which experience has shown that the courts are unlikely to impose more than a nominal penalty unless there are exceptional and aggravating circumstances. In such cases I normally advise that a caution will suffice.

h. *General*

In some cases, I think it is proper to have regard to the attitude of a complainant who may have gone to the police in the heat of the moment—as in many husband/wife assault cases—but later expresses a wish that no action be taken. Usually in such circumstances I would not prosecute unless there was suspicion that the change of heart was actuated by fear or the offence was of some gravity.

My attitude would be the same in the case of, for example, a comparatively minor theft or criminal damage if the owner of the property expressed a wish that there should be no prosecution.

Finally if, having weighed such of the above factors as may appertain to the case, I am still in doubt as to whether proceedings are called for, I would throw into the scales the good or bad character of the accused, the attitude of the local community and any information about the prevalence of the particular offence in the area or nationally. Should doubt still remain, I consider that the scales should normally be tipped in favour of prosecution as if the balance is so even, it could properly be said that the final arbiter must be the court.

Consistency of prosecution policy and practice:
Note by the Director of Public Prosecutions

I have been asked to provide factual data to illuminate particular arrangements for, and effects of, centrally directed measures to ensure consistency of prosecution practice. At the outset, I should make it clear that my statutory duties (now contained in section 2 of the Prosecution of Offences Act 1979) do not include the giving of advice on general prosecuting policy. Section 2(1)(b) places on me the duty "to give such advice and assistance to chief officers of police, justices' clerks and other persons (whether officers or not) concerned in any criminal proceedings respecting the conduct of those proceedings" as may be prescribed by the Attorney General. General prosecuting policy is not, in my view and that of my predecessors, a "criminal proceeding" and consequently it has not been the practice of this Department to offer unsolicited advice on matters of general prosecuting policy. The occasions on which the Director offers unsolicited advice to the police are very limited. On the other hand, I can see no particular difficulty about offering such general advice, if that duty were placed upon me. Indeed, as I indicated in paragraph 260 of my first Memorandum,[1] this is a way of improving uniformity of policy which I would favour.

From time to time I do by invitation attend ACPO regional and other conferences of senior officers and discuss general prosecuting policy. For example, in November 1977 I spoke at the ACPO Seminar on Public Order with particular reference to demonstrations. In August 1977 I advised ACPO at their request on topics arising out of a regional conference; these concerned the charging of a less serious offence in appropriate cases, the proper use of the charge of affray, and the responsibility of those concerned in the prosecution for the acceptance of a plea of guilty to a lesser charge. My Principal Assistant Directors and Assistant Directors attend conferences for senior detective officers at which they advise on more detailed and specific matters of investigatory and prosecuting practice. I and my senior officers also give a number of lectures each year to detectives of all ranks up to and including that of superintendent at which we frequently explain our policies and give advice on a variety of matters.

Some measure of uniformity of prosecution practice is also promoted by applying consistent policies to the cases which are referred to me. My role in these cases will vary. It may involve advising against proceedings; or advising

[1] Written evidence of the Director of Public Prosecutions to the Royal Commission on Criminal Procedure.

that there should be a prosecution in which event either I may assume responsibility for the conduct of the case or I may leave the prosecution in the hands of the police granting, where necessary, my consent.

Pre-trial reviews in the Crown Court

Note by the Lord Chancellor's Department

In October 1974 at the Central Criminal Court an experimental scheme was introduced to hold pre-trial reviews in selected criminal cases. The scheme, for which semi-formal rules were drafted, was intended to eliminate avoidable waste of time in the hearing of complicated cases and its application was thus initially confined to complicated fraud cases expected to last a number of weeks. Any case, however, for which the trial date had been fixed might be set down for review on the application of the solicitor for any party, or on the initiative of the court itself, to identify the essential matters in issue and avoid the unnecessary attendance of witnesses or production of exhibits at the trial itself.

2. The procedure was subsequently adopted in various forms for the Crown Court in each Circuit and generally has been found to be of most assistance in long or complicated cases. Some Circuits have issued "practice notes" of their own on how the procedure should be used and, in particular, the North Eastern Circuit combined its procedure with a "plea day" scheme. Under this scheme cases where the Court has been notified that the defendant intends to plead guilty and cases where the likely plea is in doubt are generally listed in the fifth week after committal for the plea to be taken. If, in the event, a plea of not guilty is entered the court may then proceed to a pre-trial review in suitable cases. In the case of notified pleas of not guilty the procedure adopted is similar to that on other Circuits.

3. No final conclusion has been reached on the best form of procedure to be adopted generally and the current schemes are still being evaluated. It does appear, however, that it is in the larger cases where the issues are complex and the evidence is extensive that the most worthwhile reductions occur in the amount of preparation required before trial and in savings in court time. Indeed, a number of the original "practice notes" have already been modified to reflect this. Copies of the latest notes about arrangements at the Central Criminal Court and in the North Eastern Circuit are attached. Practice Rules in similar terms to those of the Central Criminal Court have been issued by the Presiding Judges of the Western, Midland and Oxford, and Northern Circuits.

4. It is difficult to assess the proportion of cases in which a pre-trial review would produce worthwhile savings. To be worthwhile, the savings achieved on

preparation and trial work must naturally exceed the additional cost of the review itself. On this basis, the proportion of cases in which worthwhile savings would be achieved is likely to be relatively small. For example, in the first six months of 1978, 23.5 per cent of all contested trials in the Crown Court lasted for less than three hours, and 70 per cent lasted for less than nine hours. Some savings might be achieved if a two-day case (approximately ten hours) were reduced to one day or even 1½ days, but these would be small given the cost of the pre-trial review itself. Consequently it is probably only in cases likely to last more than two days that the pre-trial review would generally be an economic proposition, as the daily sums of money involved are greater and there is a real possibility of significant savings in time.

CENTRAL CRIMINAL COURT

Practice Rules

On the direction of the Recorder these Practice Rules replace the existing rules on and after 21 November 1977.

They give a greater flexibility in regard to the number and type of cases which may be listed for Practice Directions.

Richard Grobler

Courts Administrator

The Practice Rules

1. Any case may be listed for practice directions within those Rules upon an application in writing made to the Court by solicitors acting for any party, or by any unrepresented party, provided that a copy of the application is sent at the same time to all other parties and provided that the Court is satisfied that the case is fit for such practice directions. If no party makes application the Court may list the case for such practice directions of its own volition.

2. The Court shall determine the time and place of the hearing.

3. At least 14 days' notice of hearing shall be given, unless the parties agree to shorter notice, and that notice shall not be given on a date earlier than 14 days after the preferment of a bill of indictment.

4. *(a)* Hearings for practice directions under Rule 5 may be dealt with in Chambers before any Judge of the Court.

   (b) A represented Defendant shall be present at hearings in Chambers unless he elects not to attend.

   (c) Hearings for directions and orders under Rule 6 and the making of orders under Rule 7 shall be held and made in open Court by the Judge allocated to try the case.

   (d) All Defendants shall be present in Court at hearings under Rule 4(c) except with the leave of the Court.

   (e) Hearings under Rules 4(a) and (c) shall be attended by Counsel briefed to conduct the case on trial or in special circumstances

Counsel specifically instructed to deal with the matters arising under Rules 5 and 6.

5. At a hearing under Rule 4(a) Counsel will be expected to be able to inform the Court,

(a) of the pleas to be tendered on trial;

(b) of the prosecution witnesses required at trial as shown on the committal documents and any notices of further evidence then delivered and of the availability of such witnesses;

(c) of any additional witnesses who may be called by the prosecution and the evidence that they are expected to give; if the statements of these witnesses are not then available for service a summary of the evidence that they are expected to give shall be supplied in writing;

(d) of facts which can be and are admitted and which can be reduced to writing in accordance with section 10(2)(b) of the Criminal Justice Act 1967, within such time as may be agreed at the hearing and of the witnesses whose attendance will not be required at trial;

(e) of the probable length of the trial;

(f) of exhibits and schedules which are and can be admitted;

(g) of issues, if any, then envisaged as to the mental or medical condition of any Defendant or witness;

(h) of any point of law which may arise on trial, any question as to the admissibility of evidence which then appears on the face of the papers and of any authority on which either party intends to rely as far as can be possibly envisaged at that stage;

(i) of the names and addresses of witnesses from whom statements have been taken by the prosecution but who are not going to be called and, in appropriate cases, disclosure of the contents of those statements;

(j) of any alibi not then disclosed in conformity with the Criminal Justice Act 1967;

(k) of the order and pagination of the papers to be used by the prosecution at the trial and of the order in which the witnesses for the prosecution will be called;

(l) of any other significant matter which might affect the proper and convenient trial of the case.

6. At a hearing under Rule 4(c) in open Court, the Judge who is to try the case may hear and rule upon any application by any party relating to the severance of any count or any Defendant and to amend or provide further and better particulars of any count in the indictment. The Judge may order particulars relating to any Count to be delivered within such time as he may direct.

7. The Judge may make such order or orders as lie within his powers as appear to him to be necessary to secure the proper and efficient trial of the case.

8. Subject to the provisions of sections 9 and 10 of the Criminal Justice Act 1967, admissions made under Rule 5 may be used at the trial.

No 297

11 November 1977

Directions by the Presiding Judges of the North Eastern Circuit

In accordance with section 4(5) of the Courts Act 1971 and on behalf of the Lord Chief Justice and with the concurrence of the Lord Chancellor I revoke my directions of 5 October 1976 in respect of all cases committed for trial to the Crown Court on the North Eastern Circuit on or after the 16 January 1978 and for them I direct instead:

1. (1) Within three weeks from the date of committal, or such longer period as may be specified by the court if notice has been given under paragraph 2 of these directions, it shall be the duty of the solicitor acting for each defendant in a case to give to the court listing information in the form set out in Appendix 1. [Not attached]

   (2) In the absence of such information or if the information indicates that a plea of guilty is likely or that the plea is unpredictable, subject to court vacations and paragraph 3 of these directions, the listing officer will list the case for plea in the course of the fifth week following the week of committal, having taken into account the convenience of all concerned. Such fifth week shall be known as the plea week. The listing officer may list the case earlier with the consent of the parties or where the interests of justice so require.

   (3) If such information indicates that a plea of not guilty is likely, the listing officer will list the case for trial in the normal way. Before he does so he may, having regard to the circumstances of the case, the information he has received and the convenience of all concerned, list the case for pre-trial review or require the solicitor and counsel acting for a party to give to the court a signed certificate in the form set out in Appendix 2. [Not attached]

2. (1) If any party to any proceedings will not be ready or will find it inconvenient to proceed by the plea week, it shall be the duty of the solicitor acting for him to give to the court and to all other parties, within three weeks from the date of committal, notice in writing stating

   (a) the reasons why the party will not be so ready or will find it inconvenient;

   (b) the earliest time when he will be so ready or will find it convenient;

   (c) whether the case is likely to proceed as a plea of guilty or not guilty.

   (2) A solicitor acting for a party receiving notice in accordance with sub-paragraph (1) above may within 24 hours of its receipt (excluding

Saturday and Sunday) give to the court and to all other parties a counter-notice in writing opposing or seeking to vary the adjournment sought.

(3) Any notice and any counter-notice given under the preceding sub-paragraphs shall be considered by the court who may order that the case shall remain in the list for the appointed plea week or that it shall be listed at some other time. The court will notify the parties and other interested persons of the decision.

3. Where the interests of justice so require the court itself may take a case out of the plea week list. The court will notify the parties and other interested persons of its action and will inform them of the day when the case will be listed.

4. If on arraignment in a case listed for plea a defendant:

(a) pleads guilty to the whole of the indictment, or pleads guilty to a lesser charge or to part of the indictment and such plea to the lesser charge or part of the indictment is acceptable to the court, he will be dealt with at the time he pleads subject to:

(i) the interests of justice;

(ii) any application from a party to the proceedings;

(b) pleads not guilty, a pre-trial review will be held, unless the judge otherwise orders.

5. If a case proceeds to pre-trial review under paragraph 4(b) of these directions or is listed for pre-trial review, counsel, who should be counsel briefed to conduct the case at the trial or counsel otherwise appropriately instructed, should be in a position to assist the court in estimating the probable length of the trial, and, subject to his duty to his client, to inform the court of such of the matters set out below as are relevant:

(a) the name and availability of any prosecution witness who will be required at the trial and whose evidence is contained in the committal documents or in any notice of further evidence already delivered;

(b) any additional witness who may be called by the prosecution, his availability and the evidence which he is expected to give;

(c) the order in which it is intended to call the prosecution witnesses;

(d) any alibi not disclosed in accordance with section 11 of the Criminal Justice Act 1967;

(e) any fact which is or likely to be admitted in accordance with section 10 of the Criminal Justice Act 1967;

(f) the availability of any defence witness;

(g) any question which may arise at the trial as to the admissibility of evidence;

(h) any issue which may arise at the trial as to the mental or medical condition of any defendant or witness;

(i) any point of law which may arise at the trial and any authority which relates to it;

(j) any other significant matter which may affect the trial of the case.

Unless the judge otherwise orders the above matters (a)–(j) shall be dealt with in chambers and unless he elects not to attend the defendant shall be present whether the judge sits in open court or in chambers.

6. At a pre-trial review the judge may deal in open court with any application for

(a) the severance or amendment of any count in the indictment;

(b) further and better particulars of any count in the indictment;

(c) the separate trial of any defendant;

and may make such orders as appear to him necessary to secure the proper and efficient trial of the case. If the judge on the application refuses to make an order such refusal shall not preclude a further application on the same matter to the trial judge, if different.

7. In these directions a "judge" means a judge of the High Court, a Circuit judge or Recorder.

LESLIE BOREHAM
A presiding judge of the North Eastern Circuit

Dated 3 December 1977

Some examples of existing practice in pre-trial disclosure of
evidence in cases to be tried on indictment
(Extracted from the Report of the Working Party on the
Disclosure of Information in Trials on Indictment)

... 12. Within the office of the Director of Public Prosecutions there is no
laid-down policy but the practice, with minor variations, is along the following
lines:

(a) When an edited statement is served for the purposes of a committal,
the defence are given a copy of the original statement or statements
upon which the edited version has been based. This is usually done at
the committal but may sometimes be done shortly before or shortly
after it.

(b) If the Director's Office is not serving a statement which clearly might
assist the defence or calling the maker of the statement, the
professional officer in charge of the case may supply his name and
address soon after the committal or may decide to ask Counsel to
advise regarding this and all other statements not served.

(c) When, after committal, Counsel is sent his brief he is always asked to
advise "whether the prosecution has any duty to make available to the
defence information on any matters dealt with in Archbold's current
paragraph 443". His attention may be directed to any statements
which might be of particular interest to the defence and he will be
informed of any names and addresses already supplied.

(d) In response to this, some Counsel will almost invariably advise that all
names and addresses should be supplied even if it is apparent that
many of the statements are wholly irrelevant to any conceivable line
of defence; others are more selective and do try to confine themselves
to those which might be of some assistance.

(e) If the defence ask to see any statements, this will usually be acceded
to on a Counsel to Counsel basis unless prosecuting Counsel considers
that there are particular reasons why certain ones should not be
disclosed. However it is usually the case that defence Counsel are not
given sight of any statements until, or very shortly before, the
commencement of the trial.

(f) If there are an exceptionally large number of statements, arrangements
are sometimes made between committal and trial for the defence
Solicitor to peruse these at the local police station and to be given a
copy of any in which he expresses an interest.

(g) If a witness is to give evidence at the committal at the instigation of the prosecution, his statement will not normally be included in the bundle of statements served on the defence. If however his evidence materially differs from that statement, a copy will thereupon be given to the defence so that they may cross-examine him upon it.

(h) Previous convictions of prosecution witnesses are not normally disclosed unless Counsel so advises. Sometimes this will be done during the trial on a Counsel to Counsel basis. The tendency however is not to disclose unless the previous conviction, eg for perjury, is clearly relevant and it is also apparent that the evidence of the witness will be challenged.

(i) A copy of Forensic Science reports, including opinions of handwriting and similar experts, is always supplied at or soon after the committal.

(j) At or soon after the committal the defence, on request, will also be supplied with the name and address of any witness, whether or not such witness has attended an identification parade, who is known as having stated that he saw, or as being likely to have seen, the criminal in the circumstances of the crime, together with a copy of any description of the criminal given by such a person. This is in accordance with an answer by the Attorney General in Parliament on 27 May 1976.

13. (a) The Solicitor's Department of the Metropolitan Police adhere to a policy which, in 1974, was formulated in the following terms:

"Initially the prosecution should inform the defence of the names and addresses of the witnesses whom they do not intend to call but not provide statements unless they have a statement which of itself would tend to show the prisoner to be innocent. In such a case the statement should be provided. If after providing the names and addresses the defence request copies of the statements of such witnesses then these should be provided unless the prosecution have a compelling reason for keeping the statement to themselves, for example if the statement is that of a witness whom the prosecution suspect the defence may threaten to make him change his evidence.

Previous convictions of prosecution witnesses will be disclosed Advocate to Advocate both at the Magistrates' Courts and the Crown Courts, even when there is no request for the information, in accordance with the dicta in *R v Collister and Warhurst*. In addition if a request for such information is made by defence Solicitors prior to the hearing, the information will be given in a letter sent by Recorded Delivery. In cases of exceptional urgency the information may be given over the telephone. It is considered that it is right that the defence should have this information in advance if they request it so that they may with their Counsel properly consider the strategy of their defence. It is emphasised that information should be given in advance only when requested.

Difficulty sometimes arises when the police are not sure that one of the witnesses is identical with a person having a criminal record. In such cases a reply to a request for information about the character of prosecution witnesses should be carefully worded, for example 'Mr............ has been convicted on two occasions viz........... there may be convictions recorded against other prosecution witnesses and if this proves to be the case information will be given as soon as possible'.

Reference to the disclosure by Counsel to defending Counsel of the previous convictions will continue to be made in briefs in view of the possibility that some defending Solicitors might fail to inform their Counsel of the information given to them or that the defendant might change his Solicitor prior to the trial."

(b) In order to bring other matters to the notice of the defence, before the committal proceedings if possible, the Solicitor's Department of the Metropolitan Police follows the practice set out below:

(i) In general, copies of statements made by witnesses whom the prosecution have decided shall give oral evidence in committal proceedings are provided to the defence, and whenever an edited statement is used in such proceedings a copy of the original statement is supplied to the defence. There are occasions when no such disclosure is made, but, in such circumstances, the defence are notified that an edited statement is being used.

(ii) In cases involving disputed evidence of visual identification, any material discrepancies in first descriptions provided by eye-witnesses who are being called for the prosecution are revealed to the defence. Further, details of any person not called by the prosecution who has said that he saw the offender are also provided. Copies of any statements made by those persons, and of any descriptions given by them, are also supplied.

(iii) A copy of any Forensic Science report in the possession of the prosecution is given to the defence irrespective of whether the maker is called for the prosecution.

(iv) Details of previous convictions of a co-defendant are supplied on request, but not otherwise.

Whenever a copy of a statement of a witness for the prosecution has not been supplied to the defence, and that witness gives evidence which is inconsistent with the contents of his statement in some material particular, a copy is supplied to the defence while the witness is in the witness box so that he can be cross-examined upon it.

14. The practice followed by the Chief Prosecuting Solicitor for Greater Manchester is as follows:

(a) A Principal Prosecuting Solicitor decides which of the persons whose statements are submitted are to be used as prosecution witnesses; whether or not the proceedings are *prima facie* suitable for committal proceedings under section 1 of the Criminal Justice Act 1967; whether or not, in any event, copies of all or any of the statements of the prosecution witnesses should be served on the defence and whether or not any of the statements requires editing. If editing is required this is done by the Principal Prosecuting Solicitor who is checking the file.

(b) It is not standard practice to deliver to the defence copies of the statements of persons who are not to be called as witnesses by the prosecution nor copies of the originals of edited statements, nor is it standard practice to disclose automatically such of the contents of original statements as may have been excluded in editing. Each case is considered on its own merits and, if the Chief Prosecuting Solicitor considers that it is appropriate to do so, he will disclose to the defence any material parts of the contents of a statement that it would help them to have or even deliver a copy of the statement itself should the occasion warrant it.

(c) In the case of committal proceedings where a witness is to be called to give oral evidence, whether or not a copy of his statement will be served under section 2 of the Criminal Justice Act 1967 is decided by the Chief Prosecuting Solicitor having regard to the purpose of calling the witness in person and any other relevant criteria. In such a case where a witness, a copy of whose statement had not been served on the defence, gave oral evidence which differed materially from that statement a copy of the statement would be made available to the defence for him to be cross examined on it.

(d) Where a material statement has been taken from a person who it is not intended to call as a prosecution witness at the trial and a copy of whose statement is not to be served on the defence, the name and address of that person will be tendered to the defence after the committal proceedings. Similarly the name and address of any person known to the Chief Prosecuting Solicitor who in his view might be of some assistance in establishing a conceivable line of defence (even if that person has not made a written statement) will be supplied to the defence on request. In particular, on request the defence will be supplied with the names and addresses of any person whether or not he attended an identification parade who is known by the Chief Prosecuting Solicitor to have stated that he saw or to have been likely to have seen, the criminal in the circumstances of the crime, together with a copy of any description of the criminal given by such person. Any such information is normally supplied after committal. Counsel is always informed of the Chief Prosecuting Solicitor's decision in such matters and is commonly asked to advise whether or not further disclosure would be proper.

(e) Where the defence ask to be notified of the previous convictions of prosecution witnesses, it is the practice of the Chief Prosecuting Solicitor to arrange for details of any such convictions to be made available at Court on the date of trial. It is not his practice actively to enquire whether or not a witness has convictions without special reason nor is it his regular practice voluntarily to disclose previous convictions of prosecution witnesses unless Counsel so advise or the conviction is clearly relevant, for example, for perjury and it is apparent that the evidence will be challenged.

15. It will be apparent from the outline of the policies set out in the last three paragraphs that there are considerable variations in matters of detail. Doubtless many other variations are practised by other prosecuting solicitors but we have not considered it necessary to explore this further.

Section 48 of the Criminal Law Act 1977

48. (1) The power to make rules conferred by section 15 of the Justices of the Peace Act 1949 shall, without prejudice to the generality of subsection (1) of that section, include power to make, with respect to proceedings against any person for a prescribed offence or an offence of any prescribed class, provision

(a) for requiring the prosecutor to do such things as may be prescribed for the purpose of securing that the accused or a person representing him is furnished with, or can obtain, advance information concerning all, or any prescribed class of, the facts and matters of which the prosecutor proposes to adduce evidence; and

(b) for requiring a magistrates' court, if satisfied that any requirement imposed by virtue of paragraph (a) above has not been complied with, to adjourn the proceedings pending compliance with that requirement unless the court is satisfied that the conduct of the case for the accused will not be substantially prejudiced by non-compliance with the requirement.

(2) Rules made by virtue of subsection (1)(a) above

(a) may require the prosecutor to do as provided in the rules either

(i) in all cases; or

(ii) only if so requested by or on behalf of the accused;

(b) may exempt facts and matters of any prescribed description from any requirement imposed by the rules, and may make the opinion of the prosecutor material for the purposes of any such exemption; and

(c) may make different provision with respect to different offences of different classes.

(3) It shall not be open to a person convicted of an offence to appeal against the conviction on the ground that a requirement imposed by virtue of subsection (1) above was not complied with by the prosecutor.

Printed in England for Her Majesty's Stationery Office by
Brown Knight & Truscott Ltd, London and Tonbridge
Dd 0594276   K28   1/81